The Enigma of 1989

The Enigma of 1989

The USSR and the Liberation of Eastern Europe

Jacques Lévesque

Translated from the French by Keith Martin

UNIVERSITY OF CALIFORNIA PRESS
Berkeley · Los Angeles · London

University of California Press
Berkeley and Los Angeles, California

University of California Press, Ltd.
London, England

Library of Congress Cataloging-in-Publication Data

Lévesque, Jacques.
    [1989, la fin d'un empire.   English]
    The enigma of 1989 : the USSR and the libera-
tion of Eastern Europe / Jacques Lévesque ; translated by Keith Martin.
        p.   cm.
    Includes bibliographical references and index.
    ISBN 0-520-20631-2 (cloth : alk. paper)
    1. Europe, Eastern—Foreign relations—
Soviet Union.   2. Soviet Union—Foreign
relations—Europe, Eastern.   3. Europe, Eastern—Politics and government—1945-1989.
4. Soviet Union—Foreign relations—1985-
1991.   I. Title.
DJK45.S65L4813   1997
327.47047'09048—dc21   96-52426

Printed in the United States of America
9 8 7 6 5 4 3 2 1

The paper used in this publication meets the minimum requirements of American National Standards
for Information Sciences—Permanence of Paper for
Printed Library Materials, ANSI Z39.48-1984.

Originally published as 1989, La fin d'un empire:
L'URSS et la libération de l'Europe de l'Est (Presses
de la Fondation Nationale des Sciences Politiques:
Paris, 1995).

Contents

PART III. THE GREAT PROJECT'S RUIN

Acknowledgments
and Notes on Sources

This project was made possible by the Killam Foundation and the Social Sciences Research Council of Canada. The Killam grant allowed me to devote two years entirely to the research necessary for completing this work.

The research primarily concentrated on the gamut of sources published in the USSR during the Gorbachev period. In addition, I was able to obtain important documents from a variety of sources in Russia. These include unpublished documents from the Communist Party Central Committee, the USSR Presidency of Gorbachev, and the Ministry of Foreign Affairs. Documents which were taken by Mikhail Gorbachev and his close associates are kept at the Gorbachev Foundation's Institute for the History of Perestroika, where they can be consulted with special authorization; they were used very extensively by Gorbachev and his assistants to write their respective memoirs.[1] These documents, however, represent only a fraction of the archives relating to the Politburo and the presidency, which are currently in the Presidential Archives; in principle, these will not be accessible to the public for another twenty years.

To fill this gap, I conducted a large number of interviews between 1991 and 1995 with many of the most important actors and with witnesses who had a particularly strategic view of the events in question. In

1. Except for those of Gorbachev and Cherniaev, the memoirs were published in Moscow, in very limited editions and with little circulation. Since they were based on scattered documents transferred to the institute, large periods of time and certain important events frequently get little or no attention.

Moscow, several of Gorbachev's closest assistants and advisers on international affairs in general, and on Eastern Europe in particular, were interviewed. These include Aleksandr Yakovlev, Vadim Medvedev, Georgii Shakhnazarov, and Vadim Zagladin. Mikhail Gorbachev himself agreed to answer a series of questions that I submitted to him. There were also exchanges with two men who worked as deputy directors of the International Department of the CPSU Central Committee in 1989: Andrei Grachev (who also served as Gorbachev's spokesman in 1991) and Valerii Musatov (responsible for relations with the countries of Eastern Europe). There were also numerous long interviews with directors and researchers at the three institutes of the USSR Academy of Sciences, who gave me the most important assistance in analyzing the policies this book examines. The institutes are, first, the Institute of the Economy of the World Socialist System, directed by Oleg Bogomolov, as well as the Institute of Europe of Vitalii Zhurkin and the Institute of the U.S.A. and Canada. of Georgii Arbatov. Beyond the directors, I would like to thank several researchers at these institutes, in particular Marina P. Sil'vanskaia, Viachislav Dashichev, and Sergei Karaganov, for the invaluable assistance they rendered me.

My research was not limited to the former USSR. It was also important to evaluate how the signals and instructions from Moscow were received and interpreted in each of the East European countries. In Poland, I conducted interviews with General Wojciech Jaruzelski; Mieczyslaw Rakowski, former prime minister and general secretary of the Communist Party during 1989; Jozef Czyrek, the Party official responsible for international affairs; and with several leaders of Solidarity. Special thanks must go to Dr. Adam Bromke for arranging these meetings. In Hungary, interlocutors included Janos Kadar's successor, Karoly Grosz; Matyas Szürös, the former head of the Communist Party's International Department and President of Parliament in 1989; other high functionaries in the International Department; and with the current minister of Foreign Affairs, Laszlo Kovacs, who was deputy minister in 1989. In Bulgaria, interview partners were Todor Zhivkov's successor, Petar Mladenov; the Bulgarian prime minister in 1990, Andrei Lukanov; and Dimitar Stanichev, head of the International Department of the Communist Party in 1989. In Romania, I interviewed Silviu Brucan, the "éminence grise" of the National Salvation Front, which took power in December 1989; the former minister of Foreign Affairs, A. Nastase; and, as in the other countries, with researchers in international affairs at the Academy of Science.

In Czechoslovakia, the former Communist leaders were far less willing to be interviewed. In fact, they systematically avoided interviews. Fortunately, it was possible to have discussions with high officials of the Foreign Ministry and with Jaromir Sedlak and Oskar Krejci, the special council and assistant, respectively, to Lubomir Strugal and Ladislav Adamec, the last two Communist-era prime ministers. Jaromir Sedlak even prepared a long research report on issues relevant to this book, as they pertained to Czechoslovakia. As for East Germany, given the enormous and incomparable quantity of documents and memoirs which were published following German unification, interviews did not appear to be necessary. My research assistant, Laure Castin, a doctoral candidate at Université Paris I, indexed this literature and translated those parts which were most directly relevant to this research. Gorbachev's extensive memoirs had only appeared in German at the time this work was completed, and she patiently translated interminably long passages from them. Viktor Obst translated the Czech sources, while Jan Grabowski did the same for Polish, Bronislav Nicolov for Bulgarian, and Andrei Stoiciu for Romanian sources.

I would like to thank them as well as Keith Martin, the translator, and also Daniel Dignard, Rémi Hyppia, Jean-François Thibault, and Jean-Bernard Parenteau, who worked as my assistants from 1991 to 1995. My hope is that this work is at least somewhat worthy of the efforts and contributions that so many people gave to this project; I am profoundly grateful to them.

Introduction

The Meaning of Events That Changed the World

1989 was an extraordinary year, a year when the world watched breathlessly as the Berlin Wall fell and, one by one, the Communist regimes of Eastern Europe tumbled—a year which truly changed the face of the world. The resulting shock to the international system was so profound that we still cannot determine how the new international order will be configured. In fact, the twentieth century, with its great struggles and issues, ended in 1989.

The most surprising event of that fateful year was not, in itself, the collapse of the East European regimes. The tragic events in Hungary in 1956, the Prague Spring of 1968, and the Polish crisis of 1981, with the sudden and dramatic rise of Solidarity, had demonstrated the great fragility of these regimes. The most remarkable and least expected event of 1989 was, in fact, the Soviet Union's attitude and behavior toward the changes taking place in Eastern Europe. That behavior was all the more surprising given that Soviet foreign policy had always been at its most rigid and intolerant with respect to Eastern Europe. Though this fact tends to be overlooked today, we ought to recall that the Soviet regime was still essentially intact in 1989. The Communist Party of the Soviet Union (CPSU) still held power in *all* of the Soviet republics, and no declarations of sovereignty had been made by any authorities on Soviet territory. In short, the disintegration of the USSR had not yet begun, and its armed forces were still solidly in place in Eastern Europe.

The "permissiveness" of the USSR must therefore be considered the great enigma of 1989. It is Soviet behavior that made it possible for such a fundamental transformation in the world order to take place peacefully. This is without precedent in modern history. In fact, war was not only avoided, but the changes took place without *any* major international tension. This is why studying the enigma of 1989 is so interesting and important. Moreover, such a study relates to another enigma that concerns the end of the USSR itself and "the Gorbachev endeavor," by which I mean his entire reform project. How could a political undertaking produce results that were so manifestly contrary to its architects' objectives and interests, without these architects themselves using their full range of powers to end the process? In addition, the interests at stake were those usually considered by political scientists to be the most fundamental interests of political elites. How could a regime with a full arsenal of powers at its disposal and with such a long tradition of violence and repression collapse so meekly?

Very little in the Soviet legacy is remembered, in the current context, as having been positive. With some irony, the way the USSR separated itself from its empire and its own peaceful end may seem to be its most beneficial contributions to history. These episodes are, in any case, masterpieces of history.

This book is dedicated to examining the questions raised above. It does not directly address the collapse of the East European regimes, which numerous works, often written in the midst of these events, have studied, with respect to the region or to specific countries. My central interest is in elucidating the policies and behavior of the Soviet Union toward Eastern Europe during the Gorbachev period. This includes examining the approaches, expectations, and objectives upon which Soviet initiatives and attitudes were based. The answers to these questions will clearly provide important insights into the ambitious designs of Gorbachev's foreign policy and into the murky changes that were transforming the Soviet political system.

The extreme rapidity of the events which engulfed Eastern Europe and the Soviet Union forced political analysts to concentrate on the most current events and possible immediate implications. As a result, they could not step back and put Soviet behavior in 1989 into proper perspective, nor could they explain its deeper causes and meaning. Soviet actions were generally interpreted at the time as a "cutting loose" or abandonment of a burden which had become too cumbersome. As will be shown in the pages that follow, this interpretation is largely mistaken.

Mikhail Gorbachev's policies in Eastern Europe during this critical period were an integral part of a much larger project. He sought to transform the international order in Europe by a *controlled* overcoming of the continent's division. From that controlled process (which demanded a gradual democratization of Eastern Europe), he expected the greatest benefits for the USSR. In spite, and even because of, the doubts and resistance of his conservative opponents, Gorbachev and his team believed that a reformed socialism in Eastern Europe was viable. They were convinced that by taking the initiative in democratizing these regimes, reformist Communist leaders could retain control of the process. When things began to unravel in Eastern Europe, Gorbachev's team first tried to deny the depth of the changes that were taking place and then tried to rationalize them in terms of their own emerging social-democratic view of the world. If they did not use force to interfere, it was to avoid compromising the basic tenets of the grand design in which they had invested so much, for example through spectacular proposals and unilateral disarmament measures. Seen in this light, Soviet behavior in 1989 represents the height of credibility of the USSR's new foreign policy and Gorbachev's most dramatic "hour of glory" on the international scene. Ironically, the sudden collapse of the East European regimes destroyed Gorbachev's European policy by removing the levers he needed to execute it.

The research presented here investigates the coherence and structure of Gorbachev's East European policy by examining his initiatives in Eastern Europe and their place in the larger framework of Soviet foreign policy. I have, however, also studiously avoided the trap of ex post facto reconstructions that might give political actions greater coherence than they actually had. For this reason, the pages that follow will also elucidate the role which improvisation, contradictions, and the absence of clear choices played in the developments of 1989. This component is crucial for constructing a satisfactory explanation of Soviet policy during the period.

While the focus is on explaining Gorbachev's policy toward Eastern Europe and, above all, on the place of that policy in the larger international context, this is clearly not a sufficient explanation of all the causal factors involved. Soviet foreign policy in the Gorbachev period highlights what is always true of foreign policy: it is largely a derivative of domestic politics. Hence, frequent reference will be made to the links between these two policy areas. In addition, in order to fully comprehend the causes of Soviet behavior in 1989, studying a deeper level of domestic policy is necessary. Two fundamental and related areas of investigation must be mentioned in this regard.

First, the decades-long persistence of the USSR in maintaining the regimes of Eastern Europe, despite constant resistance and high economic and political costs, must be understood in the framework of the particular system of legitimization underlying Soviet rule. Rather than being based on popular suffrage, its legitimacy rested mainly on the affirmation of socialism's historical superiority over capitalism and the conviction that this system represented the future of humanity. The existence of a "world socialist system" demonstrated, to the Soviet leadership and its populace, that the October Revolution and the Soviet regime were not accidents of history but rather possessed a universal value and importance. Gorbachev's search for a different, more democratic, system of legitimization made it possible for the Soviet leadership to absorb the shock of the East European regimes' collapse. In this sense, my examination of Soviet policy toward Eastern Europe sheds important light on the changes taking place not only in its foreign policy but also in the USSR's domestic political system.

Second, a necessary condition for executing Soviet policies toward Eastern Europe in the late 1980s was the Soviet regime's adoption of a new view of the world and of its role in it. This world view, which I term an "ideology of transition," bore the imprint of Marxism and Leninism, despite the fact that it was superseding those ideologies. The new world view exhibited a Promethean ambition to change the existing world order, based on new, universal values. In typically Leninist and voluntarist fashion, it overestimated the possibility for shaping and channeling the course of international events. Gorbachev and his team were convinced that they had understood the important characteristics of an emerging new world order and planned to give the USSR a renewed political and moral leadership role in international affairs through their new ideology. As will be shown, this ideology of transition (which will be explored below) had two specific functions. First, it served as a support which allowed the new Soviet leadership to take the risks inherent in its East European initiatives. Second, the ideology's mobilizational and inspirational character (accompanied by the successes Gorbachev achieved on the international scene through 1989) helped neutralize conservative opponents within the USSR. Understanding the ideology of transition thus helps explain how the monumental changes of 1989 could be achieved without any major international crisis.

The East European regimes' unexpected collapse in 1989 removed the initiative Mikhail Gorbachev had held on the international scene until that time. Consequently, the ideology of transition, his support and weapon, was thrown into disarray. The collapse of those regimes greatly contributed to his loss of control over the domestic political situation in the Soviet Union itself, which he had commanded fairly well until then. Only after the fall of the allied Communist regimes did Gorbachev's foreign policy, which had been the most successful sphere of *perestroika,* became the object of open criticism, especially by the military.

The factors mentioned above explain why the events in Eastern Europe—and Soviet policies pertaining to them—constitute the breaking point between the success and failure of Gorbachev's great, historic endeavor.

PART I

The Place of Eastern Europe in Gorbachev's Political Project

CHAPTER ONE

Gorbachev's Foreign Policy and the Nature of His Enterprise

THE INHERITANCE AND THE PRIORITIES

When Mikhail Gorbachev took power in March 1985, nothing suggested that, seven years later, the USSR would have ceased to exist. Certainly, the new Soviet leader inherited numerous and difficult problems. The situation in the USSR, albeit not very enviable, did not seem desperate—at least in the short run.

For twenty years, the Soviet economy's growth rate had been declining slowly but constantly. In 1985, the rate was about 3 percent per year, according to the statistics known by the leaders and admitted at the time. Even if such a growth rate was comparable to those of several Western economies, it was definitely insufficient for the Soviet Union to catch up with—let alone surpass—those nations, as the Soviet regime had always promised. Increasing growth rates through a heavier mobilization of resources and the work force was no longer possible. The alternative, which would have been improved labor productivity and technological innovation, was structurally incompatible with the Soviet economic system. In addition, the growth rate, while superficially similar to that of Western economies, obscured one important fact: in the most strategic areas of global economic development, the Soviet Union had not only lost any hope of catching up with the West but was falling ever further behind.

Therefore, it was not imminent collapse but rather a continual decline that threatened the Soviet economic system. History has frequently shown that the decline of a great power can span a very long period of time. It is precisely the measures which Gorbachev and his associates undertook to redress the USSR's economic situation and to renew its international competitiveness that precipitated its unexpected economic and political collapse. The choices they made in this regard were far from being inevitable or predetermined—which explains the interest involved in analyzing their program.

Many more political initiatives than strictly economic ones were undertaken in the attempt to redress the economic situation. We will come back to the meaning of this paradox. It should be pointed out at the onset, however, that one would not be guilty of economic determinism for believing that the USSR's economic situation and problems were the most fundamental cause of *perestroika* and Gorbachev's undertaking, though they are also totally inadequate as a full explanation for his grand design. Any reading of Gorbachev's speeches in 1985 and 1986 is sufficient to demonstrate his initial preoccupations and motivations. He constantly and purposefully dramatized the economic problems in order to mobilize the Party apparatus and the Soviet population and to convince them that urgent measures were needed to correct the situation—measures which, at the time, were still largely undetermined. In other words, had there not been economic "stagnation," the need for democratization would have been put in far less pressing terms. If the political changes were initially conceived to support economic restructuring, they subsequently were "autonomized," becoming goals unto themselves with their own dynamic. To a lesser extent, the same phenomenon was observable in the sphere of foreign policy.

Since World War II, and even before, Soviet power and influence internationally had been incommensurate with the size and general performance of its economy. Its political and ideological clout on the international scene, which began to exhaust itself at the end of the 1960s, was gradually replaced by its growing military might, thus compensating for the economic attributes of power.

Long before Gorbachev's accession to power, international politics had been the area of the USSR's most remarkable achievements. Its catching up on the military level with the Western powers, and most notably with the United States, had progressed successfully, and more quickly than most expected. By the early 1970s, the USSR had become a military superpower on a par with the United States, a fact which the American leadership grudgingly acknowledged. Without going into the fastidious and ongoing debate about the importance and comparative cost of Soviet military expenditures,[1] it is easy to understand the enormous drain they represented on the USSR, simply on the basis of the considerable discrepancy between the U.S. and Soviet GNP. The Soviet Union's best human, technical, and material resources were siphoned off by the military sector. This primacy of political and strategic goals over economic considerations thoroughly reflected the Soviet regime's fundamental characteristics, a point to which we shall return below.

With its 1980 invasion of Afghanistan, the Soviet Union reached the apex of its international power. The previous decade had witnessed an expansionist thrust of Soviet power and political influence unparalleled since the end of World War II. It was achieved through vigorous political and military support for diverse armed interventions undertaken by the USSR's Third World allies. Their actions, conditioned by their own strategic interests, shifted the geopolitical balance significantly in favor of the USSR.[2] Certain events merit being briefly recalled, if only to put into perspective the dynamic nature of Soviet power and the dominant perception of it at the time.

In 1971, India attacked Pakistan with Soviet support, taking advantage of its civil war and finalizing Pakistan's dismemberment. Through its decisive assistance, the USSR consolidated its alliance with India, to the detriment of the interests of China and the United States, Pakistan's traditional allies. Cuba's armed intervention in Angola in 1975, supported by Soviet airlifts, assured victory for the pro-Soviet Popular Movement for the Liberation of Angola and checked South Africa's own military actions. This success, the fragility of which was universally underestimated, considerably increased Cuban and Soviet stature in Africa. Two years later, Cuba again intervened massively (and, as before, with assistance from the USSR), this time to prevent the dismemberment of Ethiopia, the United States's erstwhile regional ally.

The strategic positions the Soviet Union acquired in Africa during the second half of the 1970s seemed to open important new possibilities for

---

1. On the difficulties and the question's quasi-intractability, see Carl G. Jacobsen, *The Soviet Defense Enigma: Estimating Costs and Burdens* (Oxford: Oxford University Press, 1987).

2. Each of its actions was driven by a remarkable estimation of the weaknesses of its enemies, both direct and indirect, allowing the Soviet Union to minimize the risks involved. See Jacques Lévesque, "L'URSS et l'activité militaire de ses alliés dans le tiers-monde," *International Journal* 37 (2), Spring 1982, pp. 285–307.

the expansion of its naval power, which had undergone a period of spectacular growth in the preceding years. From the coast of Angola, for example, exerting pressure on shipping lanes around the Cape became distinctly feasible. Even more menacingly, the Soviet presence in Ethiopia and South Yemen could allow it to flex the increasingly strong muscle of its fleet in a region of vital economic importance for the West.[3]

In 1978, three years after the Saigon regime's fall had sealed the U.S. defeat in Vietnam, the Hanoi regime scored a new and important victory with the help of its Soviet allies. After signing a mutual assistance treaty with the USSR and having received new armaments from it, Vietnam invaded Cambodia, putting an end to the Pol Pot regime and establishing hegemony over all of Indochina. Shortly thereafter, Vietnam ceded the former U.S. base at Cam Ranh Bay to the Soviet Union. The USSR subsequently enlarged the base, and it became its most important military installation outside the Soviet Union, playing a pivotal role in balancing both China and American naval power in Asia.

Direct military intervention was the path the Soviet leadership chose to deal with Afghanistan in 1979. This time, its action shocked the world and provoked a major international crisis. The invasion of Afghanistan came on the heels of armed interventions by Soviet allies elsewhere in the Third World, which had somewhat obscured Soviet expansionism. This time, the case was utterly blatant. More importantly, however, the Soviet invasion began only months after the fall of the Shah in Iran, the United States's staunchest and most powerful ally in the region. In the context of the Western oil "psychosis" that had begun in 1973, Washington interpreted the invasion of Afghanistan as a major strategic thrust toward the Persian Gulf; the next step would be the subjugation of Iran or a new dismemberment of Pakistan.[4] The invasion of Afghanistan, and the military and political successes which preceded it, appeared to a growing number of observers as well-defined steps toward the implementation of a vast plan for world domination that had been prepared with great skill and cunning.[5] The more alarmist among them

3. On projections and the depth of Western concern resulting from the expansion of Soviet power in Africa, see Richard B. Remnek, *Soviet Military Interests in Africa in the 1980s* (U.S. Army War College, 1986).

4. See the tenor of reports made to President Carter by the head of the National Security Council: Zbigniew K. Brzezinski, *Power and Principle: Memoirs of the National Security Adviser, 1977–1981* (New York: Farrar, Strauss & Giroux, 1987), p. 567.

5. Hélène Carrère d'Encausse makes this point explicitly in her book, *Ni paix ni guerre* (Paris: Flammarion, 1986). To the question she poses: "Is such a growth of power the result of a coherent strategy which one can define in terms of its methods and goals?", she

claimed that the USSR had gained general military superiority over the West, even in the area of strategic thinking, and that it had practically already won World War III without a shot being fired.[6]

If the West overestimated Soviet strength and capacities, the same was true of Moscow.[7] Its international successes had contributed significantly to legitimizing the system, masking the gravity of its problems and allowing the postponement of difficult choices.

Nonetheless, beginning in 1980, the neglected economy began to take revenge on the USSR's political achievements abroad. Having just reached the summit of its influence, signs of the Soviet Union's decline appeared, though no one at the time could foresee the rapidity of that decline. First and foremost, it was the serious economic and social crisis which struck at the very heart of the "world socialist system," in Eastern Europe's largest country, Poland, that highlighted these problems. Its economic crisis turned into a virtual political collapse. While not Poland's first crisis, the 1980–1981 one was of an unprecedented magnitude. Most disconcerting of all, after thirty-five years of repeated efforts, the regime had not only been incapable of solidifying its hold on power but found itself on the brink of total disaster.

Elsewhere, it became clear quite quickly that the USSR was unable to consolidate the new allies acquired during the 1970s, not only on an economic level (which was nothing new) but, more importantly, on a military level. In Angola, Mozambique, Afghanistan, Cambodia, and Nicaragua, regimes allied with the Soviet Union faced guerrilla wars, and, for the most part, their military position deteriorated. Wherever possible, the Reagan administration, while simultaneously pursuing a massive rearmament program, also provided growing levels of military aid to the regimes' opponents. For their part, Soviet leaders began to realize that it was far more expensive to maintain a regime in power than to destabilize it. In short, the USSR found itself in a position

---

answers in the affirmative. In conclusion, she states: "Brezhnev may be forgotten by his successors, temporarily erased from the history of his country—a frequent practice in the USSR—but that doesn't matter. He has assured himself of a place in the pantheon of geopolitics" (pp. 366 and 379).

6. See Cornelius Castoriadis, *Devant la guerre* (Paris: Le livre de poche, 1983); Edward Luttwak, *La stratégie de l'impérialisme soviétique* (Paris: Anthropos, 1985).

7. As of 1975, the Soviet foreign minister, Andrei Gromyko, was writing that the USSR and the global "forces of peace" had become strong enough to "determine the direction of international political matters." See Andrei A. Gromyko, "Programma mira v deistvii" (The Program for Peace in Action), *Kommunist*, 14, September 1975.

of overextension at a time when its own economic capacities were diminishing.

Yuri Andropov's short tenure was marked by a few limited steps to redress the domestic situation while simultaneously making efforts to reduce Soviet commitments in the Third World. His intention, however, was to do so *selectively,* solidly maintaining Soviet commitments to those regimes which were most important to it, so as not to appear to be capitulating or even ceding to U.S. pressure. Simply maintaining positions in a situation where the adversary is increasing his pressure can, however, require new commitments. This is what happened in Angola, Syria, and Vietnam, for example.

At the same time, with respect to the global strategic military balance, Andropov showed as much determination as both his predecessor and his immediate successor to maintain the closest possible parity with the West. Hence, the most important diplomatic issue for the USSR in the first half of the 1980s became the "battle of the Euromissiles," as absurd as that may now seem. Soviet obstinacy on this issue is very telling. From the Soviet perspective, the stationing of U.S. missiles in Europe was a means for the United States to bypass the SALT agreements,[8] which had enshrined strategic parity between the two superpowers. These new missiles could reach the Soviet central strategic systems, without the United States having to use its own intercontinental missiles. Andropov's final concession in 1983 to prevent the deployment of the new U.S. missiles was his offer to reduce the number and payload of Soviet SS-20 missiles in Europe to the combined level of French and British missiles. The persistent refusal of the West to include French and British nuclear weapons in the European strategic equation seemed to the Soviet leadership to be an intolerable assault on the principle of strategic equality. The *status* of the USSR as an *equal* superpower, purchased at such a high price, was at stake, and the Soviet leaders clung to it, regardless of any other considerations. This led Yuri Andropov and Andrei Gromyko to end all arms control negotiations and dramatize the deterioration of Soviet-U.S. relations, in the illusory hope that the West could not get by without some modicum of detente and cooperation with the Soviet superpower and that negotiations would be resumed on a basis acceptable to the Soviets.[9]

8. While the U.S. Senate had not ratified SALT II, due to the Soviet invasion of Afghanistan, Washington did abide by the treaty's provisions for many years.

9. See Jacques Lévesque, *L'URSS et sa politique internationale. De Lénine à Gorbatchev* (Paris: Armand Colin, 1988), pp. 353–361.

Meanwhile, Ronald Reagan had launched his famous Strategic Defense Initiative (SDI), which he himself had dubbed "Star Wars." This project threatened Soviet-U.S. parity even more and risked drawing the USSR into a new arms race at an incredible cost, given that the new technologies involved in SDI were ones which the Soviet economy was particularly poorly equipped to develop.

These factors illustrate why, upon Gorbachev's accession to power, the main items on both the domestic and international agendas pertained to the economy. The Soviet Union's economic capacity to support its foreign policy was diminishing constantly. It rapidly became clear that Gorbachev intended to subordinate foreign policy to the imperatives of correcting the domestic economy to a far greater degree than his predecessors. The priority given to the economy was to impact directly on foreign policy, and both Mikhail Gorbachev and Eduard Shevardnadze were most explicit and eloquent on this point.[10] Logically, therefore, foreign policy should have been seriously downsized compared to domestic economic policy, in terms of importance, attention, and articulation.

Despite that, however, the new foreign policy was articulated far more quickly than economic policy and was innovative much sooner. It also became a far more coherent and better defined project than economic policy ever was to be. Up until the beginning of 1990, foreign policy also probably remained Gorbachev's main preoccupation and was the sphere in which he enjoyed his greatest successes. It was as if the primacy of politics over economics remained an iron law of the Soviet system, even in flux—a law which the leaders, despite their own intentions, could not escape.

---

10. In an important speech for internal use which Shevardnadze gave before the personnel of his ministry, he said: "If the thesis that the goal of diplomacy is to create a favorable environment for domestic development is accurate—and, without a doubt, it is—we must recognize that our straggling behind and the constant decline of our stature is also partially our fault."

"Outside of the borders of the USSR, you and I represent a country which in the last fifteen years has constantly lost ground compared to other industrialized nations. . . . We have frequently encouraged, and sometimes even caused, massive material investments in hopeless foreign policy projects, and we recommended actions which, either directly or indirectly, cost the people dearly, even up to now. Our principal duty is to ensure that our state does not incur additional expenses for the maintenance of its defense capabilities. . . . This means that we must search for ways to limit and reduce the military rivalry, to eliminate elements of confrontation in our relations with other states, and to suppress conflicts and crisis situations. . . . We must increase the profitability of our foreign policy and attempt to reach a situation where our interrelations with other states put the least possible burden on our economy." See *Vestnik Ministerstva Inostrannykh Del SSSR* 2, 1987, pp. 30–34.

ELEMENTS OF CONTINUITY
FROM THE INHERITANCE

In order to understand the dimensions and purpose of Gorbachev's foreign policy, we must at this point briefly stress some of the elements that characterized the Soviet regime.

To take into account the uniqueness and peculiarities of Leninist regimes, Kenneth Jowitt developed a conceptual approach based on Max Weber's writings concerning types of legitimate domination.[11] This approach is particularly useful for understanding several of the fundamental features of these regimes, which show remarkable similarities irrespective of such radically different cultural contexts as those of Russia and China, for instance.

According to Max Weber, history has produced three broad types of domination or power: a "traditional" domination "resting on an established belief in the sanctity of immemorial traditions and the legitimacy of those exercising authority under them";[12] a more modern form of domination, termed "rational-legal," "resting on an belief in the legality of enacted rules and the right of those elevated to authority under such rules to issue commands"; and a "charismatic" domination, which rests on support for an individual because of his or her "heroic," "exceptional," or "extraordinary character," and a capacity to produce "miracles," whatever the nature of those may be. For Weber and others inspired by his thinking, this last concept has an important, and often unexpected, heuristic value for explaining revolutionary phenomena through the ages and, quite simply, for understanding "political innovation."[13] We might add that by its very nature, charismatic power abhors legal rules and frameworks, economic calculations, or "routine."

To be clear, these three types of power did not, for Weber, grow out of each other, nor was there any particular or necessary order of succession of the three throughout history. All three were conceived as

---

11. Jowitt's first important work on this approach was *The Leninist Response to National Dependency* (Berkeley: Institute of International Studies, University of California, 1978), which he later developed broadly and which exercised an important influence on the study of Communist regimes in the United States. That text was reprinted recently in a collection of essays developing those same concepts: Kenneth Jowitt, *New World Disorder: The Leninist Extinction* (Berkeley: University of California Press, 1992).

12. Max Weber, *Economy and Society: An Outline of Interpretative Sociology,* 3 vols., ed. Günter Rothet and Claus Wittich (New York: Bedminster Press, 1968), p. 215.

13. Julien Freund, "Le charisme selon Max Weber," *Social Compass* 23 (4), 1976, pp. 383–396.

"ideal types," as he points out: "The forms of domination occurring in historical reality constitute combinations, mixtures, adaptations or modifications of these 'pure' types."[14] Charismatic domination, in particular, is prone over time to a "routinization," that is to say, to an evolution toward one of the two other broad ideal types.

According to Jowitt, Leninist regimes constitute a historically new form of charismatic domination. Their uniqueness lies in the fact that they integrate, in a situation of permanent conflict and tension with them, potent modernizing imperatives and important elements of rational-legal domination, which they seek to be transcending. This explains Jowitt's deliberate use of the contradictory term "charismatic-impersonal" power to describe these regimes. It is the Party which is the agent of charismatic power and the bearers of the "heroic" enterprise, producing "miracles," even if the regime is often dominated by one individual who shares in the charismatic glow. In order to accomplish its "exceptional" mission, the Party calls for combat and sacrifice (specific characteristics of charismatic power), but also practices the cult of scientific and economic progress and calls for empirical research, organization, and rigorous, carefully regulated discipline. It is within these conflicting imperatives that we begin to appreciate the particular configurations which shaped the dynamic and evolution of Leninist regimes. For instance, these imperatives explain one characteristic trait of the regimes, which is the combination of optimism and unbridled idealism on the one hand, with cold, calculating, often even cynical realism and pragmatism on the other.

According to Weber, charismatic domination is "specifically foreign to the economy." It may, therefore, at first glance seem contradictory for Jowitt to classify Leninist regimes as modes of charismatic domination, while simultaneously affirming that economic development is one of their fundamental preoccupations. But this is precisely what illuminates their approach to economic development. It was conceived and organized as a heroic enterprise, outside of the calculations and rules of "ordinary" economics. We need only recall the way in which the collectivization of agriculture and the five-year plans under Stalin, the "Great Leap Forward" in China, or the "Grand Zafra" in Cuba were conceived and carried out, and the "miracles" they promised. Under Nikita Khrushchev, the same approach is revealed in his Virgin Lands scheme, which intended to solve the agricultural sector's problems; and in the 1961 program for "large-scale construction of Communism," which

14. Weber, *Economy and Society,* p. 954.

promised that Soviet living standards would surpass those of the U.S. in the 1980s. This approach accounts for the propensity to gigantism in industrial enterprises and the common negligence of light industry and commercial networks, which were deemed less likely to rapidly produce "grandiose" and mobilizing results. *In short, it explains the tendency for Leninist regimes to give primacy to politics, even in economic matters.*

All of the above considerations are aimed at developing a better understanding of the genetic code of Gorbachev's pattern of behavior (and that of his entourage), while stressing that they are clearly not mere repetitions of past experiences.

Given the banalization or "routinization" which, according to Weber, eventually beset charismatic domination, the longevity of the Soviet regime—or rather its capacity to retain various attributes of this type—may seem surprising. The regime did not, however, escape banalization. As Jowitt points out, Leninist parties need an environment of struggle in order to preserve their cohesion as charismatic organizations.[15] Brezhnev's era, however, was marked by the absence, on the domestic level, of combat and "exceptional" tasks. The regime experienced its greatest slide toward a "neo-traditional" form of power. This characterization points to the regime's efforts to preserve Marxist-Leninist orthodoxy and its "rites" in the functioning of the economy, the political apparatus, and public life as if these were an unalterable inheritance—despite their growing incapacity to deal with the problems facing the economy and society.[16] The Party had simply become the sum of its members' interests. Without a doubt, only its successes in the international sphere could sustain and legitimize the exceptional character of the regime's "mission."

Mikhail Gorbachev and his team did not simply intend to reconnect with the "heroic" origins of the Soviet regime and the October Revolution in order to bring the USSR out of the era of "stagnation" (*zastoi,* as they termed it). They did, of course, constantly repeat that intention,

---

15. Kenneth Jowitt, "Soviet Neotraditionalism: The Political Corruption of a Leninist Regime," *Soviet Studies,* 3, July 1983, pp. 275–297; reedited and reprinted in Jowitt, *New World Disorder,* p. 126.

16. For an original and stimulating analysis that builds on the approaches of Weber and Jowitt in order to explain, in a remarkably innovative way, the great milestones of the development and application of Marxism, from Marx to Gorbachev, see Stephen E. Hanson, "Gorbachev: The Last True Leninist Believer," in Daniel Chirot, ed., *The Crisis of Leninism and the Decline of the Left* (Seattle: University of Washington Press, 1991), pp. 74–99.

and not only to defend against or mislead Communist conservatives. They wanted to invigorate the Soviet economy by putting it on a new basis, hence restoring the USSR's international competitiveness. *Symptomatically, however, that effort rapidly became a vast political struggle, calling for the mobilization of the entire society. Politics became the key instrument for bringing about economic reforms.* Gorbachev's own comments on this subject are particularly poignant: "Politics is without a doubt the most important aspect of any revolutionary process, and that is equally true of *perestroika.* This is why we are giving priority to political measures, to a broad and authentic democratization, . . . and to the active participation of the masses in the management of the nation's affairs."[17]

It should be noted, however, that the search for political solutions to economic problems, while typical, was not an obligatory outcome dictated by the nature of the Soviet regime. China, which was emerging not from a period of stagnation but rather from the latest version of the voluntaristic Cultural Revolution, pursued economic reform in a purely pragmatic fashion, first allowing peasants to take back their land. Its leaders did not embark on any large social mobilization and had no pretense of beginning a new revolution or developing a new, more "socialist" socialism than that which preceded it. In the Chinese case, one could term this a "modernist banalization" of the regime, which certainly threatens its integrity. Several economists in the USSR favored a similar pragmatic approach, but a consideration of whether such an effort could have succeeded in the Soviet Union, as in China, lies outside the scope of this book.

The fact is that Mikhail Gorbachev wanted to put in place a totally new model of socialism, building on a realistic assessment of the vicissitudes that had beset previous experiences. Conscious of the "command economy's" impasse, he planned to borrow mechanisms from the market economy in order to create a mixed economy in which the state (or socialist) sector would remain dominant but would be reinvigorated by the presence of the private and cooperative sectors and by new rules of interaction. This was the meaning of the reforms introduced in 1987. Gorbachev, like the Italian Communist Party in the 1970s and early 1980s, was looking for a "third way."[18] He remained deeply convinced

17. Mikhail Gorbachev, *Perestroika: Vues neuves sur notre pays et le monde* (Paris: Flammarion, 1987), p. 71.
18. See *Socialismo Reale e Terza Via* (Rome: Editori Riuniti, 1982).

of the October Revolution's founding principles and of their exceptional virtues. This is reflected in his statement that, "Socialism has proven that it possesses, as a societal system, immense potential for resolving the most complicated problems encountered in social progress. We are convinced that it has the ability to perfect itself, that its possibilities will offer us many more *revelations.*"[19]

Various expressions used by Soviet leaders in this period would undoubtedly have put a smile on Max Weber's face. Commenting, for example, on Gorbachev's continued faith in being able to save the Union, even after the August 1991 coup attempt, his spokesman of the time, Andrei Grachev, wrote: "He had become so good at convincing the rest of the world of his ability *to perform political miracles* that perhaps he eventually believed it himself."[20]

If *perestroika* as an ideology and an "heroic project" was typically Leninist in its impulse and general style, its objectives and several of its methods were at variance with fundamental features of the Soviet regime. In retrospect, the most remarkable of these discontinuities was the refusal to use violence, which characterized *perestroika* from beginning to end. One could, of course, invoke the bloody repressions in Lithuania and Latvia in early 1991. Given the magnitude of what was at stake, however, these incidents were so minor that they actually tend to confirm my point. Even Western democracies are more willing to resort to violence to preserve their territorial integrity or existence. The refusal by Gorbachev and his entourage to use violence and repression are so striking that they reveal a fundamental option of an ideological character. It was so strong that even the putschists of August 1991 (emerging from among the right wing of his associates) did not dare open fire in order to prevail. Given Gorbachev's frequent declarations that he would not hesitate to use force if necessary, it must be noted that it is only in retrospect that the absence of violence became so remarkable. Gorbachev's declarations remained only political weapons.

Another fundamental break with Soviet tradition, related to the one outlined above, concerns democratization and the role of the Party. Certainly the term "democratization," as a slogan, had long been present in Soviet rhetoric, and that is why it took some time for the process to be taken seriously, not only abroad, but also in the USSR itself. Without

19. Gorbachev, *Perestroika*, p. 123; emphasis added.
20. Andrei Grachev, *L'histoire vraie de la fin de l'URSS* (Monaco: Éditions du Rocher, 1992), p. 11; emphasis added.

renouncing the leading role of the Party, Gorbachev began to speak of political pluralism for the Soviet Union in 1987. Only slowly and confusingly did the importance of this ambiguous, if not contradictory, concept become clear. Through this process, he began to redefine the Party's exclusive place and role in the state, the economy, and society. To do this, he allowed various independent groups to appear on each of those levels, while simultaneously trying to maintain the Party's position as political arbitrator. Gorbachev was convinced that socialist culture had sufficiently permeated Soviet society to allow such changes to take place without calling into question the ability of a thoroughly reformed Party to keep a central position in the system.

In their search for a new model of socialist pluralism, the new leaders of the CPSU and their circle of intellectuals were engaging themselves in a process of social-democratization, more or less without being conscious thereof.[21] While there had been previous efforts in this direction within the world Communist movement, their scale and consequences were far less important. Indeed, the Italian Communist Party had undergone a tortuous, difficult, and divisive social-democratic mutation in the late 1970s and early 1980s, searching for a "third way" between the Soviet model and social democracy.[22] We will come back later to this comparison with the Italian Communist Party's experience and its kinship with Gorbachev's enterprise. In the Soviet case, the "heroic" character which enveloped the quest for a new utopia was undoubtedly an indispensable condition for the implementation of the process of mutation which, of course, had begun to germinate among different Soviet intellectual circles[23] well before Gorbachev's accession to power. I have termed Gorbachev's project a new utopia, in its global dimension—in fact, precisely because of that dimension. As will be shown, several of

---

21. It may suffice to cite just one recent, and particularly revealing, testimonial. In the present context, numerous Russian intellectuals have found it opportune to portray themselves as "always" having been democrats unable to come out of the closet before. Georgii Arbatov, one of the chief practitioners of both the ideology and practice of *perestroika*, has no such pretense. In his 1993 memoirs, he writes: "In the spring of 1985, I was a Communist, with doubts and disappointments, but still a convinced Communist. . . . I still have not lost my faith in the core of a socialist ideal that is much closer to the social-democratic variant than to the Bolshevik one." Georgii Arbatov, *The System: An Insider's Life In Soviet Politics* (New York: Random House, 1993), pp. 352, 358.

22. See Jacques Lévesque, *Italian Communists versus the Soviet Union: The PCI Charts a New Foreign Policy* (Berkeley: Institute of International Studies, University of California, 1987), pp. 27–42.

23. On the ideological and political origins of Soviet innovations under Gorbachev, see Allen Lynch, *Gorbachev's International Outlook: Intellectual Origins and Political Consequences* (New York: Institute for East-West Security Studies, 1989).

its elements often rested on a very realistic analysis of international issues and interests.

DISARMAMENT AS AN EMPIRICAL NECESSITY AND STANDARD-BEARER OF THE GRAND DESIGN

Even before Paul Kennedy's best-seller appeared on bookstands,[24] Gorbachev and his closest advisers had realized that military overextension and disproportionately large military expenditures (compared to the general economic performance of a state) were among the clearest indicators of any great power's decline. As a logical result of this, and of subordinating foreign policy to the most fundamental objective, resuscitating the Soviet economy, the first task in the international arena had to be disengaging the Soviet Union from the arms race and from armed conflicts in which it was directly or indirectly involved. These were goals that seemed easily identifiable and would permit a relaxation of the international situation, allowing the USSR a more favorable climate for pursuing economic reforms.

Soviet disengagement from armed conflicts in the Third World was somewhat delayed by the fact that it necessitated the consent of many allies and parties resolved] concerned. Hence, issues relating to disarmament took center stage. To expedite matters, Soviet leaders could have taken immediate steps, by simply reducing their military expenditures and reallocating their resources, bypassing the field of foreign policy. This was both too simple and too difficult. On the one hand, the weight of the Soviet legacy and Gorbachev's perception, albeit in flux, of the Soviet Union's place and role in the world, made this option impractical. On the other hand, we should remember that the USSR's situation did not appear desperate to anyone at the time.

Military power was the area in which the Soviet Union excelled, above and beyond all other fields. After all, it was Soviet performance and competitiveness in this sphere that secured it recognition by the United States as an equal power with equal rights at the beginning of the 1970s and its influence in the world at large. The entire, dominant Soviet political culture highly prized military power. Even if Gorbachev and those intellectuals involved in supporting and structuring his project understood the limits and costs of military might better than their pre-

24. Paul Kennedy, *The Rise and Fall of the Great Powers* (New York: Random House, 1987).

decessors, and were ready to downsize it, they intended to do so by sacrificing as little of the USSR's international power and influence as possible. In order to do so, they needed to bring the United States back to the arms control negotiating table.

While awaiting better tools, military power and armaments were the most effective ones the USSR could use to influence U.S. behavior. Therefore, Gorbachev chose arms control and disarmament as a means for changing the international situation. They became the main instrument of his foreign policy and gave him the stature he enjoyed on the international scene until 1989. *From simple necessity, disarmament became more than a program on its own. Gorbachev's grand design and the messianic, innovative character of his international policy all crystallized around the modalities and finalities of arms control, its related issues, and the multifaceted advantages the USSR hoped to gain from it.*

When Nikita Khrushchev proclaimed to the 20th CPSU Congress in 1956 that war was no longer inevitable, despite the continued existence of imperialism, he not only broke with the teachings of Lenin; his declaration also signalled a serious downsizing of the antagonism between the Soviet Union and the United States. Khrushchev pointed out, however, that this had happened because of the USSR and the socialist camp's power, and particularly its military strength, which had made imperialist leaders "more reasonable." This belief or faith in the educational and other "virtues" of Soviet military power were even reinforced during the Brezhnev era. It was held to be responsible for almost all the achievements made in managing East-West relations. From this vantage point, there could never be too many weapons; they were, one might say, "like money in the bank." Of course, arms control agreements were deemed useful for limiting costs and avoiding unpleasant surprises. But the treaties were to be concluded on the basis of the strictest parity, a parity sought not only in relation to the United States, but also between the USSR and the rest of the Western world and even China. Its stance in negotiations on Euromissiles had clearly demonstrated this. In areas where there was no agreement, the stockpiling of weapons, even on a unilateral basis, could only produce multifaceted advantages. This is why the program to develop the SS-20 missiles in Europe had been started and considered useful in the mid-1970s—although detente was then at its strongest on the continent.

As the question of the Euromissiles was at the center of Soviet diplomacy from 1980 to 1983 and was the subject of the first agreement concluded by Gorbachev, it is very revelatory on several levels. An analysis of this issue allows us to understand the differences in approaches and behavior that distinguished Gorbachev from his predecessors and the broader implications of those differences.

In 1983, the Soviet Union ended all arms control negotiations in progress with the United States, following the Reagan administration's refusal of the latest Soviet offers and the beginning of the U.S. Euromissile deployment. Subsequently, the USSR announced that it would increase the number of the already redundant SS-20s and would proceed with the deployment of new short-range missiles in Czechoslovakia and East Germany. Moscow intended these measure to be a demonstration of the ease with which it could surpass the United States in a European arms race and that it was in American interests to conclude mutually acceptable agreements with the USSR. It was a "tit for tat" approach. With a particularly hard-nosed adversary, the Soviets deemed it useful to double the stakes.

Realizing that the Soviet Union was in a weak negotiating position compared to the United States and that time was not on their side, Gorbachev and his team judged that attempts to impose or insist on absolute parity with the United States as a military superpower would be in vain. Since they did, however, intend to conserve as equal a status as possible, the U.S. "Star Wars" initiative—particularly destabilizing both in terms of the military equilibrium and of costs—became Gorbachev's main obsession. Since Gorbachev was being stonewalled on this issue, he hoped that the early conclusion of a treaty on Euromissiles would create a dynamic.

The Reagan administration was the worst U.S. partner Gorbachev could have gotten for achieving any type of mutually advantageous arms control agreement. At the beginning of 1986, he basically accepted the zero-option proposal on Euromissiles initially proposed by President Reagan in 1981. This was an important concession, given that it implied renouncing the principle of strict and rigid parity, which had been the battle cry of his predecessors. Just as Gorbachev dropped the demand to include British and French missiles in the European strategic equation, the United States presented new demands.

In May 1986, as Gorbachev was preparing to accept the zero-option proposal, the United States announced that it intended to exceed the ceilings fixed by the SALT II treaty which, while unratified, had been respected up until that point. Several U.S. senators and military experts warned the administration against a complete disregard of SALT II. They suggested that the Soviet Union was in a much better position than the

United States (given that its production lines were already in place) to rapidly and inexpensively multiply its number of intercontinental missiles, thereby surpassing the United States in that area by a significant margin. Not only did the Soviet Union not engage in any such reprisals, but it never even threatened to do so. Gorbachev was convinced that the USSR no longer had the means to continue engaging in "tit for tat" behavior. It also would have contradicted the general approach begun in 1985, which was to remain uninterrupted, despite the obstacles it encountered.

This approach consisted of putting in place what one might called a controlled avalanche of propositions on arms control, each of which was accompanied by often unilateral concessions approaching U.S. demands. In the absence of U.S. concessions, the idea was to put the Reagan administration increasingly on the defensive, with respect to both European public opinion and the U.S. Congress; it would hence seem like an anachronistic government, unable to seize great historical opportunities. It was the exact reverse of a "tit for tat" approach. In order to finally "seal" the treaty on Intermediate Nuclear Forces (INF), signed in December 1987, Gorbachev was obliged to accept terms forcing the Soviet side to destroy twice as many missiles and three times more nuclear charges than the United States.[25]

To justify this approach against domestic criticism, Gorbachev and his allies began speaking, in 1986, of "new thinking," the famous *novoe myshlenie,* which became their main objective and slogan in the sphere of foreign policy. The same year, they presented the idea of "reasonable sufficiency." The reformers argued that in the nuclear age, an understanding of parity in the framework of compensating every missile with another was absurd, since the military arsenals of both superpowers were already colossal and excessive, and more than capable of destroying the other state.

If Gorbachev enjoyed great success on the level of international public opinion, it was because his approach reflected a view long held by most people to be common sense. They had watched, with feelings of impotence and growing frustration, a seemingly endless, destructive arms race. That is why the USSR under Gorbachev appeared to be the power willing to reverse the absurd logic of the arms race. Its policy was all the more impressive, its impact stronger, as it was seen as the free (and reversible) choice of a stable superpower. Incidentally, there is no doubt

---

25. See Thierry Malleret and Murielle Delaporte, *L'Armée rouge face à la perestroika* (Brussels: Complexe, 1991), p. 222.

that if the USSR had remained a stable superpower, the pressure of international public opinion on the U.S. government would have grown, given that it was already on the defensive in the face of Gorbachev's proposals in 1987–1988.[26]

Having an effect on international public opinion and taking into account its potential influence became essential components of Gorbachev's policies. This was not, in itself, something new. During the Brezhnev era, for example, the USSR had bet on the pacifist movement in Europe and sought to encourage it. But it was the first time the Soviet Union did not merely rely upon propaganda but showed itself ready to pay an important price in terms of "the real thing"—missiles. Its concrete behavior did indeed have an important effect on public opinion.

Could it be that Gorbachev was simply making a virtue of necessity by dismantling surplus missiles which had become too costly? While those considerations certainly played a role, there was more to it than an preoccupation with the economy. It should be noted that the Euromissiles (and nuclear weapons in general) were only a small part of its military spending and hence were not what was costing the Soviet Union most dearly. By contrast, nuclear weapons had always captured the attention of world public opinion. Major reductions in expenditures, while necessary, were only a medium-term objective; in any case, it took two years of political and diplomatic efforts to reach a single treaty, the INF accord. Arms control as an instrument for restructuring the international order became at least as important a goal as restoring the

26. A comparative study of opinion polls shows a particularly striking and revealing evolution in Germany, where the "Gorbachev factor" was at its strongest. In 1984, 47 percent of the population saw the Soviet military menace as important, while 52 percent felt it was not serious. In 1987, only 29 percent still saw it as important, and 69 percent believed it to be negligible. The following year, the perception of an important menace had dropped even further, to 19 percent. See Klaus Wittmann, "The Challenge of Conventional Arms Control," *Adelphi Papers*, Summer 1989.

In the fall of 1987, a Soviet leader was classified, for the first time in the history of the Gallup polls, as one of the ten persons most admired by Americans. The next year, at the end of 1988, Gorbachev placed second on that same list. As early as 1987, 76 percent of Americans believed that chances for peace with the USSR had considerably improved. See George Gallup, Jr., *The Gallup Poll: Public Opinion 1988* (Wilmington, 1989), pp. 5 and 263; Gallup, *The Gallup Poll: Public Opinion 1989* (Wilmington, 1990), p. 3.

In France, where the negative image of the USSR had been far stronger than in the rest of the Western world for several years, the number of those assessing "the Soviet Union's policy in the world" as being positive went from 18 percent in 1986 to 42 percent in 1989. In the fall of 1988, Mikhail Gorbachev placed second behind François Mitterrand in response to the question, "Among great heads of state and government of the 1980s, which are the two the most significant?" See "Le choc Gorbatchev," in SOFRES, *L'état de l'opinion 1990* (Paris: Le Seuil, 1990), p. 63; and SOFRES, *L'état de l'opinion 1988* (Paris: Le Seuil, 1989), p. 217.

domestic economy. In this connection, international public opinion was given a role that reached beyond the issue of disarmament. In typically Leninist fashion, Gorbachev tried to transform a relative weakness into a source of power. He planned to recoup on the political playing field the military ground he had surrendered.[27] In his predilection for politics and his eagerness to give the USSR a new "heroic" mission, Gorbachev was convinced that he could give it a new political and moral leadership role in international affairs.

Before analyzing other areas of Gorbachev's foreign policy undertaking, it may be useful to emphasize a few other innovations within "new thinking," related to questions of security and disarmament, which helped structure the overall initiative.[28]

In the West, the new approach to arms control negotiations outlined above was initially understood as a mere tactical change or as the adoption of more subtle means toward achieving the same historical objectives. If only to be able to last and enhance its cohesion, however, this approach necessitated or presupposed a significant reevaluation of the adversary and of the nature of relations with it. This reevaluation began to appear on a small scale quite early, in the documents of the 27th CPSU Congress of February 1986, which were reference documents par excellence in the tradition of the system. Up to that point, Soviet theory had maintained that imperialism, by its very nature, was solely responsible for the arms race, which it had imposed on the USSR. In his speech to the Party congress, Gorbachev stated that security could no longer be assured by unilateral measures "especially when they are to the detriment of the other party. Each party must feel as secure as the other. . . ."[29] His statement reflected a new recognition that the West had legitimate

27. Commenting favorably on the INF treaty, Sergei Plekhanov, then vice-director of the Academy of Sciences' Institute of the USA and Canada, recognized that the USSR had made the greatest concessions and justified them as a political investment in the future. "The more one puts into an investment, the greater the return one can expect." Foreign Broadcast Information Service, Soviet Union, Daily Report, 1 December 1987, p. 3.

28. On the relations between security and the overall project, see the work of Lilly Marcou, who understood the entire structure of this undertaking very early on: *Les défis de Gorbatchev* (Paris: Plon, 1987), pp. 113–142.

29. See "Politicheskii doklad tsentral'nogo komiteta KPSS" (Political Report of the Central Committee of the CPSU), *Pravda,* 26 February 1986.

Later, when such things could be said much more directly, a close aide to Gorbachev, V. Zagladin, declared during a debate: "We long committed ourselves to proving that socialism was the principal force of global development. Can we then still pretend not to be responsible for the arms race, to say it was imposed on us? The two do not add up. There must be an internal logic." Another participant immediately responded to Zagladin: "We must not forget, however, that imperialism was and is a source of military danger

security interests. What is more, he implicitly admitted that the Reagan administration's massive rearmament program was perhaps not solely due to the bellicose nature of imperialism, but also a product of Soviet actions in the 1970s. The behavior of the United States, he implied, could be altered without relying mainly on Soviet military power. Gorbachev insisted that "security can only be mutual." On several occasions, he underscored his view that interdependence had become a fundamental fact of the modern world, and not only in the area of security.

An entirely new Soviet vision of the international system emerged on the basis of a new understanding of Soviet interests and from an important revision of the *conception* of the adversary—its interests, the depth of its antagonism, and the ability and means to influence its behavior. It is necessary to highlight here the main features of this new vision.

Even if new ideas acquire great importance and have a significant effect in a context of crisis and delegitimization of old ideas and traditions,[30] they obviously are not a sufficient explanation for the behavior and policies to be examined here. These ideas do, however, provide a framework and some of the tools necessary to achieve a deeper understanding of Soviet policies.

THE SEARCH FOR A NEW INTERNATIONAL SYSTEM

The new ideas and concepts presented above began to emerge in 1986, in a language still largely shaped by traditional, anti-imperialist phraseology. This was even the case for Gorbachev's speech to the 27th Party Congress, which explains why it could then be interpreted in two different ways. Over time, however, it became clear that the sections cited above were, in fact, the operative ones. They gave way to further elaboration that was mostly completed in 1987 and 1988, a comparatively

---

in our era; it is the initiator and principal promoter of the arms race. . . . The thesis of equal responsibility is an invention of anti-Soviet propaganda." See *La Vie internationale (Mezhdunarodnaia Zhizn'),* 7, July 1988, pp. 3–21.

In the same journal, published by the Ministry of Foreign Affairs, A. Kozyrev, the future foreign minister of Russia, wrote shortly thereafter: "At the height of stagnation, our 'response' went beyond their 'actions,' which definitely harmed our own interests. In this regard, the issue of medium-range missiles in Europe and Asia merits special attention." See "La confiance et l'équilibre des intérêts" (Confidence and the Balance of Interests), *La Vie internationale,* 11, November 1988, pp.. 3–11.

30. See Douglas W. Blum, "The Soviet Foreign Policy Belief System: Beliefs, Politics and Foreign Policy Outcomes," *International Studies Quarterly,* 37 (4), December 1993, pp. 373–394.

short period of time. The developments they brought about became the dominant discourse on international issues by 1988.

The general and "programmatic" thesis that the world was becoming ever more integrated acted as a framework or base for most of the conceptual changes and new policies. Soviet theoreticians and political leaders were thereby joining an established school of international relations among Western thinkers. This school had, for years, argued against the exponents of the so-called realist paradigm, pointing to the process of internationalization in economic and technological development, the formation of a world political culture, and the evolution of international institutions and organizations. All of these factors, they held, were replacing the traditional balance of power between nations as the foundation of the world order.[31]

This was the meaning of Gorbachev's 1987 comments on an "interconnected, interdependent and essentially integrated" world.[32] Eduard Shevardnadze saw in it a "tendency which is now becoming more and more evident and central"; the conclusions he drew from it explicitly repudiated one of the fundamental Soviet theses of the past, as he stated that "the rivalry between our two systems can no longer be considered the main tendency of our period."[33] The rivalry was certainly not denied, but it was considerably downsized and removed from center stage.

The belief in movement toward global integration flowed from the notion of interdependence which Gorbachev constantly invoked. On several occasions, he illustrated his point as follows: "The nations of the world today resemble a group of mountain climbers hanging on the same rope. They can either climb to the summit together or plummet into the

31. See V. Kubalkova and A. A. Cruickshank, *Thinking New about Soviet "New Thinking"* (Berkeley: Institute of International Studies, University of California), 1989, pp. 63–70. On the emergence of a "world community" and the meaning of this concept, see G. Morozov, "Mirovoe soobshchestvo i sud'by mira" (The World Community and the Destiny of the World), *Mirovaia Ekonomika i Mezhdunarodnye Otnosheniia,* 10, October 1986, pp. 3–16.

32. Gorbachev, *Perestroika,* p. 197.

33. See "Doklad E. A. Shevardnadze" (Report by E. A. Shevardnadze), *Vestnik Ministerstva Inostrannykh Del SSSR,* 15, August 1988, pp. 27–46. He drew from this that it was no longer the class struggle which should govern the USSR's foreign policy. Even if Gorbachev had been explicit on this point (cf. *Perestroika*), he did not easily achieve consensus on this issue. Even in the summer of 1988, Yegor Ligachev criticized, in an oblique way, the discourse which had become the dominant one: "We rely on the class character of international relations. To put the question any other way will only generate confusion in the spirit of the Soviet people and among our friends abroad" (*Pravda,* 6 August 1988).

abyss together."[34] By this, he was mostly referring to interdependence in security matters, but he also saw it operating in the fields of conflict management and economic relations.

Among the moving forces of the integration process—which the USSR as much sought as it recognized—the Soviets saw "universal values" and "interests common to all of humanity," which, they argued, transcended the class struggle. Human rights, in the Western sense of the term, became one of those universal values. Gorbachev naturally placed the preservation of peace, above all through arms control and arms reduction (which continued to be seen as more pressing needs), at the top of the list of most important common interests. In current conditions, he said, "Mankind has lost its immortality," and its anxieties have grown as a result. Soviet authors claimed that the arms race was creating new kinds of economic problems for the United States, as well. In this regard, they mentioned the growing U.S. budget deficit and the decreasing competitiveness of its economy when compared to that of Japan.[35]

The Soviet leadership put the growing gap between the Third World and industrialized countries on the second level of common interests and problems requiring urgent attention. According to Gorbachev, the gap was a "time bomb" for all of humanity. Together with Soviet commentators, he pointed out that the United States and the rest of the Western world had an interest in solving the most urgent problems, if only to avoid the grave threat that the colossal Third World debt posed for the stability of international financial institutions. Among possible common solutions, Gorbachev proposed that an important percentage of the funds saved through disarmament be dedicated to economic development in the Third World.[36] This was, of course, also a way to gain Third World interest in and pressure for disarmament (at least disarmament of the superpowers).

The environment was the third common problem frequently invoked by Soviet leaders and analysts. More and more, they argued, this had

34. See, in particular, *Pravda*, 19 August 1986; *Pravda*, 11 April 1987; Gorbachev, *Perestroika*, p. 199.

35. See Kubalkova and Cruickshank, *Thinking New about Soviet "New Thinking."*

36. See his speech to the Forum for a Non-nuclear World, *Pravda*, 29 August 1987. For an approach to this question that attempts to be theoretical, see "Kontseptsiia vzaimosviazi razorujeniia i razvitiia—tezisy IMEMO AN SSSR" (A Conception of the Correlation Between Disarmament and Development—Theses of the Institute of World Economy and International Relations of the USSR Academy of Sciences), *Mirovaia Ekonomika i Mezhdunarodnye Otnosheniia*, 8, August 1987, pp. 3–9; in the same issue, I. Ivanov, "Demilitarizatsiia mirovoi ekonomiki—nasushchnaia neobkhodimost" (The Demilitarization of the World Economy, an Urgent Necessity), pp. 9–21.

become a global problem, requiring common approaches and solutions supported by all states.

The most frequently used slogan used to describe the proposed cornerstone for a new international system (and for solutions to common problems) was "the balance of interests." This was juxtaposed against the "balance of power," which had been the basis of an international order now judged to be anachronistic.[37] To assure an orderly transition to the new world order already taking shape and to provide the "balance of interests" with an adequate framework, it was deemed necessary to accentuate integrational tendencies already at work. This was to be accomplished by reinforcing international organizations, above all the United Nations. Reinforcing the role of the United Nations hence became one of the most important preoccupations of Soviet diplomacy and policy. Even if arms reduction, economic and technological cooperation, and the resolution of regional conflicts obviously first had to be obtained at the level of the nations concerned, the UN would still have be vital. It would provide a stable framework and rules for "global security" and cooperation, as well as the instruments for regulating conflicts. The Soviets proposed gradual transfers of sovereignty to reinforce UN and international law, and claimed that, in any case, the idea of absolute national sovereignty was outdated. A significant number of Soviet writings were dedicated to these questions.[38]

At first, the USSR's defense of the United Nations was dismissed in the West as a simple propaganda exercise, at which Gorbachev seemed to be a master. There was clearly more to it. The seriousness of his interest was already evidenced by the fact that the Soviet Union had paid $200 million in arrears to the organization. The USSR saw the strengthening of the UN as a medium- and long-term interest. To the extent that

37. See A. Dobrynin, "Za bez'iadernyi mir, navstrechu XXI veku" (Toward a Nonnuclear World for the 21st Century), *Kommunist*, 9, 1986; R. Bogdanov, "De l'équilibre des forces à l'équilibre des intérêts," *La Vie internationale*, April 1988, pp. 87–94; and A. Kozyrev, "Confidence and the Balance of Interests," pp. 3–11.

38. See, in particular, the writings of Vladimir Petrovskii, deputy minister of Foreign Affairs, responsible for the United Nations: "OON i obnovlenie mira" (The UN and the Transformation of the World), *Mirovaia Ekonomika i Mezhdunarodnye Otnosheniia*, 4, April1988, pp. 3–10; "Sovetskaia kontseptsiia vseobshchei bezopastnosti" (The Soviet Concept of Global Security), *Mirovaia Ekonomika i Mezhdunarodnye Otnosheniia*, 10, October1986, pp. 3–14.

One article, attributed to G. Shakhnazarov, president of the Soviet Association of Political Science and a close adviser to Gorbachev, concluded in a very optimistic fashion: "We are seeing, ever more clearly, that it is not a new hegemony which is emerging, but a 'world concert' without a conductor." See "Le monde est-il gouvernable?" *La Vie internationale*, March 1988, pp. 19–28.

the Soviet Union wanted to gradually disentangle itself from international conflicts and reduce its forces abroad, it certainly did not intend to leave the field open for the United States or to facilitate the establishment of a *Pax Americana*. Hence its interest in the reinforcement of the UN. Transferring sovereignty and responsibility to international organizations might even affect the United States's greater power to a larger extent than its own. In the pursuit of this policy, the USSR hoped to find allies in the Third World and among international public opinion, thanks to an emerging "world political culture." It also sought support among middle powers, even from allies of the United States, who often complained about the Reagan administration's attitude toward the United Nations. Putting the United States on the defensive was therefore one of the goals of the Soviet initiative.

Here again, one might be tempted to summarize and see the new vision of the outside world and of the USSR's role in it as merely being a vast exercise of rationalization or legitimization of necessities imposed on the Soviet Union. The analysis above may even seem to point toward such a conclusion. It would, however, be a unidimensional one.

First, it must be pointed out that the perception of interests (and, even more so, of the best methods for pursuing them) is not *given* and does not appear on its own. If the Soviet leaders' new perception of the USSR's interests certainly influenced their reading of the international situation and trends, the reverse is also true, to a significant degree. In other words, their view of the world also influenced the redefinition of their interests and, above all, of the best way to pursue them. Educated in a Marxist tradition, Soviet leaders and their circle of intellectuals thought (with all the wishful thinking involved) that they had grasped "profound new tendencies of historical development," the most promising social and political trends for anchoring the Soviet Union's place and interests, and the most effective means to pursue them.[39] This explains how their world view acquired an operational character on its own and the reason for our interest in it. They were truly convinced that their undertaking was part of "the direction of History" and that it corresponded to the inter-

---

39. Shevardnadze, in this connection, told the Soviet diplomatic corps: "If the thesis is correct that nations can realize their potential by following historical logic and social evolution (and there can be no doubt about this), then our national interests make it our duty to be one of the unifying forces in the world and to help promote the principles of integration . . ." (*Vestnik Ministerstva Inostrannykh Del SSSR*, 15, August 1988, pp. 27–46).

ests of humanity as newly perceived; hence the reason why this "hero-ic" enterprise was pursued with so much vigor and determination.

Given that the methods used to bring this project to fruition can shed light on its nature and true importance, it will be useful to explain them in greater detail.

Two analysts of Soviet foreign policy in the Gorbachev era, V. Kubalkova and A. A. Cruickshank, have demonstrated convincingly how it was influenced by the theoretical legacy of Antonio Gramsci, one of the founders of the Italian Communist Party.[40] The strategy Gramsci suggested to his party was based on an analysis of the causes of the socialist revolution's defeat in Italy and the rest of the Western world in the early 1920s, as opposed to the Bolshevik victory in Russia. He began by stating that a fundamental difference existed between East and West. The weak development of a civil society in Russia, he noted, meant that the state "was everything" and conquering it was sufficient for carrying out the socialist revolution.[41] The situation was completely different in the West, where civil society formed an even stronger line of defense for the established order than the state. As a result, the Party had to con-centrate its efforts on gaining positions of power throughout civil soci-ety over the long term. In order to establish its position in the areas of culture and ideas, and in social organizations, it had to take into account the great aspirations of the largest segments of society, beyond the realm of merely economic interests. Gramsci paid particular attention to intel-lectuals, who would have a central role to play in creating a new "his-torical bloc."

The world view and foreign policy of the Gorbachev team did indeed appear to be inspired by Gramscian teachings.[42] No longer is it the bal-ance of forces between the two states (or between the two camps) that is judged to be the determinant of the future of the world order. In order to accentuate and reinforce the tendencies toward global integration, the

40. Kubalkova and Cruickshank, *Thinking New about Soviet "New Thinking,"* pp. 86–90.

41. See Jean-Marc Piotte, *La pensée politique de Gramsci* (Paris: Anthropos, 1970), chap. 6, pp. 161–192.

42. The rediscovery and use of Gramsci during the Gorbachev period was not limited to foreign policy. One of the ideologists of *perestroika*, the political analyst Andranik Migranian, inspired by Gramsci, insisted that one of the basic tasks on the domestic level was the development of a civil society outside of the Soviet state, through the creation of autonomous organizations, which would be better able to sustain a true socialist culture. See P. Flaherty, "Perestroika Radicals: The Origins and Ideology of the Soviet New Left," *Monthly Review,* 40 (4), September 1988, pp. 19–33.

elements of consensus in the emerging global political culture needed to be enlarged. Hence the qualitatively new importance given to international public opinion, to ideas, and to intellectuals.

In their search for the foundations of a wide consensus, the Soviets borrowed extensively from currents of Western thinking to formulate the most central elements of their "new thinking." Even the very term "new thinking" was attributed by numerous Soviet authors to Albert Einstein; Shevardnadze cited him in order to underscore that "we must rise above differences which . . . are so infinitely small compared to the danger that threatens us all."[43] Similarly, the concepts of "reasonable sufficiency," "nonoffensive defense," and "common security" were borrowed from recommendations made by the Palme commission (headed by Olof Palme, former Social Democrat prime minister of Sweden) to the United Nations at the beginning of the 1980s. Other elements came from the North-South program developed under the leadership of Willy Brandt, ex-chancellor of Germany and a fellow Social Democrat. Many Soviet intellectuals later to be found in the think tanks of *perestroika* had taken part in the work of the Palme and Brandt commissions. The Soviets did not try to hide the sources of their inspiration; on the contrary, they used them to support their point that the "new thinking" was an approach and program which transcended the two state systems and allowed them to implement them together. By drawing upon the ideas of Europe's social democrats and liberal thinkers in the United States, the Soviets believed that they were contributing to the emergence of a new "historical bloc" at the international level. They were persuaded that their new objectives' "universal value," importance, and mobilizing potential would establish the intellectual and moral superiority, and the effectiveness, of their new foreign policy. For this purpose, and in breaking with traditional propaganda exercises, they demonstrated their readiness to give concrete guarantees, not only in the area of arms control and the United Nations, but also in the search for solutions to regional conflicts, conducted under the rubric of "national reconciliation."

It was not only for heuristic reasons that Antonio Gramsci was a major inspiration for Soviet reformers in the development of their enterprise. Gramsci considered the role of intellectuals and ideas to be highly important. Given that the majority of them were intellectuals them-

---

43. *Pravda*, 11 June 1988, cited by Kubalkova and Cruickshank, *Thinking New about Soviet "New Thinking,"* p. 75, and for a reference to other Soviet authors on the intellectual impact of Einstein, p. 27.

selves, Gramsci legitimated and comforted the promoters of "new thinking" both socially and politically.

At the same time that Kubalkova and Cruickshank brilliantly exposed the innovative nature of Gorbachev's foreign policy, they insisted that it remained entirely in a Marxist, and even a Leninist, framework. As late as 1989, they wrote that his policy represented "new means for the achievement of essentially unchanged ends—namely, the historically preordained replacement of capitalism by socialism."[44] But are the means not becoming often more important than the end, especially when that end appears to be ever more distant? They refused to see that "new thinking" represented a trail leading out of Marxism-Leninism.

The USSR had frequently called upon social democracy and peace movements in the past in order to achieve medium-term objectives. The clearest indicator that something fundamentally new was taking place were the events that were going on simultaneously in Soviet domestic politics in 1987–1988, beginning with the limited democratization of the Party and the reduction of its role. The relationship with social democracy, therefore, was no longer simply one of instrumentalization, but also one of osmosis. This was accompanied by a reevaluation of Western democracy, and the acceptance that it could, in certain cases, "represent a synthesis of class interests."[45] These factors help explain the qualitatively new trust Soviet leaders placed in public opinion.

At the beginning of the 1980s, several years after formulating its policy of "historic compromise," the Italian Communist Party had proclaimed that the great schism between Communist and socialist parties was "historically outdated." It refused to participate in any meetings of the international communist movement and worked toward the formation of a much more broadly based "Euro-Left." In this regard, its main partner was the German Social Democratic Party, with which it shared views on a vast array of issues, most notably on Europe and East-West relations. The Italian Communist Party, which had come close to a total break with Moscow in the early 1980s, became Gorbachev's most frequent interlocutor among Communist Parties after 1985.[46] Under its influence, the Soviet leader ended once and for all the practice of holding separate meetings of the international communist movement. As a

44. Kubalkova and Cruickshank, *Thinking New about Soviet "New Thinking,"* p. 103.

45. See *International Affairs*, 11, November 1988, pp. 3–11.

46. Lévesque, *Italian Communists*, pp. 42–49.

result, the 1987 celebrations for the anniversary of the October Revolution in Moscow became the largest gathering of Communist Parties,
socialists, and other leftist movements.[47]

The new Soviet view of the world and of the USSR's most appropriate instruments of policy were, as a whole, an integral part of what I
have termed the ideology of transition, developed and put in place
by Gorbachev and his entourage. We have seen how this new vision
broke from Marxism-Leninism, while simultaneously retaining its
imprint in the global and messianic character of the project. It should be
emphasized that this second aspect is as important as the first. The global, messianic character served two functions. First, it was a decisive and
galvanizing factor for the political energies of the new leaders, something
that was absolutely necessary to implement a program as risky and far-
reaching as this one. Second, through the new world leadership that it
promised the USSR—and which was partially realized until 1989—it
also helped in large measure to disarm skeptics and opponents within
the Soviet political apparatus.

In the previous pages, we have sketched out the general framework
into which the USSR's policy toward Eastern Europe was placed. In so
doing, my analysis gave special attention to the elements of coherence,
innovation, and finality in its foreign policy, at the risk of losing sight of
its contradictions and hesitations. These latter dimensions were far more
prevalent in domestic politics than in foreign policy, where innovation
was more easily achieved. Since Soviet policy toward Eastern Europe
was situated somewhere between foreign and domestic policy, these
dimensions must be reintroduced and analyzed. Otherwise the course of
this policy would already seem to be entirely mapped out. Also, if Gorbachev undoubtedly played a decisive role in the process of change in
the USSR, he remains the most ambiguous person among the reformist
leadership. It is also a reflection of his function at the top of the system
that he himself incorporated the hesitations and contradictions which
permeated Soviet policy toward Eastern Europe in particular.

47. On the necessity of overcoming the differences between Communist and socialist
parties, and on their growing convergence, see Iu Krasin, "Novoe myshlenie vo vzai-
mootnosheniiakh kommunistov i sotsial-demokratov" (New Thinking in the Relations
between Communists and Social-Democrats), *Mirovaia Ekonomika i Mezhdunarodnye
Otnosheniia*, 4, April 1988, pp. 23–34; I. Shadrina, "Sotsintern v 'eru Brandta' i aktu-
al'nye problemy mirovoi politiki" (The Socialist International in the "Brandt Era" and
Current Problems of World Politics), *Mirovaia Ekonomika i Mezhdunarodnye Otnosheniia*, 6, June 1987, pp. 3–14.

CHAPTER TWO

The European Initiative

EUROPE'S ATTRACTION

Having put the main objectives and meaning of Gorbachev's foreign policy into perspective, one intermediate step must be taken before focusing on the policies directly concerning Eastern Europe. Though these policies must be understood in light of the overall dynamic of Gorbachev's undertaking, they were more narrowly conditioned by his European initiative. Just like the Soviet Union itself, Eastern Europe was to become part of the "common European home": this theme became one of the principal slogans of Soviet foreign policy and the leitmotif of its policy toward Europe.

Europe took pride of place in *perestroika*'s political imagery and in the alchemy of the ideology of transition which it put in place. In the treatment of that ideology, we have stressed its Marxist-Leninist heritage, which provided its form and part of its content. At this point, one should outline a dimension that is specifically of Russian heritage, acting as a catalyst for Soviet policy and illuminating the European initiative of Gorbachev's team.

One of the old debates, thought to have ceased, resurfaced with surprising vigor in the USSR under *perestroika* and has become even more pronounced since the collapse of the Soviet Union; it is of particular significance for the questions which interest us here. The debate had pitted Russian Slavophiles against Westernizers in the nineteenth century and crossed all currents of Russian political life until the triumph of

Stalinism extinguished them. This debate rested on a deep sense among the Russian intelligentsia of Russia's profound estrangement from Europe, having been cut off from it by centuries of Mongol domination. The depth of this gap was also well understood abroad. One of the most illustrious to underline it was Karl Marx, who wrote that "Russia was making Europe fear the threat of a barbaric invasion."

The Slavophiles saw Russia's difference as a part of its authenticity and power which ought to be cultivated, and they intended to do so. The Westernizers, on the other hand, believed that Russia's social, economic, and political peculiarities were obstacles that needed to be eradicated in order for Russia to fully enter the mainstream of world civilization, that is, European civilization. One might say that this opposition crossed all Russian political currents in one way or another. In other words, there were Slavophiles and Westernizes among conservatives as well as among revolutionaries. The populists (*narodniki*), for example, wanted to rid Russia of tsarist rule, but also considered it historical good fortune that the Russian peasantry had escaped the corrupting influence of European mercantilism and capitalism. Therefore, they argued, true socialism would be easier to establish in Russia than in Europe, given the communal traditions among the Russian peasantry. Conversely, the first Russian Marxists and the Mensheviks both saw those same traditions as barriers to the victory of socialism; to make such a victory possible, Russia needed to develop democracy, capitalism, and a strong working class.

This cleavage could also be found among Bolsheviks themselves. In this respect, Lenin can be considered a Westernizer, to the extent that he believed the Russian revolution could not survive if it were not quickly followed and salvaged by a European revolution. Stalin's "socialism in one country" and his insistence upon the Soviet model as the only possible socialist model, by contrast, reflects a notion of Russia as Europe's road to salvation, to the future, and not vice versa. In Stalinism, therefore, we witnessed the most complete form of revolutionary and messianic Slavophilism. At the time, Karl Wittfogel opined that collectivizing agriculture and forbidding peasants to leave the land were equivalent to a restoration of serfdom, and that the Stalinist regime represented a vast regression to the "Asiatic mode of production" and to "Oriental despotism."[1] Incidentally, most of the intellectuals who developed and

---

1. See Karl Wittfogel, *Le despotisme oriental* (Paris: Minuit, 1964).

defended *perestroika* came to similar conclusions regarding the Stalinist heritage.[2]

Perestroika can legitimately be seen as a new version of the battle between Westernizers and Slavophiles. Among the top Soviet leaders, the new leaders were, in a ranked order of their "Europhilism," Yakovlev, Shevardnadze, and Gorbachev. They quickly came to the conclusion that the failure of the Brezhnev regime was mainly, though not exclusively, in the economic sphere. Following in the footsteps of the nineteenth-century Westernizers, they believed the USSR's salvation to lie in its reinsertion into Europe, in the areas of economics, politics, and social values. The main slogans of *perestroika*—"democratization," "human rights," the valorization "of the role of the individual," and "reducing the role of the state"—can also be seen as measures to bring the USSR closer to Europe, which was again considered the standard-bearer of the mainstream of world civilization.

Even for Aleksandr Yakovlev, whom the conservatives considered the main "liquidator" among reformist leaders, it was clear that the USSR would still be a socialist state at the end of the reform process. That socialism, however, would be characterized by democracy and pluralism, and be imbued with Western values.[3] Summarizing *perestroika* as an urge toward Europe would be a simplification, but not a caricaturization. This fascination with, or nostalgia for, Europe was especially strong among intellectuals, the *instituchniki,* who inspired and defined *perestroika*. It favored and accompanied the social-democratization of the CPSU.

The purpose of this extensive contextualization was to underscore the very high priority that the USSR's European policy progressively took on for Gorbachev. Furthermore, it was intended to point out the deeper meaning of slogans, such as the "common European home" and the necessity of "transcending the division of Europe," which were initially taken to be basically empty propaganda.

---

2. See notably, L. Ionin, "Konservativnyi sindrom" (The Conservative Syndrome), *Sotsiologicheskie issledovaniia,* 5, 1987.

Anatolii Sobchak, an academic who joined the party in 1988 and became mayor of Leningrad in 1991, writes: "We have erected a 'Great Wall,' which, for decades, has isolated us from Europe . . ." and "we must return to the heart of European civilization . . ." in Anatolii Sobchak, *Khozhdenie vo vlast'* (*The March to Power)* (Moscow: Novosti, 1991); translated into French (Paris: Flammarion, 1992), pp. 252 and 242.

3. See Aleksandr Yakovlev, *Ce que nous voulons faire de l'URSS. Entretiens avec Lilly Marcou* (Paris: Le Seuil, 1991); Aleksandr Yakovlev, *Muki prochteniia bytia—perestroika: nadezdy i real'nosti* (*Perestroika and the Torments of Being: Hopes and Reality)* (Moscow: Novosti, 1991).

Of course, Gorbachev, Shevardnadze, and others responsible for Soviet foreign policy did not foresee totally suppressing the division of Europe. That could not be a realistic, operational goal. Their objective was to attenuate and gradually reduce the division, without knowing exactly to what extent. It was the process itself which was seen as being more beneficial than its indeterminate end point.

THE THREE LEVELS OF EUROPEAN RECONCILIATION

Before examining the articulation and evolution of the Soviet leaders' European policy through the end of 1988, it may be useful to outline its main features. In this respect, one can say that the Soviet leaders operated on three *relatively* separate levels in order to bring about a rapprochement of the "two Europes." In order of importance, those three levels were the military, economic relations, and the societal level. On the first two levels, the leadership intended to operate by multiplying the number of "bloc to bloc" negotiations and agreements.

As on the general international plane, military issues were the Soviets' first priority and main instrument for attenuating the division of Europe. Again, the arms race, which had been the main tool of influence, was replaced by disarmament, with the same goals. Soviet leaders decided that the accumulation of weapons was the basis of the greatest distrust and most serious anxieties. By first operating on this level, they hoped to establish the confidence necessary to bring about pan-European reconciliation. This priority also matched their intention to find ways of reducing the economic burden of military expenditures, though this goal, as indicated above, became a medium-term, not an immediate objective.

On this level, therefore, the Soviet Union planned to reduce tensions through successive arms control and arms reduction agreements between NATO and the Warsaw Pact. The old rhetoric on the simultaneous dissolution of the two blocs and on their harmful character almost completely disappeared from Soviet discourse. It was replaced by an affirmation of the blocs' utility, for an undefined period of time, as a stabilizing factor reassuring both sides. The progressively "disantagonized" blocs would become the foundation of European security. They were to become less military and more political, while still serving as the basic infrastructure for a new pan-European security construct.[4] Since the

4. In characteristic fashion, two members of the Foreign Affairs ministry wrote the following for the journal of their ministry in 1988: "We must admit that the security system

structuring of a new European order was to be achieved gradually, and in tandem with important disarmament treaties which would necessarily take time to negotiate, this was a relatively distant goal. As a result, it was not the subject of very precise conceptualizations on the part of Soviet analysts and politicians. Starting from established realities and institutions, they proposed reinforcing the Conference on Security and Cooperation in Europe (CSCE), without defining its future contours. Even at the beginning of 1989, the director of the Academy of Sciences's Institute of Europe foresaw quite distant steps. The first was to have been completed in 1992 through the intensification of cooperative measures, using the framework already put in place by the CSCE. He also foresaw the "development of permanent supranational organizational structures"[5] beginning in the year 2000.

On the second level, the Soviet leadership also planned using "bloc to bloc" agreements to progressively reduce the gap between the two European economic blocs.[6] Here, we again find the paradox described in the previous chapter. Since Gorbachev continually underscored the urgency of fixing the Soviet economy, one would have expected economic relations with Europe to occupy center stage in his efforts to reinsert the Soviet Union into Europe. Instead, given that this task was more complex and difficult, and possible successes slower to achieve, the USSR's main efforts concentrated on military issues. The conviction was that their resolution would have positive repercussions on economic relations with Europe, which were not altogether neglected and remained a central goal.

The development of "bloc to bloc" agreements between the EEC (European Economic Community) and CMEA (Council for Mutual Economic Assistance) implied, at the start, a change of Soviet attitudes toward the EEC. Until Gorbachev's assumption of power, Moscow had steadfastly refused to recognize the EEC. It was seen as an instrument

---

in Europe will long continue to rest upon the *coexistence of the two military blocs*. Security will be reinforced as a result of modifications in their mutual relations. But the blocs will not be dissolved, and the very idea of the blocs will continue." M. Admirzhanov and M. Cherkasov, "Les étages de la maison commune de l'Europe," *La Vie internationale,* 12, December 1988, pp. 28–39; italics in the original text.

5. See V. Zhurkin, "Obshchii dom dlia Evropy" (A Common Home For Europe), *Pravda,* 17 May 1989.

6. "The goal of constructing the 'common European home' is to overcome the economic and political division between the EEC and CMEA," declared the director of the Soviet Foreign Ministry's European department (Foreign Broadcast Information Service, Soviet Union, Daily Report, 9 September 1988).

for reinforcing monopolistic capitalism devoted to serving as the economic infrastructure of NATO, undermining the sovereignty of European states and, as a result, limiting the USSR's maneuverability in Europe. After 1985, that estimation was reversed, initially as a pragmatic adjustment, but soon thereafter as part of a new Soviet evaluation of trends at work around the world. Mikhail Gorbachev proposed the establishment of relations with the EEC in 1985; by May of 1987, he was arguing for a revision of "dogmatic approaches" toward the EEC.[7] Soon, the organization was being understood and described as a reflection of "the fundamentally progressive tendency toward reinforcing the interdependence of states";[8] it was also credited with having contributed to a reduction of the risk of conflict in Western Europe. With respect to its pursuit of economic and political integration, the EEC was described as a "laboratory" for the whole of Europe.

In June 1988, a joint declaration was published by the EEC and CMEA, in which the two organizations recognized each other formally, a step the Soviet leaders wanted to see as the basis for developing a pan-European market. The delay was due to the EEC's reluctance to deal directly with CMEA, for fear of giving it anything at all resembling a status of equality. It was not until August 1988, therefore, that the USSR established full diplomatic relations with the EEC. The Soviet leadership was perfectly aware of CMEA's weaknesses compared to the EEC, which were largely due to an insufficient degree of integration that could not even begin to compare with the EEC. Though the Warsaw Pact and NATO could negotiate on equal footing, the Soviets knew that the terms were far less favorable for them in the economic area.

The 1987 ratification of the West European treaty creating a single market and the perspective of "the Europe of 1992," while considered a positive evolution, augmented Soviet anxieties and impatience regarding the weakness of East European integration. The leadership feared that any possible widening of the economic gap might lead the countries of Eastern Europe to be drawn into the EEC's orbit *separately,* based on the very different relations each of the states enjoyed with it. Therefore, to avoid this eventuality, accelerating Eastern Europe's economic inte-

7. See *Vestnik Ministerstva Inostrannykh Del SSSR,* 1, August 1987, p. 6.
8. See "Evropeiskoe soobshchestvo segodnia. Tezisy Instituta mirovoi ekonomiki i mezhdunarodnykh otnoshenii AN SSSR" (The European Community Today. Theses of the Institute of World Economy and International Relations of the USSR Academy of Sciences), *Mirovaia Ekonomika i Mezhdunarodnye Otnosheniia,* 12, December 1988, pp. 5–19.

gration became a more pressing concern.[9] Integration, however, could not be deepened without a certain degree of homogeneity in the member states' economic structures, particularly with regard to the autonomy of enterprises vis-à-vis the planning organisms. Yet the difference between those states oriented toward reform and others ruled by conservatives was growing. Western Europe's rendezvous with 1992 must be seen, in this light, as a factor explaining the impatience the Soviet leadership began to show more directly toward the conservative regimes of Eastern Europe at the end of 1988 and beginning of 1989, a point to which we shall return.

The third level for attenuating the division of Europe was related to the social and political order of the societies. Soviet leaders—of all political stripes, incidentally—were keenly aware of the fact that the nature of the regimes in the USSR and Eastern Europe was an important cause for the division of Europe, regardless of the specific foreign policy they were pursuing. For Gorbachev and his chief lieutenants, the democratization of socialism in the Soviet Union and Eastern Europe was expected to play a very important role in reducing the division of Europe. They also saw quite clearly that democratization would necessarily have a positive effect on disarmament and on economic relations with the West, to the benefit of the USSR. This is why *glasnost'* and democratization became very distinct instruments of foreign policy, to such a point that some Western observers saw this as their main raison d'être.[10]

While the Soviet leadership believed that bringing the two parts of Europe closer on this level was necessary and useful, it obviously was out of the question to do so through negotiations, let alone "bloc to bloc" talks. First of all, the issues centered around domestic policies that were officially nonnegotiable. Beyond that, there was no consensus

9. "Don't these developments, and the general economic influence of the EEC, bring to light the centrifugal forces in the socialist camp? To avoid that, a serious restructuring of the CMEA member states' system of interaction must be undertaken. . . . Time is of the essence. If, in the near future, our states do not organize their "common socialist market" . . . we will not be able to found future relations between the European Community . . . and the CMEA as a whole . . . on the basis of equal rights and parity" (Admirzhanov and Cherkasov, "Les étages de la maison commune de l'Europe," pp. 28–39. For another, very critical, evaluation of CMEA from the same period, see V. Spandarian and N. Shmelev, "Problemy povysheniia effektivnosti vneshneekonomicheskikh sviazei SSSR" (Problems of augmenting the efficiency of the USSR's foreign economic relations), *Mirovaia Ekonomika i Mezhdunarodnye Otnosheniia*, 8, August 1988, pp. 10–26.

10. This was the case with Françoise Thom who, even in 1989, argued that democratization in the USSR was nothing more than a vast effort to intoxicate the Western world in order to convince it to reinvigorate the Soviet economy. Françoise Thom, *Le moment Gorbatchev* (Paris: Le livre de poche, 1990).

between the USSR and its East European allies on democratization; in fact, the majority of its allies were hostile to such reforms.

With time and the development of *perestroika*, the most reformist Soviet officials began to see an accentuation of the democratization process not only as a trump card, but even as a necessary condition for making the most significant advances on the two other levels outlined above. In a text written on this subject in the autumn of 1988, the Institute of Europe's deputy director, Sergei Karaganov, was very explicit on this issue.[11] Andrei Kozyrev, at the time assistant director of the Foreign Ministry's Office of International Organizations, even wrote in November 1988: "The link between domestic policy and foreign policy is an axiom of political science. This is why the world community's interest in the domestic affairs of a country is natural, legitimate, and even necessary."[12]

How far should and could a rapprochement of these societies go? For Soviet reformers, that question called forth another: how to undergo profound transformations and still remain one's self. More than a question, it was a dilemma. The resolution was to be found in the idea and hope (or illusion) that *perestroika* ultimately meant "more socialism," to use Gorbachev's expression.

Bringing the two parts of Europe together was seen, by the Soviets, as involving a symbiotic relationship between the two adversaries. In other words, from the Soviet perspective, the West itself was to undergo a certain degree of transformation, even if its scope was not expected to be as great. While Communist Parties were losing ground throughout Western Europe, Gorbachev and his advisers believed that a broader Left, going well beyond those parties, would definitely gain greater influence, in part specifically as a result of the changes transforming the USSR's domestic and foreign policies. The Soviet leaders counted on such consequences, especially in West Germany.

Here again, the Italian Communist Party's experience and evolution are useful for understanding the changes in the USSR. At the time of the "historic compromise," the Italian Communist Party had already renounced the idea of triumphing over the enemy. In a balance of power that appeared to be more advantageous than that of the USSR in the 1980s, it proposed a new relationship with its adversary, through which

---

11. See Sergei Karaganov, "Towards a New Security System in Europe," in V. Harle and J. Livonen, eds., *Gorbachev and Europe* (New York: St. Martin's Press, 1990).

12. A. Kozyrev, "La confiance et l'équilibre des intérêts, *La Vie internationale,* 11, November 1988, pp. 3–11.

the Italian Communist Party expected to transform its opponent, while also accepting to be transformed itself. It hoped that, in the process, it could keep the best of itself. Just as in the case of the USSR some years later, the most distrustful enemies of the Italian Communist Party saw its intention as "embracing to better strangle" and as "the kiss of death." We have now seen in what direction events proceeded.

What the most reformist Soviet officials contemplated at the end of 1988 was somewhat similar to the "convergence theory," the old Western idea of the 1960s, though understood in a more dialectic way in Moscow. Karaganov, for example, wrote that the future pan-European security system "will not be socially or politically homogeneous despite a growing similarity" between its constituent parts. In this regard, he invoked the "socialization" of capitalism in Western Europe and the "growth of political democracy in East Europe."[13] Mikhail Gorbachev's view of affairs in 1988 suggested that there were still to be important differences between the "two Europes." During a discussion with the general secretary of the Italian Communist Party in which he revealed his conception of pluralism and democracy in the USSR, Gorbachev stated that the propagation of independent social and socioeconomic organizations was all the more important in a one-party regime. The role of the Party in the state and society was to be reduced by their presence; democratization would be guaranteed by sustaining them alongside the Party, and by democratizing the Party itself. The CPSU would, however, "remain the principal motor" of the process, as it had been up to that time.[14]

As will be shown in greater detail below, various signs and developments, including a new step toward democratization in the USSR, marked an important turning point in Soviet policy toward Eastern Europe during the second half of 1988. But before addressing it, it may be useful to put the Soviet conception of the "common European home" into the context of its dynamic and historical evolution.

THE COMMON EUROPEAN HOME: HOW TO REUNIFY EUROPE AND YET KEEP "TWO EUROPES"

As one of the principal children of *perestroika*, the concept of a "common European home," its content, and Europe's attraction evolved

13. Karaganov, "Towards a New Security System in Europe," p. 47.
14. See Antonio Rubbi, *Incontri con Gorbaciov—i colloqui di Natta e Ochetto con il leader sovietico* (Rome: Editori Riuniti, 1990), p. 190.

together with the concept of *perestroika*. In fact, the term itself appeared
before the advent of *perestroika*. The content and meaning therefore had
to change. Similarly, with the development of *perestroika*, Europe came
to assume an ever more central role in Soviet foreign policy. At the beginning of Gorbachev's tenure, from 1985 through 1986, when democratization was not yet on the agenda, the United States was the Soviet leadership's main preoccupation, given "Star Wars" and the importance of
nuclear arms control.

From 1987 into 1988, Europe came to occupy a central, and growing, place in Soviet policy. One sign, among several others, was the creation of the Academy of Sciences's Institute of Europe in early 1988; the
institute was to play an important role in clearing up ambiguities in the
"common home" concept. Gorbachev himself had suggested creating
the institute the year before. He made the suggestion in a private conversation with his advisers, during the course of which he also expressed
his conviction that Europe was decisive for the future of *perestroika,*
"even for our internal policies."[15] The new institute's mandate for
research and consultation was explicitly pan-European. In other words,
it overlapped the jurisdiction of the much older Institute of the Economy of the World Socialist System, directed by Oleg Bogomolov and one
of the loci of "new thinking." In April 1988, the CPSU Central Committee department responsible for relations with ruling Communist Parties was abolished, and its mandate transferred to the International
Department. The Central Committee progressively lost its quasi-exclu-
sive responsibility for ties to Eastern Europe, which shifted to the Ministry of Foreign Affairs.

In 1987, and even in 1988, two important questions contributed to
nurturing doubts abroad about the novelty of Soviet intentions concerning the "common European home." The first had to do with the
place and role of the United States in Europe, and the second, with the
ambiguity surrounding the concept's central objective.

A significant proportion of Moscow's discourse on the "common
home" suggested that Soviet leaders were mainly interested in it as a way
of getting Western nations to sanction and recognize the political status
quo in Eastern Europe as definitive, which had been one of Soviet diplomacy's traditional goals. Mikhail Gorbachev wrote that the East Euro-

15. See the testimony of Anatolii Cherniaev, one of his principal assistants on foreign
policy: Anatolii S. Cherniaev, *Shest' let s Gorbachevym: po dnevnikovym zapisiam* (Six
Years with Gorbachev: From Journal Notes) (*Moscow: Progress Kul'tura,* 1993), pp.
140–141.

pean states "have made their choice" between capitalism and socialism, and the European process could only be built "on the basis of recognizing and respecting that reality."[16] Other Soviet officials were more specific and went much further. In particular, they noted that "the consolidation of socialism on German soil" was "an integral part of the common European home's foundation." They even went as far as demanding that Western states provide "guarantees" for the maintenance of Eastern Europe's political order.[17] Furthermore, Gorbachev was deliberately ambiguous about the Brezhnev Doctrine until the second half of 1988.[18] Though he of course never openly invoked it, the Soviet leader also refused to disavow the doctrine explicitly, even when urged to do so. In March of 1988, on the occasion of his trip to Yugoslavia, Gorbachev had insisted on the necessity of "unconditional recognition by the world community of the right for each people to choose its destiny."[19] An American journalist interviewed him shortly thereafter, asking whether his comments in Belgrade meant that a repetition of events in Hungary in 1956, or in Czechoslovakia in 1968, was impossible. Gorbachev responded by avoiding the question: "I can only reiterate what I said before and, generally speaking, there is nothing I can add to it. I would only say the following: interference, from whatever source, is inadmissible."[20] During the same period, he also spoke of the need "for a certain degree of integration"[21] between the two parts of Europe.

This ambiguity can be understood as a function of the differences between more reformist and less reformist leaders and analysts: while the former underscored the elements of integration, the latter concentrated on the preservation of the "socialist choice." From this angle, the ambiguity of Gorbachev's comments could be seen as a clumsy synthesis between diverging visions. But the ambivalence also emanated from Gorbachev himself, and reflected the dilemma indicated above,

16. *Perestroika,* p. 280.

17. "The ideological confrontation of the two systems, represented by their respective blocs, determines their aspiration to have *guarantees for their socio-political security, to maintain the system in place,* assuring the internal stability of each state. *The Europeans should reflect upon the measures likely to reinforce these guarantees*" (Admirzhanov and Cherkasov, "Les étages de la maison commune de l'Europe," italics added).

18. The Brezhnev Doctrine was the name given to the Soviet claim (made after the invasion of Czechslovakia in 1968) that the socialist community had a duty to intervene to protect socialism when it was threatened in a given country.

19. *Pravda,* 17 March 1988.

20. *Pravda,* 23 May 1988.

21. *Perestroika,* p. 282.

concerning the future of socialism in the USSR. His approach recalled that of the West German Social Democrats in the early 1970s, who thought it necessary to reassure the Soviets by recognizing the political status quo in Europe, in order to better transform and overcome it with time. It was a profoundly contradictory ambition, at least on the surface. Gorbachev demanded to be reassured about preserving socialism in East Europe in order to take the risks of working towards its transformation.

In the end, with the exception of those concerning the Brezhnev Doctrine, it was not declarations, but the tortuous advances toward democratization in the USSR and Eastern Europe which gradually removed the cloud of ambiguity hanging over the "common home."

The whole notion of gradual sociopolitical changes, not only in Eastern Europe but in both parts of Europe, with due respect for the framework of "disantagonized" blocs and the geopolitical interests of the great powers, was far from new, even if it was a new concept for the Soviet leadership. It was exactly the vision of Europe put forth by the Italian Communist Party in the mid-1970s, and largely shared by Germany's Social Democrats.[22]

The other great ambiguity in initial Soviet discourse concerned the place of the United States in the "common European home." In other words, was this a project which sought to marginalize the role of the United States in Europe by constantly contrasting the USSR's belonging to Europe to the extra-European character of the United States? Was it here again, as some Western observers argued, a new term to support traditional objectives of Soviet diplomacy?

It should be pointed out that those traditional objectives were, themselves, ambiguous. On the one hand, the previous Soviet leaders wished for a U.S. military retreat from Eastern Europe, and hence the end of NATO. On the other hand, however, they preferred preserving the American presence and U.S. military control of Western Europe to a militarization of Germany, which might have implied the latter's access to nuclear weapons, and to the emergence of an integrated common defense system in the western part of Europe. They preferred bipolarity. From their point of view, the ideal solution would have been a progressive ero-

---

22. On the Italian Communist Party's vision of Europe, see Lévesque, *Italian Communists,* pp. 10–20. On the German Social Democrats' conceptions of East-West relations, see Timothy Garton Ash, *In Europe's Name: Germany and the Divided Continent* (London: Jonathan Cape, 1993), pp. 28–48, 312–334.

sion of U.S. military engagement in Europe, proceeding sufficiently slowly so as not to induce the emergence of a new anti-Soviet bloc. While the Soviet leadership probably had few illusions about the chances of realizing such an objective in the foreseeable future, they also did not miss any opportunity to exploit differences and conflicts of interest between the United States and one of its European allies, or between the United States and Western Europe as a whole.

In 1986 and 1987, while affirming that the United States had a role to play in Europe, the Soviet leadership frequently contrasted their interests and concepts of a European order with those of the Americans.[23] Mikhail Gorbachev's vision of a "common European home" occasionally took on an anti-American coloration altogether typical of Soviet intellectuals' gushing about a Europe still considered to be the summit of world civilization. In one particularly colorful example, he contrasted European culture with "mass culture" coming from the other side of the Atlantic and expressed shock "that a profoundly intelligent European culture, so deeply shaped by humanism, is beating a retreat before an uncontrollable deluge of violence and pornography, a wave of base sentiments and vile thoughts."[24]

During the second half of 1988, with the Soviet Union increasingly impatient to accelerate disarmament in Europe, the ambiguity concerning the role of the United States completely disappeared. If exploiting cross-Atlantic differences had given (and could continue to give) the Soviets momentary advantages, it was deemed necessary for the advancement of their European initiative to remove the distrust of the United States and its most committed European allies, who could block the process. In recognizing themselves the ambiguity of their previous positions, and its potential harmfulness, Soviet analysts stated: "If the United States does not participate in the construction of the common European home, the idea risks being still-born."[25] Gorbachev himself

23. See, in particular, the article by the future secretary of the Gorbachev Foundation: A. Likhotal, "Na evropeiskom napravlenii" (On Europe's Orientation), *Mirovaia Ekonomika i Mezhdunarodnye Otnosheniia*, 7, July 1987, pp. 3–6.

24. *Perestroika,* p. 301. His comments appeared to be directly inspired by Aleksandr Yakovlev's ideas formulated in the latter's book on the United States published in 1984 and were undoubtedly edited by Yakovlev himself. In his memoirs (published in the USSR in 1991, and later translated into English), Ligachev wrote that "almost all of the general secretary's speeches on international affairs . . . were prepared by Yakovlev" (Yegor Ligachev, *Inside Gorbachev's Kremlin* [New York: Pantheon, 1993], p. 122).

25. Admirzhanov and Cherkasov, "Les étages de la maison commune de l'Europe," pp. 28–39.

declared that "a weakening of the alliances" might "increase distrust and harm disarmament."[26]

This evolution was comparable to the evolution of the Soviets' position on European integration. Not only economic integration, but also the possibility of political union was deemed positive, to the extent that it would be easier for a Europe speaking with one voice to advance the construction of the "common home" more effectively. Uneasiness was, however, expressed with respect to the realization of a West European political union. The leadership feared that it might "cement the economic, and perhaps even spiritual, basis of Europe's political division."[27] The perceived solution was not to put brakes on West European integration, but to accelerate measures leading to a rapprochement between the two parts of Europe. At the same time, the possibility of an independent military integration of Western Europe continued to be seen as the worst of all possible outcomes, given that it might deepen and make permanent the most antagonistic division within Europe.[28]

Soviet analysts began to find all sorts of advantages for preserving the presence of the United States in Europe and for its participation in the European process.[29] This could help, they suggested, reduce "the fear of the 'Soviet menace' on the part of the Europeans." More interestingly, their statements indicated the belief that, in the past, Europe had always been less anti-Soviet than the United States, and that the preservation of close political and strategic links between Europe and the United States could only have a moderating, if not to say civilizing, effect on U.S. foreign policy.[30] More generally, we can say that accepting the presence and role of the United States in Europe went hand in hand with the growing affirmation of a world view in which East-West tensions and

26. *Pravda*, 12 March 1988.

27. Karaganov, "Towards a New Security System in Europe," p. 45.

28. See V. Stupichin, "En effet, rien n'est simple en Europe," *La Vie internationale*, May 1988, pp. 61–65. See also "Evropeiskoe soobshchestvo segodnia. Tezisy Instituta mirovoi ekonomiki i mezhdunarodnykh otnoshenii AN SSSR" (The European Community Today. Theses of the Institute of World Economy and International Relations of the USSR Academy of Sciences), *Mirovaia Ekonomika i Mezhdunarodnye Otnosheniia*, 12, December 1988, pp. 5–19.

29. See G. Vorontsov, "Ot Khel'sinki k 'obshcheevropeiskomu domu'" (From Helsinki to the "Common European Home"), *Mirovaia Ekonomika i Mezhdunarodnye Otnosheniia*, 9, September 1988, pp. 35–46.

30. See Sergei Karaganov, "Les États-Unis et la 'maison commune de l'Europe,'" *La Vie internationale*, 8, August 1989, pp. 19–30. To appreciate the considerable change in Karaganov's (deputy director of the Institute of Europe) opinion on this issue, compare this article to another he wrote one year before: "La 'maison commune de l'Europe' vue dans l'optique militaire," *La Vie internationale*, 8, August 1988, pp. 69–77.

the contradiction between socialism and capitalism were becoming less antagonistic.

For our purposes, it should be stressed that the American presence in Europe and NATO's stability were explicitly described as guarantors of the Warsaw Pact's stability and of the Soviet Union's role in it. This preoccupation became even clearer at the beginning of 1989, as the process of democratization took a decisive turn in Poland and Hungary. Vitalii Zhurkin, director of the Institute of Europe, stated at the time that, just as the USSR was no longer calling into question the stability of NATO, "in equal measure, that should be applied to Eastern Europe, and we, in turn, have the right to count on a similar approach on the part of the West."[31]

In light of the above, it is quite clear that the Soviet leadership intended to keep its allies and alliance system. These represented a crucial element in their European policy. We also see how, in concert with Western states and international organizations, they thought it possible to control the process of bringing the two parts of Europe closer together. Gradualism, a step-by-step approach, and relative reciprocity were to serve as guarantors thereof. One can observe here a typical legacy of the Leninist approach, based on the conviction that an omniscient political leadership can channel the course of events and control social processes.

It was believed that the rapprochement and controlled integration of the two parts of Europe would provide the USSR with the greatest benefits and advantages, notably in the economic sphere. But, there again, the means for achieving those goals were mainly political.

In contrast to its great continental and global designs, Gorbachev's policy directly relating to Eastern Europe at first seemed banal and hardly innovative. This was true until the grand design overwhelmed day-to-day policies.

31. "Obshchii dom dlia Evropy" (A Common Home for Europe), *Pravda*, 17 May 1989.

CHAPTER THREE

The Meaning of Soviet Immobilism in Eastern Europe

From 1985 to the Summer of 1988

SOVIET LAISSEZ-FAIRE POLICIES

During the first years of perestroika, even a superficial political obser-
vation was sufficient to note a clear disparity between the general orientation of Soviet foreign policy and that being directed toward Eastern
Europe. As innovative and dynamic as Soviet policy toward the United
States, Western Europe, and the resolution of Third World conflicts was,
policies touching upon Eastern Europe did not seem to have undergone
any significant change. At the most, perhaps, there appeared to be a rec-
tification of style.

In 1986, when the broad new outlines of Soviet foreign policy began
to be defined, it was the slogans of a domestic policy which had not yet
found its ultimate course that seemed to apply to Eastern Europe. At the
time, the call was still for increased discipline, and it was uskorenie,
"acceleration," more than structural reforms, that dominated discussion
of economic policy and was seen as the remedy for "stagnation." The
Soviet Politburo, following a CMEA summit meeting, called for the
"acceleration of socioeconomic development" in Eastern Europe.[1] Just
as it sought to increase the quality of production domestically through
methods of administrative control, the USSR became more demanding
of its economic partners in Eastern Europe and their deliveries, and it
appeared that CMEA was to undergo serious reinforcement from above.

---

1. *Pravda,* 14 November 1986.

From 1987 onward, it became clear that the search for economic change in the USSR would build upon the notion of greater autonomy for enterprises and that glasnost' had effectively transformed itself into a watchword and instrument of democratization. Henceforth, a discrepancy between Soviet domestic developments and its East European policy began to crystallize. In other words, the new leadership not only appeared not to have a real program of transformation for Eastern Europe, but it also did not seem to make any particular effort to promote steps toward democratization in those countries where they were most needed.

Mikhail Gorbachev, upon coming to power, had certainly shown obvious sympathy for the leaders of the two least conservative states in the region, Poland and Hungary. In his meetings with Janos Kadar and the Hungarian leadership, he (contrary to his predecessors) very directly and warmly praised the reforms which Hungary had begun implementing several years before. He did not, however, cite them as examples for other countries to follow. Very rapidly, General Jaruzelski became his preferred partner among East European leaders, and this, of course, was no accident. The top of the Soviet political apparatus had not completely trusted Jaruzelski in previous years. He was reproached for not having implemented a true "normalization" after 1981, and in particular for not trying to destroy the Solidarity trade union but instead wanting to find a modus vivendi with it while making concessions to the moderate elements in the opposition.[2] After his first meetings with General Jaruzelski, Gorbachev gave him clear signs of full confidence. He even tried to help reinforce Jaruzelski's authority among the Polish population against the more conservative, "Sovietophile" elements of the Polish party. In 1986, for example, General Jaruzelski became the first Polish leader granted authorization to make an official visit to Lithuania. Given the Poles' nationalism, their sense of history, and continued attachment to memories of the old Polish-Lithuanian kingdom, this visit, which was given extensive coverage by the Polish media, helped Jaruzelski reinforce the image he was cultivating of a national, patriotic figure.

At the same time, during his meetings with other leaders, such as Erich Honecker, Gustav Husak, or Todor Zhivkov, nothing in Gorbachev's public speeches indicated that he was not supporting them or the policies

---

2. See Georges Mink, "La montée des périls en Pologne," *Notes et Études documentaires,* 4737–4738, 1983; "Pologne en 1983–1984," *Notes et Études documentaires,* 4767, 1984.

they were following in their respective states. One could possibly interpret explanations and justifications of perestroika he gave during his
speeches made in their presence as indirect criticism of his dialogue partners, but he never pressed them to adopt similar policies. Yet, a few clear
signs to this effect would have been all that was necessary at the time to
give the potential forces for change in the "fraternal parties" strong
encouragement. Everything therefore seemed to indicate that, while Gorbachev had a special affinity for his more reformist partners in Eastern
Europe, he also was very willing to do "business as usual" with the conservative leaders, who formed the majority within the Warsaw Pact.

If one can speak of any change in Soviet policy toward Eastern Europe
during this initial period, it was essentially limited to a clearly expressed,
and basically fulfilled, willingness not to interfere in the internal politics
of these states. Even if a statement of such a policy was nothing new, following through on it was. From the beginning of his tenure, and even
behind closed doors, Gorbachev stated that each socialist state was free
to choose its own path and that diversity in this area was something
perfectly normal. In a speech he gave before personnel from the Ministry
of Foreign Affairs in May 1986, he declared that, given past errors,
the USSR ought to "show modesty" in its relations with other socialist
countries.[3]

The principles of noninterference in the affairs of other Communist
Parties and their freedom to choose their own paths became the most
persistent rule governing Gorbachev's relations with East European
parties, practically until the very end. In other words, even if this rule
was not always evenly applied and also was used for different ends
depending on the period of time, it weighed heavily on Soviet behavior and gave it a unique orientation and shape. The application of the
rule had such a genuine meaning that the conservative leaders in Eastern Europe could use it, relatively successfully, as an important defense
behind which to hide and resist the contagion of the Soviet example.
That is why the power that this principle wielded in Moscow deserves
an explanation.

The refusal to dictate the East European parties' behavior effectively
seemed an innovative measure in 1985 and 1986, and one can understand that Gorbachev wanted to make it one of the hallmarks of his leadership. He even made a sort of "religion" out of it, or a fundamental
question of principle through which he claimed to distinguish himself

3. *Vestnik Ministerstva Inostrannykh Del SSSR*, 1, 1987.

from his predecessors.[4] However, it is difficult to believe that it was only or mainly for the "beauty of the principle" that he continued to uphold this rule in 1987 and even 1988, when it could harm the coherence of his political project, at the very moment that that project was reaching a fundamental turning point.

A first part of the explanation for Gorbachev's "laissez-faire" policy is that domestic transformations in Eastern Europe were not a priority in the order of importance and urgency of the tasks he had set forth. Arms control, East-West detente, and the restructuring of Soviet society (which was, itself, to benefit from detente) were perceived to be far more pressing undertakings.

Directly related to the first, a second element of the explanation is particularly important for the period extending up to the summer of 1988. It concerns the balance of forces at the top of the Soviet political apparatus and the freedom that Gorbachev and his reformist advisers had to maneuver. In 1987 and the first part of 1988, Gorbachev was far from having an automatic majority in the Politburo. His power was much less consolidated than that of Honecker, Zhivkov, or Ceausescu. Yegor Ligachev, who was identified, even abroad, as the head of the conservatives, remained second only to Gorbachev in the Party apparatus; and the Politburo continued to include several potentates from the Brezhnev era. Eduard Shevardnadze and the Ministry of Foreign Affairs had little hold on relations with Eastern Europe, which remained the preserve of the Party apparatus and the Defense Ministry. Soviet ambassadors in those countries reported directly to the Central Committee. Only in the summer of 1986, almost a year and a half after Gorbachev took power, did Georgii Shakhnazarov, president of the Soviet Political Science Association and later Gorbachev's principal adviser on Eastern Europe, become deputy director of the Central Committee's Department for Liaison with Ruling Communist Parties. Shakhnazarov replaced Oleg Rakhmanin, who was one of the principal defenders of the Brezhnev Doctrine and continued to uphold it even after Gorbachev became general secretary.[5]

Valerii Musatov, who in 1987 was a functionary in the same Central Committee department up to its dissolution in 1988 and then became

4. It is in this way that he, even today, justifies himself at length in his memoirs against critics who have accused him of passivity. Mikhail Gorbachev [Michail Gorbatschow], *Erinnerungen (Memoirs)* (Berlin: Siedler Verlag, 1995), p. 847; translated from German for the author by Laure Castin.

5. See the article published in *Pravda* on 25 June 1985 under Rakhmanin's usual pseudonym, O. Vladimirov; it lashes out against all attempts to seek a basis for relations between socialist states outside of proletarian internationalism.

deputy director of the International Department with responsibility for relations with Eastern Europe, granted interviews to this author. In a first meeting, he stated that, during discussions among reformist Central Committee cadres in 1987, several of them urged that pressure be exerted on the most conservative regimes in the region to put them on the path of political reform. The closest advisers to Gorbachev, however, judged the timing to be inopportune, and even dangerous, for "opening a new front in the battle with the conservatives," he told us.[6]

The principle of noninterference and nonimposition of the new Soviet way on East European countries, as well as the relatively rigid application of this principle, reflected a political compromise at the top of the Soviet apparatus. On the one hand, the countries which wished to follow the path of reforms could do so without being hindered by Moscow (and were encouraged by Gorbachev); on the other hand, those regimes that refused to do so were to be left alone. Yegor Ligachev, who did not have any direct responsibility for relations with the fraternal parties, enjoyed publicly stating in Eastern Europe that "each country can act independently." And he added: "It was said, in the past, that the orchestra was conducted by Moscow, and that all the others should listen. That is no longer the case."[7] Coming from him, those words were doubtless reassuring for Eastern Europe's conservative leaders.

As there was, however, a consensus among the Soviet leadership on the need for the countries of Eastern Europe to improve their economic performance and make changes at that level, comments in this direction were much clearer. It was on the necessity of political reforms and, even more, of a change in East European leaders, that no consensus existed, and so it was with respect to these questions that the rule of noninterference was applied. Only in the context of a very important change in the balance of forces at the top of the Soviet political structure in 1988 did Gorbachev begin to distance himself a bit from the compromise, albeit in a very cautious and indirect manner, as we shall see.

In 1987 and 1988, as a consequence of this compromise, the gap between the different East European regimes grew, as did the variance between the USSR's policy toward the West and toward Eastern Europe. Gorbachev and his reformist advisors could, however, believe that the difference did not (yet) harm their European policy. If a certain amount

6. First interview with Valerii Leonidovich Musatov, Moscow, 4 November 1991.

7. *New York Times*, 5 November 1987, cited by Glenn Chafetz, *Gorbachev, Reform and the Brezhnev Doctrine: Soviet Policy toward Eastern Europe, 1985–1990* (Westport: Praeger, 1993), p. 71.

of democratization in the East was a necessary component of any rapprochement between the two parts of Europe, and for the construction of the "common European home," the USSR was clearly the most important and essential element of that process in the East. At first, the Soviet democratization movement was largely sufficient for advancing the process. To put the importance of the gap into perspective, we must underscore that the European initiative, which we discussed in its final form in the previous chapter, was still being shaped in 1987 and was itself the subject of ambiguities in Gorbachev's declarations. It must also be pointed out that Gorbachev's refusal to practice what the West had reproached Brezhnev for doing, could also constitute a good line of defense against possible Western criticism of Soviet passivity toward the conservative regimes in Eastern Europe.

Finally, another factor explaining Gorbachev's adhesion to the principle of noninterference must be mentioned. He was fully aware, given the historical experience of the region, that the East European regimes were more fragile than the Soviet one. Direct interventions by Stalin's successors to impose the leaders of their choice, especially in Hungary in 1956, had been destabilizing and had generated crises which proved very difficult to control, as Gorbachev knew. His refusal to demand or directly encourage the replacement of East European leaders was also a way to avoid personally taking political responsibility for the possible results of such a policy.

Curiously, while he reproaches Gorbachev for unexpected decisions, Ligachev writes in his memoirs that he found in Gorbachev a different character flaw, namely to waffle and temporize before taking a position on important questions.[8] This behavior, which may seem surprising on the part of a leader who knew how to advance things at such an unexpected pace, is confirmed by several other instances. It can undoubtedly be explained in part by Gorbachev's desire to stay as much as possible in the center, by allowing the reformist current to develop on its own and then adopting compromise measures which did not always go in the same direction.

Therefore, Gorbachev preferred to rely on the diffuse and indirect influence of the changes going on in the USSR, and to wait for changes to come from within the East European regimes themselves. Even when he later abandoned his wait-and-see attitude, the Soviet leader's method

8. Yegor Ligachev, *Inside Gorbachev's Kremlin* (New York: Pantheon Books, 1993), pp. 129–130.

of pressing for change remained marked by a desire to implicate himself as little as possible, directly and personally, especially with regard to the changing of the guard among East European leaders. As we shall see, he began very early to let his close advisers send clear signals, but simultaneously avoided involving himself personally, hence limiting his aides' effectiveness.

At the beginning of 1988, during a meeting in Moscow between the leaders of the Italian Communist Party and Gorbachev, the Italians spoke to him about Czechoslovakia, insisting on "the indispensable renewal that needed to be undertaken there, without generating a process of destabilization." Gorbachev responded, in an evasive and unconvincing manner, "that he could say that all socialist countries were in the process of reflecting on changes, the necessity of which they deemed indispensable for their society." He added that "the depth and rhythm of these changes will vary, depending on the specificity of each nation, but the process of change has been launched."[9]

In 1987, there was one single, open exception to the noninterference rule, and notably to its corollary of not commenting critically on the political choices of East European leaders; it was a revealing exception. During an official visit to Romania in May 1987, Mikhail Gorbachev, in the presence of Nicolae Ceausescu, delivered a long, weighty plea in favor of democratization which contrasted with the simple justifications of Soviet democratization he usually made during his meetings with East European leaders. Even more importantly, he made public criticisms of the cult of personality, nepotism, and the destruction of artistic heritage.[10] This atypical behavior on Gorbachev's part may be explained by three factors, given here in order of decreasing importance. First, from the very beginning of the Brezhnev era, Ceausescu had been considered a nuisance by the Soviet leadership, given his policies toward CMEA and the Warsaw Pact. He had no friends among the Soviet hierarchy, even among its most conservative members. Furthermore, his regime was the most odious of all the East European states, an international pariah. To protect the credibility of his European project, it was therefore in Gorbachev's interest to openly distance himself from the Romanian regime. Finally, during closed-door meetings between War-

9. See Antonio Rubbi, *Incontri con Gorbaciov—i colloqui di Natta e Occhetto con il leader sovietico* (Rome: Editori Riuniti, 1990), p. 191.
10. For Gorbachev's remarks, see *Pravda*, 26 and 27 May 1987. See also Édith Lhomel, "Ceausescu dit non!", *Problèmes politiques et sociaux*, 574, December 1987, pp. 23–24.

saw Pact leaders, Ceausescu was the only one who dared to confront Gorbachev directly and attack his policies.[11]

The specific, more favorable circumstances for intervention sur-rounding the changing of the guard in two East European states—one in 1987, the other in early 1988—reveal more than the Romanian case about Soviet behavior and the influence of the Soviet domestic political context on the region.

THE CZECHOSLOVAK CASE: A MISSED OPPORTUNITY

The political and ideological dependence of East European ruling circles on the Soviet Union was such that the policies Gorbachev pursued in Moscow necessarily influenced their internal political equilibrium and relations between members, even without any pressure for change from the Soviet leader. His policy choices also had a legitimizing or delegit-imizing effect on their political preferences. Of course, the effects varied from one state to another, depending on the balance of power prevail-ing in its top leadership and within the country.

In Czechoslovakia, it was Prime Minister Lubomir Strugal who sought to take advantage of the conjuncture created by Gorbachev's assumption of power. Strugal had been Prime Minister of the Czech republic at the time of the Prague Spring of 1968 but had been won over to the group which took power after the Soviet military intervention. After Leonid Brezhnev's death, he had tried, without success, to have Czechoslovakia adopt a form of "Kadarism," that is, a controlled relax-ation in the political sphere and an economic reform based on the intro-duction of market mechanisms.

After Gorbachev rose to power in Moscow, Strugal renewed his efforts, at first very cautiously. In order to do so, he established a net-work of contacts with the advisers of Kadar, Jaruzelski and Gorbachev, naturally pinning his greatest hopes on the last. Jaromir Sedlak, one of his principal advisors and collaborators, who was given the responsibil-ity of establishing and maintaining links with Gorbachev's entourage, revealed important information about this process to this author.[12] Dur-ing a 1986 stay in Moscow, Strugal came to an understanding with the

11. First interview with Valerii L. Musatov, Moscow, 4 November 1991.
12. A significant proportion of the information that follows is based on an interview with Jaromir Sedlak, given in Prague on 4 May 1993, and above all on a very long research report which he subsequently wrote for me in the framework of this project. This 1993

academician Oleg Bogomolov, director of the Institute of the Economy of the World Socialist System and a reformist adviser to Gorbachev on East European affairs. He would regularly provide Bogomolov, through an intermediary—a researcher of the institute working at the Soviet embassy in Prague—with political analyses and reform propositions from Strugal's office, in order that they might be passed on to Gorbachev's entourage and that Gorbachev might be privy to full, correct information. The Czech prime minister could certainly have used regular diplomatic channels to pass on a certain amount of this information to Moscow. However, the Soviet ambassador in Czechoslovakia, Viktor Lomakin, was not a career diplomat, had been a regional Party secretary, and was politically close to Vasil Bilak, one of the Czechoslovak leaders who had called for Soviet military intervention in 1968. Bilak, a member of the Politburo, supervised foreign affairs for the Central Committee of the Czechoslovak Communist Party (CCP) and was the Soviet ambassador's prime interlocutor. Strugal was convinced that, through this intermediary, his analyses would arrive at Gorbachev's office with counteranalyses and negative commentary. He expected the opposite to happen by going through Bogomolov's institute.

At the beginning of 1987, Gustav Husak, who was more than 70 and in poor health, decided to retire from his position as general secretary of the Czechoslovak Communist Party, without fixing a date for his retirement. So began the political maneuvers for his succession. Though clearly in the minority in a Politburo dominated by conservatives, Strugal counted on his alliance with Antonin Kapek, the first Party secretary of Prague, to carry the day. Kapek was Boris Yeltsin's counterpart, as Yeltsin held the same position in Moscow, and there were contacts between them. Strugal did bet on the "Gorbachev factor," and on support from him. On March 2, 1987, shortly before an official visit Gorbachev was to make to Prague, and for which Strugal had high expectations, the latter made an important public speech at a ceremony organized by Kapek. He stated his support for a renewal of socialism in Czechoslovakia and criticized those politicians who claimed that the new policies adopted by the USSR were not relevant for them. He pointed out that these views were all the more incom-

---

report, entitled "The Road to the Velvet Revolution," concerns the relations between the Soviet and Czechoslovak leadership between 1985 and 1990; the sources for it are his personal notes and documents available in Czechoslovakia.

prehensible as those expressing them had, only a short time before, been touting the universal value of the Soviet experience.[13]

Miroslav Stepan, one of the most conservative leaders of the Czechoslovak Party, the right-hand man of Milos Jakes, and who was later imprisoned for having ordered the violent suppression of the demonstrations of November 17, 1989, writes in his memoirs that there was great nervousness among the leaders in Prague on the eve of Gorbachev's visit, which took place in April 1987.[14] For this, they had good reason.

Indeed, among Gorbachev's advisers in Moscow, there was what Soviet observers termed a "Czechoslovak lobby" or a "Prague club," which had a favorable view of Dubcek's 1968 policies. This circle was composed of intellectuals and cadres who had served in Prague at the headquarters of the international communist movement's journal, Problems of Peace and Socialism, between the mid-1960s and early 1970s. Among its members were Anatolii Cherniaev, Gorbachev's first assistant for international affairs; his spokesman at the time, Gennadi Gerasimov; G. Shakhnazarov, who later followed Gorbachev as part of his presidential staff; and Fyodor Burlatski, editor-in-chief of Literaturnaia Gazeta. Valerii Musatov recalls the discussions which took place in the Central Committee before Gorbachev's visit to Prague. Cherniaev suggested to Gorbachev that he take advantage of his stay in Czechoslovakia to present a new evaluation of the Prague Spring. This is not surprising: was the Prague Spring not, after all, an attempt at democratization in the framework of preserving a one-party system? Musatov adds, not unexpectedly, that Ligachev was opposed to such a reevaluation which, he said, would create grave problems for the Czechoslovak leadership and possibly for the USSR itself. "Gorbachev listened attentively to Cherniaev's suggestion, without saying anything, as was often his habit, and several of us had the impression that he would say something along these lines while in Prague."[15] The Institute of the Economy of the World Socialist System had also sent a

---

13. Dissidents and former militants of the Prague Spring were impressed by the fact that Strugal avoided any negative reference to Dubcek and the 1968 events. For comments from one of them, see Milan Hübel, *Cesty k moci* (Prague: Nase vojsko, 1990), pp. 81–82, cited by Sedlak, "Road to the Velvet Revolution."

14. Miroslav Stepan, *Zpoved vezne sametove revoluce (Confessions of a Prisoner of the Velvet Revolution)* (Prague: Grafit, 1991), pp. 112–113; sections were translated for us by Jaromir Sedlak.

15. Second interview with Valerii L. Musatov, Moscow, 26 April 1993.

report on this question to Gorbachev, and it contained a recommendation similar to Cherniaev's.[16]

For his part, Strugal's adviser had received (premature) assurances from his contacts in Moscow to the effect that Gorbachev would say something positive about the Prague Spring during his visit.[17] Other signals also allowed him to believe in such an outcome. On the very eve of Gorbachev's departure, his spokesman, Gennadi Gerasimov, was asked by Western journalists what the difference was between the Prague Spring and perestroika. To this, Gerasimov answered with two eloquent words: "Nineteen years."[18]

Despite the exceptionally warm reception Mikhail Gorbachev received from the population, and a context that seemed very favorable, he greatly disappointed the veterans of 1968 and Strugal's entourage. Gorbachev did not express any sympathy for the Prague Spring. He also, however, did not fully satisfy the conservatives, who held that the events of 1968 had been a "counterrevolution," preferring himself to qualify them as "chaotic." Perhaps he thought this to be a "centrist" characterization.[19] Without a doubt, it was that same middle turf he was seeking when he stated: "I must say that we have often thought about Czechoslovakia after 1968. It is evident that there were many problems during that difficult period. But you, Czechs and Slovaks, have succeeded in overcoming them and you now have a very modern country."[20]

Vasil Bilak and the conservative majority in the Czechoslovak leadership were relieved by Gorbachev's behavior and speeches. They interpreted them as proof of weakness on his part and were heartened in their maneuvers for Husak's succession. Several months later, an occurrence in Moscow was to solidify their confidence. The event was the removal, in early November, of Boris Yeltsin as Moscow Party first secretary and as member of the Politburo. This was the punishment he endured, it may be recalled, for the frontal assault he had launched against Ligachev in front of the Party Central Committee on October 21, accusing him of being the principal obstacle to perestroika. In the face of the virulent and

16. Interview with Oleg Bogomolov, director of the Institute of the Economy of the World Socialist System, Moscow, 23 April 1993.

17. Sedlak, "Road to the Velvet Revolution."

18. Cited by Charles Gati, *The Bloc That Failed: Soviet-East European Relations in Transition* (Bloomington: Indiana University Press, 1990), p. 178.

19. In 1995, he wrote in his memoirs: "I am often asked why the Soviet Union only admitted very belatedly . . . that the armed intervention of 1968 was a mistake. The answer is simple: the Soviet Union had to change a lot before being in a position to engage in self-criticism" (Gorbachev, *Erinnerungen*, p. 879).

20. *Pravda*, 11 April 1987.

practically unanimous reaction of the speakers who rose to defend Ligachev and attack Yeltsin, Gorbachev, who had initially succeeded in delaying any punitive action, was finally compelled, several days later, to oversee the removal of the man he himself had brought to Moscow in 1985.[21] The departure of Boris Yeltsin and Ligachev's political victory changed the balance of power in the Soviet Politburo, and Gorbachev emerged temporarily weakened.

It was in this context, and in connection with the seventieth anniversary of the October Revolution, that Gustav Husak came to Moscow on November 7; he had a long conversation with Gorbachev, which the latter recounts in great detail in his memoirs. Husak confided to his Soviet counterpart that he intended to resign from his position as general secretary of the Czechoslovak Communist Party (but not as head of state) in the near future. He expressed to Gorbachev his opposition to Vasil Bilak and even to Milos Jakes (who had been linked to the suppression of the Prague Spring) as possible successors.[22] Conversely, he lauded Strugal's merits, and awaited Gorbachev's comments. The latter recalls that he had anticipated being consulted on this issue, and, for this reason, had discussed the question with the Politburo. In conformity with the decision taken there, he refused to give even the slightest advice.[23] Husak nevertheless asked Gorbachev to personally receive Strugal, who was to come to Moscow some days later for meetings with his Soviet counterpart, Nikolai Ryzhkov, and Gorbachev accepted. Given that protocol did not call for such a meeting, Husak saw this as a way of reinforcing Strugal's political position.

In mid-November—Strugal had just returned from Moscow—Bilak, who evidently understood the meaning of Strugal's meeting with Gorbachev, decided to launch an offensive in Prague within the Politburo of the Czechoslovak Communist Party, where he had a majority, to immediately settle Husak's succession.[24] Under these unfavorable conditions, Husak refused to retire. In the meantime, given the balance of power in the Party leadership and the absence of support from Gorbachev, Husak

---

21. See Michel Tatu, *Gorbatchev: l'URSS va-t-elle changer?* (Paris: Le Centurion, 1987), pp. 243–249; Roy Medvedev and Giuletto Chiesa, *Time of Change* (New York: Random House, 1989), pp. 133–148.

22. Gorbachev, *Erinnerungen.*

23. "I had foreseen the course this discussion would take; we had discussed it in the Politburo and we stuck to our collective decision. We did not want to prescribe the manner in which the fraternal parties ought to resolve their leadership problems" (ibid., p. 882).

24. The head of the CPSU Central Committee's department for relations with socialist states relates these events with more, and sometimes contradictory, details. See Vadim

began to envisage a compromise, under which he would cede his position to Jakes, in the hope that Jakes would join forces with Strugal. But Bilak was only interested in having him serve as "deputy general secretary." During this deadlock, which lasted through several meetings,[25] Husak, using the Soviet ambassador in Prague as an intermediary, asked that Gorbachev contact him by telephone. Gorbachev refused.[26]

This example is a prime illustration of Gorbachev's weakness at that time. To call a contender might have been compromising. But to phone his direct counterpart would have been in conformity with all established rules. Several of the less combative conservative Czechoslovak leaders had a very servile attitude toward the USSR, and a hint of support from Gorbachev for Husak might have modified their position. In a note to Gorbachev, Medvedev, responsible for relations with socialist countries, recommended that the former simply express his confidence in Husak.[27] Before Gorbachev could do so, however, Husak finally succeeded in pushing through his compromise solution.[28]

On December 18, the CCP Central Committee ratified the compromise. According to Strugal's adviser, the Soviet prime minister, Nikolai Ryzhkov, called his Czechoslovak counterpart, urging him to cooperate with Jakes to ensure harmony in the new leadership. Similarly, Gorbachev called Jakes to congratulate him and to encourage him to work with Strugal.[29] Moscow apparently expected Jakes to ensure political stability and Strugal to pursue economic reform. This is exactly the type of formula that Ligachev desired for the USSR itself. But Jakes, while paying lip service to the Soviets' perestroika, proved to be an ally of his party's dominant conservatives, even in the area of economic policy, and

---

A. Medvedev, *Raspad: kak on nazreval v "mirovoi sisteme sotsializma" (The Collapse: How It Happened in the "World Socialist System")* (Moscow: Mezhdunarodnye Otnosheniia, 1994), p. 147.

25. Medvedev and Gorbachev both note that the balance in the Politburo was seven to three against Husak, but ten to ten in the broader meeting of the Politburo, candidate members, and the Secretariat.

26. Medvedev, *Collapse*, pp. 147–148.

27. The text of the memorandum is in Medvedev, *Collapse*, p. 50.

28. Asked about the events in 1991, Jakes responded: "Certain comrades were not in favor of promoting Strugal, and proposed my candidacy. I was informed that this proposition was received positively by the CPSU. . . . Gorbachev was undoubtedly informed about my candidacy. By whom? Maybe by the embassy or other sources" (*Reporter*, 17, 1991, supplement, pp. 5–6; translated for us by Jaromir Sedlak). In fact, Gorbachev was informed about Husak's proposed compromise by his ambassador. The fact that he refused to give an opinion could be interpreted as tacit approval.

29. Sedlak, "Road to the Velvet Revolution."

despite the fact that he later managed to push Bilak aside. In 1988, Kapek was forced out of the leadership, and Strugal left political life.

It is missed opportunities such as this, and Gorbachev's frequent passivity toward Eastern Europe, that led Vitalii Zhurkin, one of the architects of the "common European home" and director of the Institute of Europe, to say that the Soviet leader did not have a coherent policy toward those countries.[30] We shall return to this issue. But we can already indicate, at this point, that the coherence of his European policy would end up giving a very particular configuration to his hesitation and caution regarding Eastern Europe.

THE HUNGARIAN CASE:
A TEMPORARILY ATTUNED AGREEMENT

In 1987, all the signs indicated that "Kadarism," which had been one of Eastern Europe's showcases for the Western world, had exhausted its potential. Hungary had reached the highest level of per capita indebtedness among the countries of the region. Almost 70 percent of the state's hard currency revenues were used to service its debt. Economic growth had nearly ceased, and Hungarians' standard of living had been declining significantly and constantly since 1985.[31] Janos Kadar, at 76, not only was incapable of providing any new perspective, but had become an important factor blocking change.

If the population's dissatisfaction was high, the impatience of the Party cadres, technocrats, and enterprise managers was perhaps even greater. For a limited period of time, Karoly Grosz, the new prime minister appointed in June 1987, was able to channel their discontent and to galvanize their energies. Grosz had previously shown himself to be an orthodox and rather conservative apparatchik. After his nomination to the post of prime minister by Kadar, however, he demonstrated remarkable pragmatism and dynamism in the quest for solutions to Hungary's pressing problems. It was, above all, the movement he was able to create that became quite impressive. He injected new life into parliamentary institutions, to the detriment of the Party. Ministries and various state agencies were called upon to be publicly accountable. In early 1988, he formed a coalition with Rezso Nyers, who had been the "father" of

30. Interview with Vitalii Zhurkin, Moscow, 5 November 1991.
31. See G. Schöpflin, R. Tökes, and I. Völgyes, "Leadership Change and Crisis in Hungary," *Problems of Communism,* September-October 1988, pp. 23–46.

Hungary's economic reform program but was later forced out of the Party leadership when brakes were put on the reforms. Grosz also sought out Imre Pozsgay as an ally. Pozsgay favored "socialist pluralism," though that concept was still vague at the time; he had also supported, and even presided over the founding of the Hungarian Democratic Forum in September 1987. The forum, which at the time was not a political party and which no one would have predicted would come to power in 1990, was made up of intellectuals and nationalists. Grosz had every intention to preserve the Party's leading position in the movement for renewal, which he also favored.

In December 1987, the leadership of the Hungarian Socialist Workers' Party (HSWP), following Moscow's example of several months earlier, scheduled an extraordinary Party Conference for May 1988. Gorbachev's purpose in calling the CPSU conference, which took place shortly after the Hungarian one, was to strengthen perestroika. With the May conference in mind, Karoly Grosz launched a campaign in early 1988, which ever more clearly was aimed at forcing Janos Kadar to quit the leadership of the Party. It was, Grosz told this writer, "extremely difficult to convince him to retire."[32] "Several years prior, he had thought about resigning, but, in 1988, Kadar saw himself as the captain of a ship in peril and refused to leave the helm, believing that he alone had the experience to steer it clear of the worst." Given this, the author asked Grosz whether Kadar sought support from Gorbachev, for whom he was an admired precursor. Grosz responded that Kadar "knew precisely that he could not count on any support from Gorbachev"; Grosz continued: "In 1985 and 1986, his relations with Gorbachev were excellent. But, in 1987, he became convinced that Gorbachev, through his policies, would bring a catastrophe upon the USSR. . . . As Kadar was a prominent figure in the international communist movement, he did not hesitate to repeat this opinion, not only in our Politburo, but also in front of Soviet visitors. Gorbachev knew that and believed he had only one true ally among East European leaders, General Jaruzelski."[33]

In fact, counting on his own influence, it was more the support of Gromyko and Ligachev that Kadar sought.[34] But Gorbachev was in a position to invoke the minimal consensus on the rule of nonintervention to permit the forces of change to succeed in Hungary. By all counts,

32. Interview with Karoly Grosz, Gödöllö, 1 May 1992.
33. Ibid.
34. See information obtained by G. Schöpflin and his coauthors.

Grosz was expecting at least implicit support from Gorbachev.[35] As shown above, most of Grosz's policies and directives were in the same vein as Gorbachev's, or were at most a few months ahead of the Soviet leader's own initiatives.

The advice of Medvedev, head of the CPSU Central Committee's Department for Liaison with the Communist Parties of Socialist States, was very clear. In March 1988, he sent a memorandum to Gorbachev, in which he stressed that Kadar "does not feel the changes in the mood of the public and the Party" and that "his interlocutors say . . . that he is incapable of leading the renewal of the Party's policy, and does not recognize his incapacity."[36] Medvedev recommended using the upcoming visits by Ryzhkov and Yakovlev to Budapest to convince their Hungarian partners that their country was at a turning point. He added "that it would be useful to demonstrate, in all acceptable ways, political support for Comrade Grosz."[37]

According to all indications available, Gorbachev avoided any personal involvement. When Kadar phoned him for consultations under the pretext that he did not want the Soviet leader to "learn of his decision from the newspapers,"[38] Gorbachev dispatched Vladimir Kriuchkov to Budapest as his personal emissary. Kadar was not urged to retire, but he also did not receive any encouragement to keep his position. If he still had some doubts about the Soviet leader's personal opinion, they were definitively removed by Gorbachev himself on May 19, when Kadar phoned to recount the circumstances surrounding his decision to allow Grosz to take over. He was then told: "This decision must not have been easy for you. It proves the political wisdom of the Hungarian leader, of my friend Janos Kadar. The interests of the Party and the country must be preserved. I can tell you in all honesty that I would not have expected you to take any other decision. I was convinced that you would take it when it would become necessary."[39]

Indeed, Gorbachev had every reason to be satisfied when Grosz was elected general secretary of the HSWP.[40] Imre Pozsgay and Rezso

---

35. He was informed of his intentions by his Soviet counterpart Ryzhkov, who visited Budapest in February 1988 (Schöpflin et al., "Leadership Change and Crisis in Hungary)".

36. The text of the memorandum may be found in Medvedev, *Raspad,* p. 127.

37. Ibid., p. 128.

38. Gorbachev, *Erinnerungen,* p. 857.

39. Transcript of the conversation in ibid., p. 858.

40. According to Matyas Szuros, who was Hungary's president in autumn 1989 and was the HSWP Secretariat's person responsible for international relations in 1988, Gorbachev would have preferred another, more reformist, successor to Kadar, given Grosz's

Nyers became Politburo members. And an honorary post of president of the Party was created for Kadar, which did not give him a seat on the Politburo.

Rather than direct action by the Soviet leader, it was the "Gorbachev effect" that destabilized Kadar within his party and allowed Grosz to succeed. Kadar had long been a master of the art of playing on the narrow limits of Soviet permissiveness. It was on this very field that he was beaten. If the "Gorbachev effect" was felt more decisively in Hungary than in Czechoslovakia some months earlier, this was also a result of Kadar's more liberal legacy.

The harmony between Grosz and Gorbachev only lasted briefly. Events in Hungary were to become far more precipitous than in the USSR. As we shall see, Gorbachev was able to adjust to and accept the changes more easily than Grosz. From early 1989, the Hungarian leader started to be overwhelmed by his allies and the forces he had allowed to be unleashed. If such comparisons are useful, one might say that he proved to be more a Hungarian Ligachev than a Gorbachev.

THE GORBACHEVITES' IMPATIENCE

Gorbachev's caution and his refusal to put pressure on the majority of conservative leaders in Eastern Europe to push them down the road toward democratization were far from being an approach shared by his entourage and reformist advisers. Beginning in 1987, several of them began to show their impatience with official immobilism, even in their public writings and declarations. It must be remembered that, in 1987, foreign policy was still a sphere closed to open criticism.

In an article written for the theoretical journal of the Party Central Committee, Oleg Bogomolov, director of the Institute of the Economy of the World Socialist System, cautiously criticized those in the Soviet leadership who were ready to accept reforms in Eastern Europe that were limited to economic policy. Writing about those countries, he underscored "the necessity of restructuring the political rules and social relations, without which changes in the economy and technology will

conservative past. György Aczel, a member of the Politburo in the Kadar period, was of the same opinion. They are based on the flattering comments made by Gorbachev and his entourage about Hungarian leaders other than Grosz. Among those whom Gorbachev supposedly preferred, Szuros names Pozsgay, Miklos Nemeth, Nyers, Gyula Horn, and himself. Interviews with Matyas Szuros, Budapest, 4 May 1992 and with György Aczel, Budapest, 8 May 1990.

only remain pipe dreams."[41] In another article on Eastern Europe, published in November 1987, Bogomolov wrote that "the domestic and international conditions . . . imperatively demand proceeding with transformations."[42] Writing about the diversity which existed in the socialist world, Bogomolov did not, as was customary, applaud it. He stated that it would be "from the generalization of the collective experience that an optimal model for the new society will emerge." It was clear that the "optimal model" was perestroika. While acknowledging the legitimacy of "the variety of forms and methods of socialist transformations," he commented that it was also necessary to take into account "the common needs of the socialist world's development." In a roundabout, but quite stunning way, he found himself invoking the terms of the Brezhnev Doctrine in order to demand changes in Eastern Europe. In 1988, under more favorable circumstances, he would continue to make the same suggestions.[43]

Fyodor Burlatski, chief editor of Literaturnaia Gazeta, a magazine which strongly supported perestroika, declared the following in an interview given to an Austrian newspaper, in a tone meant to be ironic: "We have given our allies so much bad advice in the past that we now hesitate to give them good advice."[44]

In closed-door discussions and debates within the leadership, the desire to move ahead more rapidly in transforming the international system was expressed far more boldly and more articulately. In this regard, it is useful to examine a particularly revealing report presented to the Ministry of Foreign Affairs on November 27, 1987, by Vyacheslav Dashichev of the Institute of the Economy of the World Socialist System, who then chaired the scientific-consultative council of the Ministry's division for socialist states.[45] His report examined the "German question," and the heart of its message was to demonstrate that the status

41. Oleg Bogomolov, "Mir sotsializma na puti perestroiki" (The Socialist World on the Road to *Perestroika*), *Kommunist*, 16, 1987, pp. 92–102.

42. Oleg Bogomolov, "Le monde du socialisme à l'étape cruciale," *La Vie internationale*, November 1987, pp. 12–23. Solidarity and relations between East European states were, at the time, an extremely sensitive issue, so much so that even Bogomolov had to acknowledge their sensitivity. In his article, he does so with a phrase that is most astonishing, given the source: "The socialist countries form the most dynamic sector of the world economy, and have done so for the past several decade."

43. See *Komsomol'skaia Pravda*, 23 July 1988.

44. *Die Presse*, April 1988, cited by Charles Gati, *The Bloc That Failed: Soviet-East European Relations in Transition* (Bloomington: Indiana University Press, 1990), pp. 76–77.

45. The text of this report was given to us by its author during an interview in Moscow on 1 November 1991. The report is entitled *Nekotorye aspekty "germanskoi problemy"*

quo between the two Germanys was fundamentally contrary to the USSR's interests, and that the latter would have everything to gain, on all levels of the perestroika process, by initiating a change of policy.

Dashichev argued that the division of Europe was expressed first and foremost by the division of Germany, which experienced the division in its most acute form. Consequently, it would not be possible to advance the process of European reconciliation very much without calling into question the status quo in Germany. He suggested that there was a dialectic link between the two questions. In other words, to find a solution to the German problem, pan-European detente also needed to be relatively far along. But in order keep the European process "open," the German question also had to be "open."[46] Following the logic of the new Soviet policy toward Europe, he openly stated that the position of the Honecker regime, which had claimed that "the German question has been definitively solved," directly contradicted Soviet interests.[47]

It was mainly, but not exclusively, due to foreign policy considerations that Dashichev believed the German question could not lie dormant indefinitely. Prophetically, and in a manner unusual even in the West, he stated that aspirations for reunification were significantly stronger in the German Democratic Republic (GDR) than in West Germany.[48] Using West German sources, he cited comparative figures that were devastating for the Honecker regime. He mentioned as examples that the difference between the two Germanys in the area of worker productivity, which had been 25 percent in 1963, had reached 40 percent in 1987, and that real income was 50 percent higher in the Federal Republic of Germany (FRG). Because of the desire for reunification, it was more urgent in the GDR than elsewhere to initiate radical reforms, in order to give the population "new horizons and hopes in socialist development."

Dashichev presented several "possible variants in the evolution of the German question from the point of view of Soviet interests," weighing the advantages and disadvantages of each. The first option was the preservation of the status quo, both within the GDR and in inter-German relations, a status quo which he saw as harboring only disadvantages. In this case, he argued that the traditional Soviet nightmare

---

(Some Aspects of the "German Problem"). Dated November 17, 1987, it was presented to and debated by the Ministry of Foreign Affairs ten days later, on November 27.

46. Dashichev, *Nekotorye aspekty "germanskoi problemy,"* pp. 18–19.

47. More literally, he spoke of "the thesis of the definitive closing (*okonchatel'noi zakrytnosti*) of the German question which GDR policy supports" (ibid., p. 20).

48. Ibid., p. 20.

would likely become reality: West European military integration, "based on the Bundeswehr and Anglo-French nuclear weapons." He foresaw accentuation of the economic and technological gap between the two Germanys and the continuation of "the 'bloc' character of international relations in Europe."[49] For Dashichev, support of the GDR's domestic and foreign policies would favor rigidity in the entire East European region, harm economic and political reforms, hinder the transformation of CMEA and put it on a new basis, and therefore be more costly for the USSR and cripple perestroika.

Among the alternatives to the status quo which he examined, Dashichev did not explicitly favor one over the other. However, the option for which he cited the greatest number of advantages was "unification" on the basis of Germany's neutrality and withdrawal from the two blocs. He had claimed, citing opinion polls, that a strong current in favor of this option was progressively and continually gaining strength in West Germany. An ever-growing number of West Germans, he stated, were realizing that the Federal Republic's Western allies were not interested in German reunification and that the "key" to it was to be found in Moscow; furthermore, neutrality would be a small price to pay for obtaining reunification. As a result, a unilateral initiative in this direction on the part of the USSR would encounter irresistible support from the German population and put the Western powers on the defensive.[50] Dashichev hence called on Gorbachev's propensity for bold initiatives, the method which had made such an impact and had so much success on the international scene in the area of disarmament, both with respect to Euromissiles and the Reykjavik summit. The benefits of a Soviet policy with this purpose were held to be numerous and important. Without Germany, NATO would lose its raison d'etre, and the Soviet Union would be in a good position to propose the immediate dissolution of the two blocs. We should recall that in November 1987, the idea of preserving American presence in Europe was not yet a consensus opinion among the reformers. Dashichev listed the certain end of U.S. military presence in Europe as one of the advantages of German reunification, and his vision of the "common European home" under this hypothesis excluded the Americans. France and England would henceforth seek better relations with the USSR, which they would see as a necessary counterweight to Germany in Europe. The EEC and CMEA could be transformed into a

49. Ibid., p. 23.
50. Ibid., p. 14.

pan-European organization for economic cooperation. Both Poland and Czechoslovakia, he stated, would be more solidly aligned with the Soviet Union to provide security for their Western borders. Finally—and this is a very interesting aspect—Dashichev claimed that this option would advance the ideas and cause of socialism in West Germany and all across Europe. This hypothesis might seem surprising, but it directly mirrors one of the theses of the Italian Communist Party, which, at the end of the 1970s, had asserted that the polarization of the international system (which it accused the USSR of reinforcing through its policy of force) strengthened the internal polarization of European societies and impeded the Left, burdened by the Soviets' image and policies, from making gains in the centrist electorate.[51] According to Dashichev, there already were very favorable conditions in West Germany for the advancement of "socialization," which would receive "an enormous boost" from reunification, bringing with it the collapse of anti-Soviet attitudes. It is clear that the socialism in question was not Soviet-style socialism. This final argument of Dashichev's was not simply a requisite lip service to socialism in a report remarkably free of propagandistic verbiage. His bold report was not directed at the conservatives, but rather to the attention of reformers, and he was using an appeal to the messianic ambition of Gorbachev's initiative to get his message across.[52]

The only disadvantage Dashichev mentioned in connection with the unification-neutralization option was that it might be considered as "a violation of the principles of socialist internationalism" with respect to the GDR.[53] And for good reason! He also suggested another option which would be far less problematic in this regard: a confederation formula between the two German states. Such an alternative would also be very advantageous for Soviet interests, he wrote. But it presupposed

51. See Jacques Lévesque, "Le Parti communiste italien, l'URSS et l'ordre international. Le cheminement du PCI depuis 1975," *Revue française de science politique,* 37 (2), April 1987, pp. 141–179.

52. As to the question of whether Dashichev himself believed in the simultaneous advancement, in East and West, toward a new democratic socialism, the Hungarian sociologist Istvan Rev's comments on the convictions of East European economic reformers may provide an adequate response. He writes: "The only way that the economic reformers could succeed in introducing some elements of the market system in the rigid world of central planning was to promise to make the planning mechanism more efficient. In the process of persuading the leadership of the Party, the reformers could not avoid convincing themselves. After a while, the majority of economic reformers firmly believed in the phenomenon of "market socialism," which combined the positive elements of the planning mechanism and of the market." Istvan Rev, "The Postmortem Victory of Communism," *Daedelus,* 123 (3), Summer 1994, pp. 159–170.

53. Rev, "Postmortem Victory of Communism," p. 25.

important reforms in East Germany. If he had built his list of advantages on this option, rather than on the previous one, his report might not have been received as negatively as it was.

Indeed, according to its author, the report unleashed a wave of criticism from his audience, even from the reformers. Only Shevardnadze, he claims, abstained from negative comments, though he also did not signal any approval.[54] For most reformers, the GDR remained one of the pillars of Soviet power and influence in Europe. They were thinking in terms of a reformed, redynamized East Germany. Even if there was no great sympathy for him, Honecker commanded respect within the Soviet political apparatus—more so than any other East European leader. The respect went so far that one Soviet diplomat claimed Honecker practically had a veto right over the USSR's German policy.[55] It was felt in Moscow that he was leading the most efficient socialist economy at the time. He arrogantly proclaimed those successes, even writing about them himself in the Soviet press. He openly and directly declared that, as a result, the GDR was not in need of any kind of perestroika.[56]

For their part, Gorbachev, Shevardnadze, and the majority of their entourage had good reasons for believing that a status quo in the German question was not an obstacle to their European policy, and that the GDR would have a full part in the "common European home." West Germany's Social Democrats (or SPD), which had in part inspired Gorbachev's European policy and were his prime partner in West Germany (with a good chance of returning to power in the fairly near future) believed that the question of German unity should be put on the back burner so as not to harm the building of European security. Egon Bahr, the SPD's chief ideologist, wrote in 1988 that "just as German unity could not be an obstacle to the European Act [of Helsinki], so it equally cannot be a condition for European security now."[57] Rather than one peace treaty for all of Germany, which he believed to be unrealistic, he

54. Interview with V. I. Dashichev, Moscow, 1 November 1991.
55. Igor' Maksimychev, "What 'German Policy' We Need," *International Affairs,* September 1991, pp. 53–64.
56. *Pravda,* 26 January 1988. Sensing the implications of the concept of a "common European home," Honecker showed himself to be very reticent about the idea, beginning in 1987. He categorically opposed the philosophy on which it was based, and stated that socialism and capitalism were as irreconcilable "as fire and water." Cited by Michael Sodaro, *Moscow, Germany and the West from Khrushchev to Gorbachev* (New York: Columbia University Press, 1990), p. 372.
57. Egon Bahr, *Zum europischen Frieden: eine Antwort auf Gorbatschow (Concerning Peace in Europe: An Answer to Gorbachev)* (Berlin: Corso bei Siedler Verlag GmbH, 1988), p. 40; translated for our research by Laure Castin. The acronym "SPD" stands for the German party name: *Sozialdemokratische Partei Deutschland.*

foresaw two parallel treaties, confirming the adherence of the two Germanys to their respective alliances. It was on the basis of accepting the status quo, that is to say of two German states and two alliances, that favorable conditions would be created, allowing the development and intensification of a new modus vivendi. This perspective corresponded perfectly to Gorbachev's approach at the time.[58]

Dashichev's ideas, however, were destined to progressively, step by step, make headway among circles within the Soviet leadership, especially as the pressure of rapidly changing events increased. Nonetheless, the leaders had already realized that it was in the USSR's interest to leave the German question at least "half-open." In other words, cloaking the future in a certain ambiguity could broaden the current of benevolence toward Soviet policy in West Germany. In this regard, the former Soviet ambassador to the Federal Republic and future head of the CPSU Central Committee's International Department, Valentin Falin, had told West Germany television in 1987 that the 1971 quadripartite agreement on Berlin "was not the last word" and that one could consider "more interesting models."[59] N. Portugalov, while discounting the idea of a German confederation as being very premature, stated that it would be better to start by creating "inter-German commissions" to settle various questions.[60] As we shall see, the idea of a confederation of the two German states was later considered, secretly. But when Gorbachev finally did propose the unification-neutralization option, he had already completely lost the initiative in international affairs and was lagging far behind the pace of events.

---

58. At the moment Dashichev presented his report, the dominant point of view in Moscow was best expressed by N. Portugalov, the Party Central Committee's specialist on Germany, who reprimanded the leaders of the German Christian Democrats in power in Bonn, and stated: "On the basis of an unconditional recognition of post-war realities, it would be possible to view the borders through different eyes, and the inter-German border could become transparent." N. Portugalov, "Der CDU fehlt das ostpolitische Bad Godesberg" (The CDU needs a Bad Godesberg for Its *Ostpolitik*), *Blätter für deutsche und internationale Politik*, 11, 1987, pp. 1392–1404; translated for our research by Laure Castin. Bad Godesberg was the site of the 1959 SPD Congress at which the party renounced its links to Marxism.

59. Cited by Sodaro, Moscow, Germany and the West, p. 353.

60. Portugalov, "Der CDU fehlt das ostpolitische Bad Godesberg."

CHAPTER FOUR

The Second Half of 1988

The Turning Point

Between the dream . . .

The objective is to create a qualitatively new model of socialism in these countries that would be truly human in its nature. This would lead to a draconian change in the role of these states in the pan-European process and in the system of East-West relations.[1]

and the nightmare . . .

The direct use of force by the USSR in favor of the conservatives would signify, in a perfectly obvious manner, the end of *perestroika,* the loss of the world community's confidence in us . . . and it would compromise the idea of socialism in all its variants.[2]

THE ACCELERATION OF *PERESTROIKA*

The Soviet leaders' behavior toward Eastern Europe began to change during the summer of 1988. At first, the shift did not seem very radical. *Direct* intervention and pressure to modify the composition of the regimes continued to be avoided. The conservative leaders were, however, treated far less tactfully. Soviet policies which directly affected them

1. Report of the Institute of the Economy of the World Socialist System, presented to a Soviet-American colloquium on Eastern Europe in Arlington, Va., in July 1988; text reprinted in Charles Gati, *The Bloc That Failed: Soviet-East European Relations in Transition* (Bloomington: Indiana University Press, 1990), p. 207.

2. "Confidential" report of the Institute of the Economy of the World Socialist System entitled *Peremeny v vostochnoi Evrope i ikh vliianie na SSSR* (The Changes in East Europe and Their Influence on the USSR), presented to the CPSU leadership in February 1989 (pp. 22, 30).

were implemented without regard for their sensitivities, despite their objections and irrespective of the problems those policies might cause them. Messages and signals, which became ever more open, were directed to them, indicating that they would either reform or suffer all of the consequences of their tardiness. This bolder Soviet behavior was not the product of events within the East European states themselves. Instead, it was the result of a clear acceleration of *perestroika* and a change in the balance of political power in the Soviet Union, which had repercussions on foreign policy.

On the domestic front, the first conspicuous event for our purposes was the 19th Party Conference, which took place from June 28 to July 1, 1988. No such "mini-congresses" had been held since the time of Stalin. It had been conceived the year before in order to give a new boost to *perestroika,* and its preparation had witnessed several political battles over the determination of its development and outcome. The conference paid off by becoming a major success for Gorbachev and the reformers. Under the slogan of creating a "socialist *Rechtsstaat,*" it adopted important measures for reducing the tutelage of the Party apparatus over the State by assigning the latter more autonomy and powers. It would allow the creation of new parliamentary institutions and permit multiple candidates for elections. There was still no question of multiple parties, but the Party apparatus lost exclusive control over the nomination of candidates. This measure, combined with the obligation imposed on Party functionaries of all levels to face the electorate, would lead to the elimination of several among them the following year.

At the end of September, following the 19th Party Conference, the most dramatic and decisive test of strength at the top of the Party since Gorbachev's assumption of power took place. A series of decisions announced on September 30, at the end of a dramatic Central Committee meeting, clearly signalled a turning point in Gorbachev's struggle for reform. First, drastic measures were announced which would reorganize the Party with a view to reducing the size of the apparatus and its instruments of control over the State. Furthermore, the "resignation" (read: divestiture) of four Politburo members who had been obstacles to the new direction in foreign and domestic policies was announced: Gromyko[3] and Solomentsev, and two candidate members, Dolgykh and

3. Gromyko, who had supported Gorbachev at the decisive moment of the Chernenko succession in 1985, could only oppose the unexpected foreign policy direction of Gorbachev and Shevardnadze, which turned its back on all that had given the USSR its international stature during his period.

Demichev. Even more importantly, two "reassignments" were made. Chebrikov, who had emerged during the previous months as an ally of Ligachev, was removed as head of the KGB and became the president of a judicial commission. Ligachev himself was stripped of his responsibility for ideology and put in charge of a commission on agricultural policy. Even though he remained in the Politburo, he had ceased to be second in the Party hierarchy.

On the other hand, Aleksandr Yakovlev was given the leadership of a new commission for international affairs, which supervised the International Department. Valentin Falin, the famous Germanist and former ambassador to West Germany, became head of the International Department, which annexed the Department for Liaison with the Communist Parties of Socialist States. Yakovlev became the de facto number two of the Party. With Shevardnadze at the head of the Ministry of Foreign Affairs and Yakovlev as his counterpart in the Party apparatus, the control over foreign policy was now in the hands of what the conservatives would later call the "leading revisionist *troika*": Gorbachev, Yakovlev, and Shevardnadze. Its control was certainly not complete, but its freedom to maneuver grew considerably after these changes in the balance of power.

It was in the sphere of European policy that the new freedom was first used. In conformity with the policy priorities outlined in the previous chapters with respect to the Soviet effort to attenuate Europe's division, it was the military level which was the first to be decisively addressed. This was done by means of a spectacular initiative, in line with Gorbachev's innovative behavior which had contributed to his success on the international stage.

In anticipation of a new round of negotiations about to begin in Vienna on conventional forces in Europe (CFE), which in the past had been going in circles for years without any concrete results, Gorbachev used his speech to the United Nations General Assembly on December 7, 1988 to announce a series of unilateral reductions to restart the negotiations on a new basis and to create a favorable context for a speedier outcome. These steps reflected Gorbachev's impatience to obtain rapid results in this area and, at the same time, his desire to begin reducing the burden of Soviet military expenditures in a faster, more significant manner. The reductions he announced amounted to 500,000 troops, or about 10 percent of the Red Army's total manpower. Within that total, and of more specific interest to us, Gorbachev announced the withdrawal of 10,000 troops from those East European countries directly bordering on

Western Europe: the GDR, Czechoslovakia, and Hungary.[4] The USSR was also to withdraw and dismantle 10,000 tanks from Europe, including 5,000 from the westernmost members of the Warsaw Pact. It should be pointed out that this last figure represented 50 percent of Soviet tanks in those countries. Finally, Gorbachev also announced the removal of 8,500 artillery pieces (out of 33,000) and 800 fighter planes (of 6,050) from Europe. Similar measures were subsequently adopted by the other states of the Warsaw Pact.

Those reductions could not, on their own, end Soviet superiority in conventional weapons in Europe. Beyond the desire to create a favorable climate for the negotiations to come, they also were designed to have an immediate political impact. The measures directly responded to anxieties which had long been held in the West concerning the offensive position of the Warsaw Pact and the quantitative disequilibria underlying it, particularly with respect to the number of assault tanks, which Gorbachev had pledged to reduce by 50 percent. The reductions were also intended to affect attack units equipped to cross rivers, amphibious vehicles, and mobile, sophisticated systems for facilitating the movement of tanks. As such, they were designed to give a specific content to the concepts of "nonoffensive defense" and "reasonable sufficiency," which Moscow had already put forth, and to increase their credibility.[5] This is why these measures had such a great resonance in Europe, and especially in West Germany, where they threw Chancellor Kohl's military policy into disarray. Kohl had been solidly behind NATO's project of modernizing short-range nuclear weapons and its refusal to negotiate with the USSR about this type of armaments.

Measures along the lines of those announced in December 1988 had already been envisaged by Gorbachev more than one year earlier.[6] If it took this long for them to be adopted, it was not only because the initiative encountered stiff resistance within the USSR and from the Soviet

4. As for the remainder, 240,000 troops were to be withdrawn from the European part of the USSR and possibly Poland, and 250,000 from its Asian part.

5. Commenting on the measure, the Soviet defense minister, General Yazov, declared: "All of this means that 'the potential for a surprise attack' which has long been used to intimidate the public in West European countries is in the process of being removed" (*Izvestiia*, 28 February 1989).

6. In his book published in autumn 1987, he stated that one needed to plan "the withdrawal of offensive weapons from the zones of direct contact in order to eliminate any possibility of a surprise attack, and a change in the overall structure of the armed forces, with a view to giving them an exclusively defensive character" (*Perestroika: Vues neuves sur notre pays et le monde* [Paris: Flammarion, 1987], p. 294). Those measures were clearly not presented, at the time, as being of a unilateral nature.

military. It was leaked, and later confirmed, that East Germany and Czechoslovakia had opposed unilateral reductions of this type during a Warsaw Pact meeting in July 1988.[7]

Solidarity between the Soviet conservatives and the leaders of those countries was not surprising, and gave them mutual reinforcement, at least tacitly.[8] Ligachev's famous August 1988 phrase (at a time when he was still responsible for ideological issues), which contradicted one of the fundamental theses of "new thinking," is most eloquent in this regard. He stated: "We hold fast to the class character of international relations. Any other formulation can only lead to disarray in the minds of the Soviet people and among our friends abroad."[9] Eastern Europe's conservative leaders were betting on an eventual victory by Ligachev in the Moscow power battles, and his "reassignment" in September 1988 was a harsh setback for them. They could only expect to be "pushed around" far more by Gorbachev and his reformist entourage.

It should be underscored that the conservative East European leaders' preoccupation was not mainly the Soviets' "free" concessions to NATO within the unilateral Soviet reductions announced by Gorbachev. The *implicit* message these measures could be interpreted as carrying was the real source of the leaders' anxiety. And, in fact, these measures could create the impression of a Soviet political and military disengagement from the East European regimes, and hence encourage opposition movements in those countries. It was, incidentally, in this way that the Soviet initiative was confusedly (mis)understood in those countries.[10]

In such conditions, it was not by accident that the acceleration of *perestroika,* and the measures that followed, brought about a repudiation of the Brezhnev Doctrine; that repudiation, while still indirect, was clearer and less ambiguous than before. In his report to the 19th Party Conference, Gorbachev elevated each country's "freedom to choose" its sociopolitical regime to the level of a "universal principle" and to being

7. From leaks gathered by the *Baltimore Sun,* 17 July 1988; cited by Karen Dawisha, *Eastern Europe, Gorbachev and Reform: The Great Challenge* (Cambridge: Cambridge University Press, 1990), p. 212.

8. And sometimes even more. In 1988, Soviet officers opposed to the unilateral reductions supposedly encouraged Eastern Europe's conservative leaders to preserve their opposition to the measures through their own contacts. Interview with A. Baev, Institute of Europe, USSR Academy of Sciences, Moscow, 5 November 1991.

9. *Pravda,* 6 August 1988.

10. In accordance with the Soviet initiative, the conservative leaders of these states proceeded with unilateral reductions of their own military forces. These reductions obviously did not have the same political connotation as the Soviets' measures

a "key concept" of the Soviet Union's new foreign policy.[11] Addressing the results of the Party Conference during a Foreign Ministry "scientific and practical conference" called to assess the Party meeting, Shevardnadze picked up on and amplified Gorbachev's comments.[12] They were amplified by several other Soviet officials.[13]

These declarations, and the importance Soviet leaders assigned to them, carried various messages to different audiences. In the context of the summer of 1988, they were directed, first and foremost, at Western political circles. From the beginning of the Gorbachev era, Western political analysts most skeptical of "new thinking" had established two litmus tests for the credibility of a fundamental change in Soviet foreign policy: withdrawing from Afghanistan and abandoning the Brezhnev Doctrine. For other and more compelling reasons, it was easier to reach a consensus among the Soviet leadership on a withdrawal from Afghanistan. The Geneva accords regarding Soviet withdrawal were signed in May 1988 but could have been completed earlier if a formula had been found to help the Soviet Union "save face."[14] During the second half of 1988, Gorbachev sought a major breakthrough in East-West relations in Europe. The proclamations about the "universality" of "freedom of choice" were part of the declarations and measures designed to facilitate that breakthrough.

At the same time, however, the same statements were intended as a signal to Soviet political and military circles that the USSR would not, under any circumstances, intervene militarily in Eastern Europe, as to do so would ruin the investments made to reorder East-West relations. For Gorbachev and his team, it was clear that military intervention in the region would be a possibly fatal blow to *perestroika* and their entire undertaking. The historic precedents served as a reminder of this. Soviet

11. He stated: "The concept of choice occupies a key place (*kliuchevoe mesto*) in the new thinking. We believe in the universality of this principle for international relations. . . . In this situation, foreign imposition of a social system or a lifestyle through any method, and even more so through military measures, is a dangerous way of acting from the past" (*Pravda*, 28 June 1988).

12. *Vestnik Ministerstva Inostrannykh Del SSSR*, 15, August 1988, pp. 27–46.

13. For example, Vadim Loginov, an official in the Central Committee's International Department, stated in an interview given to an Austrian journal: "Every people and every country has the right to choose its own economic and political social system and its own aspirations, and no one has the right, in this regard, to impose, whether it be through a revolution or a counterrevolution" (*Neue Kronen-Zeitung*, 23 July 1988, from Foreign Broadcast Information Service, 26 July 1988).

14. See Jacques Lévesque, *L'URSS en Afghanistan: de l'invasion au retrait* (Brussels: Complexe [Coll. "La mémoire du siècle"], 1990), pp. 229–245.

intervention in Hungary and Czechoslovakia had provoked an important conservative reaction in the USSR. In June 1957, due to the events
in Hungary for which he was held accountable, Khrushchev had found
himself in the minority within the Politburo, which demanded his resignation. In 1968, the repression of the Prague Spring brought about the
final blow to the economic reforms which Prime Minister Alexei Kosy-
gin had been trying to introduce.

Finally, the message was also directed at Eastern Europe's leaders.
They had already been discreetly advised that they could no longer count
on Soviet military intervention. The official proclamations cited above,
however, gave much more force to that message, and made it more difficult to reverse.

Given these increasingly plain indications, it must be asked whether
Gorbachev and his circle believed that the socialist regimes and Communist Parties could preserve their position in the region in a context
that excluded a resort to Soviet military force as the ultimate guarantee
of their grip on power. The response is self-evident, but it immediately
raises several other questions. Soviet reformist leaders were convinced
that the regimes could survive, on the condition that they reform themselves. The Brezhnev Doctrine's revocation was both a warning and a
way of pushing them toward reform. However, given that the Soviet
leaders knew these regimes were far more fragile than the Soviet system,
one can only ponder how they could possibly have believed that even
limited democratization in Eastern Europe would not lead to the collapse of those regimes.[15]

We are dealing here with one of the fundamental characteristics of the
ideology of *perestroika*. In 1988 and 1989, the voices of *perestroika*, in
particular Aleksandr Yakovlev, continually repeated that a political
party could regain legitimacy—on the condition that it demonstrated
boldness and vision by taking the initiative in making necessary, historic
changes. I would term this the "initiativist ideology," constituting one
of the most important parts of *perestroika*'s ideological structure. It
should be noted that "initiativism" had worked perfectly well for Gorbachev up until that time, and not only in foreign policy; within the

15. The concept of a renewed socialism was constantly evolving. In 1988, it was still
defined as follows: "The essence of a new model of power can be defined as a delegation
of considerable responsibility to the local level, to territorial and work collectives, and as
the expansion of pluralism in public life and the democratization of all institutions, including the avant-garde Party" (Report of the Institute of the Economy of the World Socialist
System presented to a Soviet-American colloquium on Eastern Europe in Alexandria, Va.,
July 1988; in Gati, *The Bloc That Failed*, p. 211).

USSR, he had succeeded in creating an enthusiastic movement for his policies, especially among the country's intelligentsia.

There is also another important element of *perestroika*'s ideological body that applies to Eastern Europe, and which is related to the "initiativist" component outlined above: the conviction that *perestroika* could co-opt a significant part of the opposition through its progression. In the summer and fall of 1988, when the nationalist-inspired Popular Fronts (parties had not yet been authorized) were founded in the Baltic republics, Communist Party rank-and-file members and leaders alike were encouraged to participate. In Lithuania, the majority of the founders of "Sajudis" were Communists, and the Lithuanian Party first secretary participated in the movement's founding congress. Even if the purpose was largely one of co-opting and manipulating outside forces (which formed part of a long Bolshevik tradition), these terms are not entirely adequate to fully do justice to Soviet reformers' intentions. Certainly, by "accompanying" the nationalist movements, one of the objectives was to slow down and moderate their nationalism. Contrary to pure Bolshevik tradition, however, the parties themselves intended to change and develop a new approach to national problems through their contact with these movements. Though it was not known at the time, Gorbachev's advisers were counselling him to follow the Baltic republics' example and create a Union-wide Popular Front. One of them told Gorbachev that the Party "should take matters into its hands," in other words, take the initiative, "before opposition forces do so."[16] He specifically recommended including people like Andrei Sakharov, Roy Medvedev, Gavriil Popov, and other relatively moderate opponents in the new Front. In that way, he argued somewhat naively, "the Party, acting through the Popular Front, will become its own opposition."[17]

Of course, the Soviet Union's reformist leaders were constantly cautioned by hard-line Soviet and East European conservatives that the reforms were opening the door to "counterrevolution" and could lead to the collapse of socialism. However, *this is precisely the line of argumentation that they refused to listen to and systematically opposed*, not only because it came from their political opponents, but above all

16. See the text of a memorandum addressed to Gorbachev by Georgii Shakhnazarov on 11 November 1988, reprinted in *Tsena svobody: reformatsiia Gorbacheva glazami ego pomoshchnika (The Price of Liberty: Gorbachev's Reformist Enterprise through the Eyes of His Assistant)* (Moscow: Rossika Zevs, 1993), p. 380.

17. Memorandum dated 12 January 1989 (ibid., p. 393).

because they had staked their political careers on the opposite outcome. In short, they believed that democratization and reforms not only would not lead to a collapse, but were the most efficient—the *only*—way to avoid it.

During an interview for this book, Aleksandr Yakovlev recounted a private conversation he had with Erich Honecker in 1989; the conversation is most telling. To Honecker's question why the CPSU's leadership had begun and was continuing down the path of dangerous policies, Yakovlev responded that "it is not a question of choice or political options, but of an objective, unavoidable necessity." He added: "Without *perestroika,* I told Honecker, we would eventually be confronted with a revolution that could be as violent as the October Revolution."[18] During his last visit to the GDR in October 1989, just one month before the fall of the Berlin Wall and in an already charged context, Gorbachev, in order to incite the East Germany Party to initiate reforms, declared publicly: "Only for those who do not react to the burning questions of life is there grave danger. But those who respond to their challenges and integrate them into adequate policies need not fear any problems."[19]

"Initiativism," the co-optation of important elements of the adversary, and the idea of reform as an antidote for the dangers to socialism (even a reanimation of it)—all of these constitute what must be termed, in retrospect, the reformist illusion of Gorbachev and his team. This was true with respect to both the USSR and the future of Eastern Europe. According to General Jaruzelski, Gorbachev interpreted the particularly warm public welcome he received during his visits to Czechoslovakia in 1987 and Poland in 1988 as proof of the support and enthusiasm of the populations in those countries for a reformed socialism.[20]

One should not overestimate the depth of Gorbachev's reformist illusion, at least with respect to Eastern Europe. Being the centrist he was, Gorbachev knew well that the reforms could harbor certain risks, especially in Eastern Europe, where the Communist Parties were weaker. During a February 1989 meeting between Gorbachev and the new leader of the Italian Communist Party, Achille Occhetto, the latter was even more persistent than his predecessor in trying to convince the Soviets of the necessity of putting pressure on the Czech leaders. He stressed the need to rehabilitate Dubcek and the other veterans of the Prague Spring and

18. Interview with Aleksandr Yakovlev, Moscow, 8 November 1994.
19. *Pravda,* 7 October 1989.
20. Interview with General Wojciech Jaruzelski, Warsaw, 8 May 1992.

to reintegrate them into the political life of the country. (In this connection, it is interesting to note that, one year before, the Czech authorities had given Dubcek an exit visa to travel to Italy, where he met with the leaders of the Italian Communist Party; the exit visa was issued pursuant to a request from Gorbachev's office to the Czech leaders.[21] To better convince Gorbachev, Occhetto assured him that Dubcek was "a real Communist and a true fighter for the cause of socialism," as well as "a fervent supporter of *perestroika*."[22] Gorbachev admitted that the reintegration of the Prague Spring veterans was "undoubtedly an issue he was watching with interest" and that the Jakes regime was clearly demonstrating "excessive slowness." But, he said, "the necessary changes must mature naturally." According to his Italian interlocutors, Gorbachev quickly added, as if to defend his passive attitude: "I say to all those I meet [in the Czech leadership] that the depth of the crisis is such that those who are wasting time will endure serious defeats."[23] We have here a clear example of contradictoriness found in Gorbachev's declarations. On the one hand, the changes are urgently needed, but on the other, they must mature naturally. For the leaders of the Italian Communist Party, it was obvious that Gorbachev's caution stemmed from a fear of precipitating an uncontrollable crisis in Eastern Europe, which would inevitably perturb both his foreign policy and the pursuit of *perestroika*. To impose a rehabilitation of Dubcek and his associates from abroad seemed to Gorbachev a move which might perilously destabilize the political situation in Czechoslovakia.

On this basis, Gorbachev's policy toward the conservative East European regimes in 1988 and 1989 oscillated between two contradictory tendencies: between suggestions, or indirect, but growing, pressure; and temporizing. For the reasons given above, the most prudent Soviet leaders and, to a certain extent, Gorbachev himself, frequently were concerned about avoiding "ruptures" and keeping a certain "stability" in Eastern Europe. Stability and reform were, however, at least partially contradictory concepts. Ideally, it was reform within stability that they desired. In other words, they wanted to have it both ways.

It must be noted that in the case of certain countries, and especially the GDR, the Soviet capacity to impose changes, particularly in the area

21. Interview with Jiri Hajek, Czechoslovak Minister of Foreign Affairs at the time of the Prague Spring, and later leader of the Charter 77 movement, Prague, 27 April 1992.

22. See Antonio Rubbi, *Incontri con Gorbaciov—i colloqui di Natta e Occhetto con il leader sovietico* (Rome: Editori Riuniti, 1990), p. 246.

23. Ibid., p. 248.

of leadership turnover, was limited. Honecker's control over his Polit-buro was almost total. The simple fact that Gorbachev's reformist entourage favored Hans Modrow[24] prevented him from joining the Politburo and resulted in a critical report on him being sent from the Politburo to the Central Committee in June 1989.[25] An open con-frontation with Honecker would have been necessary to force important changes in the orientation of his regime. That is, in fact, basically what happened later on in the year, when his regime, and he himself, had been seriously weakened. In the case of Czechoslovakia, more forceful pres-sure might have produced results earlier and more easily. But, as we have seen, Gorbachev preferred other methods. In 1988, during meetings of Soviet and Czech leaders on various levels, the latter were told by their Soviet counterparts that a reevaluation of the armed intervention of 1968 was just a question of time; at the same time, however, they were told that the initiative had to come from the Czech leadership itself.[26] A Czech delegation attended a closed-door annual conference in Decem-ber 1988 at the Diplomatic Academy of the Soviet Ministry of Foreign Affairs in Moscow. All of the Soviet participants, diplomats and spe-cialists of the Academy of Sciences, told their Czech audience that the 1968 invasion not only was unjustified but represented a flagrant viola-tion of international law. Even if they had not received a directive to this end, they certainly knew that they were free to express themselves in such a way on this delicate subject. The leaders of the Czechoslovak delega-tion protested against such "counterrevolutionary propaganda" and even planned to cancel their participation in the conference the follow-ing year.[27] Despite *glasnost'*, none of this debate was discernible in the Soviet press in 1988.[28]

24. See Vadim A. Medvedev, *Raspad: kak on nazreval v "mirovoi sisteme sotsializma"* (*The Collapse: How it Happened in the "World Socialist System"*) (Moscow: Mezh-dunarodnye Otnosheniia, 1994), pp. 158–159, 191–192.

25. See Michael Sodaro, *Moscow, Germany and the West from Khrushchev to Gor-bachev* (New York: Columbia University Press, 1990), p. 377.

26. Interview with Zdenek Mateika, a high official in the Czechoslovak Ministry of Foreign Affairs, Prague, 27 April 1992.

27. Ibid.

28. For example, in an interview given on the twentieth anniversary of the Soviet inva-sion, even the deputy director of the Institute of the Economy of the World Socialist Sys-tem, Leonid Iagodovskii, used ambiguous language to express his opinion about the Prague Spring. While he termed the Czechoslovak political program of January to April 1968 as having been positive, he also stated that it could not be fulfilled because of the activity of "antisocialist elements." He further stated that the 1968 program's objectives "are largely identical to the tasks of reconstruction that are on the agenda in Czechoslovakia today" (*Argumenty i Fakty,* 33, 19 August 1988).

BETWEEN SUBORDINATION AND ABANDONMENT

Neither the USSR, nor the United States, nor any other
country, can allow the success of normalization in East-
West relations to depend on . . . the occurrence of a
crisis in any country, including in a socialist country.[29]

During the second half of 1988, and even more so in 1989, Soviet policy toward Eastern Europe increasingly underwent a dual subordination:
first, to the demands of improved East-West relations, which fed ever
greater hopes; and to those of perestroika, which intensified considerably in terms of a political evolution, and only slowly evolved in the area
of economic reforms. This is to say that, despite a false impression that
our treatment of the subject may have created, Eastern Europe was a low
priority among the many pressing preoccupations facing the Soviet leadership. If this dual subordination had a structuring effect on Soviet policy toward the region, it was also a factor contributing to Soviet negligence and even inconsistency regarding Eastern Europe's own needs.

The Soviet leaders' strong priorities and the apparent calm they
demonstrated on the occasion of the East European regimes' collapse at
the end of 1989, have contributed to bringing up the notion that they had
decided to jettison these regimes well in advance. That idea is even held
by several of the direct participants in the momentous events of 1989.

In the author's interview with him, Karoly Grosz made the following
comments, which are interesting not only in connection with the above,
but also in other respects:

> When I became general secretary of the Party, I learned that there were So-
> viet nuclear weapons stationed on Hungarian soil. Even as prime minister, I
> hadn't known. Only Kadar and the defense minister were aware of their pres-
> ence. From my first meeting with Gorbachev, I expressed the wish that those
> arms be withdrawn. He made no objections, and they were, in fact, with-
> drawn. I then put it to him that it would be useful, in order to reinforce the
> Party's legitimacy with the populace and to distance us from the memories of
> 1956, for all Soviet troops to leave Hungary. He immediately acquiesced, not-
> ing that it would, however, be better to place the withdrawal in the frame-
> work of negotiations with NATO, so the USSR might obtain comparable
> American reductions in Western Europe in exchange. So, to my surprise,

---

29. Report of the Institute of the Economy of the World Socialist System presented to
a Soviet-American colloquium on Eastern Europe in Alexandria, Va., July 1988; in Gati,
The Bloc That Failed, p. 218.

every time that I asked him for something that I believed to be very difficult and delicate from the standpoint of Soviet interests in Hungary, he always said yes. I eventually came to the conclusion that he and Shevardnadze already had in mind a plan to completely disengage the Soviet Union from Eastern Europe.[30]

As we shall see, Grosz had very good reasons to feel personally and politically abandoned by the Soviet leaders, and hence to link his political destiny to that of his regime. In that regard, General Jaruzelski, who was supported by Gorbachev until the very end, has a totally different perspective. In February 1989, Grosz made a request to the USSR for urgent economic aid, including important hard currency loans, believing the request to be indispensable for the preservation of a minimum of political and social stability in Hungary.[31] His request was rejected, which only supported his impression that Hungary had been left to fend for itself.

This touches upon the fundamental point on which the thesis of Soviet "dropping" of Eastern Europe is based: that the economic burden or cost which the region represented for the USSR was incompatible with the fundamental objective of *perestroika*, the redressing of the Soviet economy.

The question of Eastern Europe's "cost" goes back a long way, and has been the subject of numerous analyses and estimates by a variety of Western economists studying the Soviet Union. Without going into the complicated details of this analysis, it may suffice to note that the problem centered on the structure of economic exchanges between the USSR and Eastern Europe which, for a number of years, had favored the latter. The Soviets were mainly exporting raw materials, which had been decreasing in price on the world market, while it imported finished products from its allies; the prices of those products had increased on the world market, but given their mediocre quality, they would not have found any other markets. This situation was somewhat modified by the increase in oil prices following the 1973 Arab-Israeli war. But to avoid too brutal a shock to the East European economies, the USSR, while increasing its prices, continued to sell them its oil at prices well below those of the world market. American economists Michael Marese and Jan Vanous have estimated that the loss of profit for the USSR, or its

30. Interview with Karoly Grosz, Gödöllö, 1 May 1992.
31. Ibid.

"indirect subsidies" resulting from various price differentials, totalled $18 billion per year at the very beginning of the 1980s.[32]

Even if the USSR could have sought to make a showcase of its "fraternal aid," such estimates were never published in the Soviet press before *perestroika*. Exchanges with fraternal states were generally presented as being "mutually advantageous." That was to change after 1987. For example, after the 19th Party Conference, in a debate between high Party and state officials that was made public, one speaker claimed that the USSR had lost $50 billion in its trade with Eastern Europe.[33] In a context where Shevardnadze was speaking of "increasing the profitability of foreign policy," one could believe that these considerations might push the Soviet leaders to divest themselves of Eastern Europe.

Though these factors had an effect on Soviet behavior, it would be absolutely misguided to see in them the key to the USSR's policies. As we have already seen, even if economic problems were the fundamental cause of *perestroika*, their concrete and immediate solution was far from narrowly defining Soviet leaders' actions. In 1988 and 1989, even the most radical reformers did not envisage—behind closed doors or in public—the abandonment of Eastern Europe. *After* the loss of the region, with the widening crisis of the Soviet regime itself in 1990, several radical reformers, who evolved with the crisis and became real "liquidators," congratulated themselves on the loss of Eastern Europe, and even favored the dismantling of the Soviet federation and system. In 1989, however, this was not the case.

To better understand the reformist leaders' approach one could compare Eastern Europe to nuclear weapons, as strange as that may sound. Both were very expensive—and deemed too expensive—for the Soviet Union. They were, however, essential attributes of Soviet power. It was necessary to reduce their cost and downsize their importance, while simultaneously seeking to gain advantages from the West for and from

32. Michael Marese and Jan Vanous, *Implicit Subsidies and Non-Market Benefits in Soviet Trade with Eastern Europe* (Berkeley: University of California Press, 1982).

33. "In the second half of the 1970s alone, imports of raw materials from the USSR at prices that were substantially below those of the world market allowed the European CMEA member states to save up to $50 billion. For our national economy, this practice has meant exporting our national product without compensation. In addition, the low price of energy and raw materials have not stimulated the creation of enterprises which consume less energy nor the appropriate reconstruction of the energy sector in the CMEA countries" ("Perestroika, XIXth Party Conference, Foreign Policy," *International Affairs*, July 1988, pp. 3–21).

the process. But it was out of the question to get rid of them, and particularly not unilaterally.

A memorandum to Gorbachev from his main adviser on Eastern Europe, Georgii Shakhnazarov, dated 10 October 1988, illustrates this point perfectly. Shakhnazarov put some questions to the Soviet leader, several of which contained implicit answers. The most important were:

- Can the socialist states get out of their precrisis situation without help from the West?
- What would be the proper price to pay for such assistance?
- Up to what point ought we encourage or accommodate ourselves to such an evolution?
- To what extent does it serve our interests to preserve the military presence of the Soviet army on the territory of a whole series of allied countries (except the GDR)?[34]

The superfluous and largely negotiable (for economic and political advantages) character given to the Soviet military presence in Eastern Europe, with the exception of the Warsaw Pact's keystone, the GDR, should be noted. At the same time, and this clearly demonstrates that the memorandum's author did not envisage Soviet disengagement from the region, Shakhnazarov asked that greater attention be paid to Eastern Europe's problems, writing to Gorbachev: "Even if we have put aside our mission as the socialist world's 'big brother,' we cannot shed our leadership role, which, objectively, will always belong to the Soviet Union, given that it is the most powerful socialist state. Whenever things have reached a crisis situation in one country or another, we have always had to come to the rescue, at an enormous political and material price. . . ." Since Soviet military intervention had been excluded, Shakhnazarov pointed out that new policies needed to be envisaged, along the lines of the suggestions he had made, and he recommended that the new International Affairs Commission of the Central Committee, headed by Yakovlev, tackle these questions.[35]

It is certain that the USSR's economic necessities led its leaders to take a much harder line toward some of their East European allies, full well

34. Text of the memorandum is reproduced in Georgii Shakhnazarov, *Tsena svobody: reformatsiia Gorbatcheva glazami ego pomoshchnika* (*The Price of Liberty: Gorbachev's Reformist Enterprise through the Eyes of His Assistant*) (Moscow: Rossika Zevs, 1993), p. 368.

35. Ibid.

knowing that this would reduce their political maneuverability. The imperatives of *perestroika* induced contradictory Soviet objectives in Eastern Europe: the search for relative political stability and a simultaneous reduction of the USSR's costs for the region. Reform, which became a new fetish, was proposed as a solution, as if it was to be a panacea and a substitute for increased Soviet aid.

On several levels, the Soviet leadership neglected Eastern Europe. There is, however, a substantial difference between neglect and abandonment.

PART II

1989: The Apotheosis of the Soviet Union's New Foreign Policy

CHAPTER FIVE

Soviet Scenarios for Eastern Europe's Future at the Beginning of 1989

On the eve of the historic year 1989, no one, be it in the West, Moscow, or Eastern Europe, foresaw the collapse of the region's socialist regimes in the months that were to follow.[1] In fact, the element of surprise is part of what made that year so memorable.

In two countries, however, the situation evolved much more quickly than elsewhere, under the pressure of political forces beyond Communist Party control, and it contained important elements of uncertainty. Not by coincidence, it was in Poland and Hungary that precisely the most reformist policies, supported by Moscow, favored such an evolution. Hence, the most crucial tests for the future of the reform process began to take shape there. In Poland, talks finally opened in Warsaw on February 6, 1989, between representatives of the Polish government and of the opposition, grouped around Solidarity, in the framework of the so-called Roundtable discussions which had been anticipated for several months. The principle of legalizing the independent trade union had

---

1. In the autumn of 1988, one particularly astute observer and analyst of Eastern Europe, Timothy Garton Ash, who was in touch with opposition circles, characterized the situation in these countries by using the term "Ottomanization." He wrote: "By Ottomanization, I mean that there is a certain analogy here with the decline of the Ottoman Empire: in both cases, we have witnessed a slow, long process of decadence marked by a disorganized, fragmented and discontinuous emancipation, both of the different states with respect to the center of the empire, and, within each country, of the society from the State." He saw in it "a very long-term historic process—a process, the outcome of which is, most definitely, practically impossible to imagine, since most empires have, up to now, fallen in the course of war . . ." (Timothy Garton Ash, *La chaudière: Europe centrale, 1980–1990* (Paris: Gallimard, 1990), pp. 263, 265–266.

already been accepted. In Hungary, in a climate of feverish social activity, groups had been allowed to form as part of a limited pluralism authorized by the regime. These groups were now transforming themselves into de facto political parties, with growing demands; the Communist Party had accepted the principle of a multiparty system, but its modalities and the rules of the game were not yet determined.

In this context, Aleksandr Yakovlev, in his capacity as the president of the Central Committee's new International Affairs Commission, sought to better inform the Party leadership by ordering the Institute of the Economy of the World Socialist System to prepare an important report. The report was to examine the political situation in the whole of Eastern Europe, as well as in each particular country, with an evaluation of possible developments and their implications for the USSR.[2] After having obtained the results of this report, Yakovlev ordered similar documents to be prepared by the Central Committee's International Department, the Ministry of Foreign Affairs, and the KGB, and organized a meeting between the authors of the four reports to compare and discuss their conclusions.

It goes without saying that these reports, which have never been published, are extremely revelatory. This author was able to obtain copies of the first three. They showcase the variety of opinions and estimations which existed within the reformist camp and help us overcome the simplistic representation of a clear-cut cleavage between two homogeneous camps. More importantly, however, they give us an invaluable indication of several parameters within which were situated Soviet leaders' expectations, attitudes, and behavior toward the historic events that took place in the following months. The reports also provide a partial response to a question frequently asked, namely about the quality of information on Eastern Europe at the Soviet leadership's disposal during this crucial period.

A RELATIVELY NONCOMPLACENT APPROACH

The report of the Institute of the Economy of the World Socialist System could be qualified, in the context of early 1989, as radically reformist. It strove to be realistic, without illusions. Even if it obviously did not foresee the rapid, domino-like collapse which was to ensue, it was the least optimistic about the chances of success of a renovated socialism, or the

---

2. Marina Pavlovna Sil'vanskaia, a senior researcher, was put in charge of preparing the report for the institute.

most realistic about its hidden traps. It noted, in several countries, the "beginning of the disaggregation of the socio-political system, without excluding possible cataclysms"; it further noted that, therefore, the difficult conditions which "accompanied the passage to a new model of socialism might lead to the drowning of the socialist idea."[3]

The report fully put into perspective the depth of the traps which East European reformers had to face. It illustrated, for example, that while it was popular pressure and demands which were pushing the regimes toward reforms, the very existence of these frustrations prevented the introduction of reforms that would necessarily impose sacrifices on the population, risking increased discontent. The need to sacrifice the interests of the traditional sectors of the working class reinforced opposition to reforms from the right wing of the respective ruling parties. At the same time, reformist leaders found it very difficult to find a new social base for themselves. On this question, the analysis brought out a fundamental difference between the USSR and Poland and Hungary, which had largely contributed to the success of *perestroika* in the Soviet Union to date. In the two latter cases, it said, "the opposition gathers the entire intellectual potential of the country."[4]

It was in Poland that the report foresaw the greatest danger of a "social rupture" and explosion. Despite this danger and the difficulties enumerated above—or rather precisely because of them—the report's author believed that the leading parties should continue to advance along the path of reforms, and notably form coalitions, making necessary concessions. They were reproached for not yet having "succeeded in seizing the initiative" due to a "lack of clarity about the perspectives of the transformation and a lack of vision of contemporary socialism."

If the analysis of the general situation in Eastern Europe was non-complacent and rather pessimistic (which was quite typical for reformist analyses that, in the case of the USSR itself, tended to dramatize the situation in order to better support the necessity for reforms), the examination of each country on its own allowed for some hypotheses about more optimistic solutions. Each country was subject to the presentation of different scenarios, which were termed "favorable" or "unfavorable," and "pessimistic" or "optimistic."

In the case of Poland, the "most favorable" scenario envisaged the success of the Roundtable, the emergence of a mixed economy, true

3. *Peremeny v vostochnoi Evrope i ikh vliiane na SSSR (The Changes in East Europe and Their Influence on the USSR)*. Report of the Institute of the Economy of the World Socialist System, February 1989, p. 1.
    4. Ibid., p. 7.

political pluralism, and the opposition's participation in governance. The worst-case scenario was a breakdown of negotiations due notably to obstruction by Party conservatives and an escalation of social conflict, leading therefore, "most probably in the spring of 1989," to the establishment of a second state of emergency, similar to the one in 1981. In that case, the author invoked the specter of "an Afghanistan in Europe."[5] One must point out, to the credit of the author, that she noted: "even the development of the most favorable scenario *does not guarantee, in the long term,* the preservation of the socialist choice."[6]

As for Hungary, across a plethora of scenarios that did not exclude an anarchical situation, the perspectives were more optimistic. In this regard, the "capacity of a reformed Party to keep the initiative" and the "step-by-step" introduction of a parliamentary system were expected. One could thus anticipate the "development of a social structure in the direction of the socialist ideal, but in a social-democratic form." It should be noted that, for the report's author, social democracy had become fully compatible with the socialist ideal. This was, in any case, the predominant view at the time within the institute which produced the report.

Not surprisingly, the states with more conservative regimes were the subject of less detailed analyses, given that the political situation there was less fluid and tumultuous. For Czechoslovakia, the prognosis was rather optimistic, albeit guarded. The author envisaged the possibility of a Jakes initiative to get rid of the more conservative elements in the Party leadership and to undertake "practical measures along the path of renewing socialism and toward broad democratization," with the help of Prime Minister Adamec (who had replaced Strugal). This is *precisely* the hope which Gorbachev was expressing at the same time to the leader of the Italian Communist Party, in the conversation cited in chapter 4. The author stated, however, that this scenario was unlikely, at least in the absence of Soviet pressure.[7] In contrast, she believed it to be "very likely, in the course of coming events, that the position of new forces in the country's political arena, such as the Socialist Perestroika Club headed by known figures of the Prague Spring who have kept to their socialist positions, will be reinforced." That group, she claimed, could

    5. Ibid., pp. 9–12.
    6. Emphasis added to indicate the nuance within the author's pessimism.
    7. The word "pressure" was doubtlessly taboo, as the author preferred to mention "prudent and skillful influence [*vliianie*]" (ibid., p. 17).

count on an important reservoir of supporters, which she estimated to number between 500,000 and 750,000.

The analysis of the Romanian case is quite interesting as it seems to be based on privileged information about the goings-on in various Romanian political circles. The report stated that, in fact, "changes in the leadership are taking place, thanks to which, once Ceausescu is replaced, sensible politicians will be able to put into practice radical reform ideas and a renovation of socialism." Rather curiously, it stated that "favorable premises" for a "dynamic restructuring and a modernization of the economy" under conditions of marketization and freeing up of economic initiatives were already present in Romania. The author estimated that Ceausescu could use the economic flexibility which the rapid (and socially costly) repayment of Romania's foreign debt had given him to increasingly satisfy the consumer needs of the population and to reduce social tensions. This hypothesis, the author continued, was rather unlikely to happen, and hence she argued that there was a fairly high probability of social unrest occurring in Romania. In such a case, "the absence of an organized opposition in Romania" and "growing discontent, not only at the popular level, but even among the leadership" meant that "changes from above" were very likely, the report concluded.[8]

As for the smallest and least important member of the Warsaw Pact, Bulgaria, the report outlined the gradual erosion of the Party's authority, in a context where "the alternative forces" were still weak. While recognizing that the leadership had introduced economic reform plans, it underscored that nothing concrete had been done to make them work effectively and that not much could be expected on that level in the immediate future. Even if the report noted that there were forces in the leadership capable of introducing an "authentic renovation" after the departure of Todor Zhivkov, it went on to state that his legacy would be "profound." In short, here, too, the situation was becoming urgent.

Apart from Ceausescu, it was the GDR's leaders that came in for the harshest criticism in the report. They were described as "dogmatic" and "sectarian," imposing on their society a "heavy-handed control through the apparatus of repression." The author stated—and, on this point, events were to prove her wrong—that, even if a nonconformist movement existed in East Germany, there were no adequate forces "to

8. Ibid., pp. 17, 18.

exercise significant pressure from below or to destabilize the situation."
She did, however, argue that there were forces within the Party apparatus capable of elaborating "a constructive program of changes." Those
elements had not yet stepped forward because they "have not received
sufficient proof that the process of change in the Soviet Union is irreversible." The report's message to the Soviet leadership on this count
could not have been any clearer. In a very important passage, the report
emphasized that the forces of change "understand that profound
reforms in the GDR cannot remain a purely domestic affair" and could
not take place except in tandem with a modification of inter-German
relations. Consequently, if the USSR wanted "a *perestroika* in the GDR,"
it would have to be prepared to revise its policy in the heart of Europe.
In that context, it ought to propose "objectives, such as the creation of
a neutral German state on a confederal basis." In the context of early
1989, the author made the very bold suggestion of a new slogan: "one
state, two systems." Further into the report, however, the author situated this scenario in a fairly distant future, arguing that it depended on
the construction of the "common European home"; she also mentioned,
as an alternative equally desirable to German neutrality, the preservation of the eastern part of a confederated German state within the Warsaw Pact, while the western part would remain in NATO.

In conformity with the views outlined above, the report recommended
a far less tolerant Soviet policy toward the conservative socialist states.
It claimed that the status quo in these countries which formed a majority in the Warsaw Pact, was harmful to reforms in Poland, Hungary, and
even the Soviet Union itself, notably by hindering the development of
economic relations on a new basis, and even contributed to the recent
decline in trade among these states. It also warned of the "internationalization" of the conservative forces, which were mutually supporting
each other and reinforcing their international contacts. The report furthermore suggested more open support for reformers in the four states
where they did not hold power, and the recalling of conservative Soviet
ambassadors and diplomatic personnel serving in Eastern Europe, arguing that they had been tacitly encouraging the East European conservatives' resistance.

Even more than the individual predictions elaborated for each state,
it was the scenario envisaged for Eastern Europe's overall evolution by
the Bogomolov institute report that was interesting and revealing, as was
the behavior it recommended the Soviet authorities follow.

The report considered an important, albeit not total, slide by Eastern Europe "into the economic and political orbit of the Western world" as being inevitable. The Soviet Union, it argued, ought to accommodate such a "neo-Finlandization" of the region and even profit from it. It should be emphasized that the author was giving the term "Finlandization" a specific meaning, and distinguished it from its traditional meaning and from the actual situation in Finland, noting two fundamental differences. First, the countries of Eastern Europe, unlike neutral Finland, would remain allies of the USSR. The report envisaged that all of these countries would voluntarily remain in the Warsaw Pact. Second, even if one of the Communist Parties were to lose power, Soviet political influence in the country and the region would remain much greater than in Finland. Here again, it should be stressed that the report considered the loss of power by one or another Communist Party to be a worst-case scenario, and certainly not a broad movement. In this regard, the report's ideal model was a return to the formula that had existed in Eastern Europe between 1945 and 1948: coalitions in which the Communist Parties would have varying influence, but always a dominant role, in the context of a mixed economy. At that time, even if Eastern Europe was already closer to the USSR, it was still an intermediary zone between East and West. The report argued that the USSR need not fear a downsizing of the East European Communist Parties' power, even their "social-democratization," since, after all, that would only be slightly different from the new socialism the Soviet Union itself was seeking.

In absolutely typical fashion, the author stated that "the Soviet Union's optimum reaction to the process in Eastern Europe" was to "participate actively in it in order to keep a certain control over it and to assure its predictability" and its "self-limitation." The report argued that "the terrain favorable to nationalist and anti-Soviet forces will be reduced . . . to the extent that the political movement will be seen as a result of our conscious decision rather than of the pressure of hostile forces." It came to this remarkable conclusion: "Therefore, it will be 'a revolution from above' which will prevent a 'revolution from below'."[9] To facilitate the "self-limitation" of the movement, it recommended that the USSR develop contacts with the forces of the "constructive

9. Ibid., pp. 27, 25.

opposition." This term was understood to mean, quite simply, any forces willing to negotiate with the existing governments.

In short, the report urged the USSR *itself* to organize and preside over the inevitable erosion of its influence in Eastern Europe, in order to better preserve a significant measure of that influence. Such Soviet behavior would also give the USSR a number of benefits in foreign policy. The acceptance of an "intermediary position" for these countries would "reinforce Western Europe's interest in supporting the economic and political stability of Eastern Europe and stimulate the disarmament process." As such, it would contribute to "partially overcoming the legacy of Yalta and the division of the world" and to "the gradual formation of a more united Europe."

The report saw the countries of Eastern Europe becoming "a common sphere of influence for the Soviet Union and the European Economic Community," due to their expected political evolution and their foreign economic relations. Consequently, it predicted that certain of these states could, even in the fairly near future, become associated with the EEC, "acting as precursors in the process of East-West integration."

This general view of affairs, it must be underlined, went much further than Gorbachev and Shevardnadze were prepared to go at the time, and especially on the last point. They envisaged East-West economic integration on the basis of greater relative equality. To achieve this, Eastern Europe was to accompany the USSR in the process, not to precede it (at the risk of leaving it aside). The Bogomolov institute's scenario therefore rested on a more pessimistic assessment of the influence the Soviet Union could preserve in Eastern Europe; it also practically acted as if CMEA were already buried, not mentioning it once throughout the report. It tried to be more realistic about the consequences of the growing decoupling the USSR's military might from its economic strength. As we have seen, the report gave better chances to the Soviet ability to preserve its political influence, considering the Warsaw Pact's survival to be guaranteed. It did not, however, foresee that, having absolutely renounced any use of military force, a serious divergence would emerge between the Soviet military presence and its political influence. But who would have believed, at the beginning of 1989, in East or West, that so much military might could lose so much political influence so rapidly?

THE MODERATING ROLE OF THE UNITED STATES

There is an essential element upon which the author of the Bogomolov institute's report counted to ensure some measure of stability in the changing geopolitical configuration envisaged for Eastern Europe. That element was the expected role and actions of the Western powers, particularly the United States. It is important to examine Soviet expectations on this count in greater detail, as they strongly influenced the Soviet leadership's behavior in the months that followed.

The report asserted that *perestroika* in the USSR and its implementation of "new thinking" had progressed far enough that "constructive" American politicians had an interest in protecting the process. This meant an altered state of affairs on several levels. The United States would not only have progressively less reasons to exploit Soviet and East European difficulties. It would also have an interest in impeding the explosion of a crisis that could endanger this vital movement of *perestroika* and "new thinking" and introduce an important element of "unpredictability" into the favorable evolution of the international system.

This expectation was far from being based on an illusion, resting instead on specific facts. In mid-January 1989, some days before the inauguration of George Bush, Henry Kissinger had come to Moscow, carrying a letter of good intentions from the new president to Mikhail Gorbachev. In his talks with Soviet leaders, and notably with Yakovlev and Gorbachev himself, Kissinger told them of a project of understanding on Eastern Europe which he had proposed to Bush on December 18, 1988.[10] He also expressed his opinion to Yakovlev that the fluidity that was beginning to characterize the situation in Eastern Europe posed threats for the USSR and the United States. Among these threats he cited the centrifugal forces that might increase in Eastern Europe and the possibility of a resurgent German nationalism, which could push West Germany to try to exploit, for its own purposes, the differences between the Soviet Union and the GDR. As a result, Kissinger suggested that high-level negotiations take place in order to reach a series of detailed accords (some of them formal, others informal) under which the USSR would undertake to not oppose the liberalization of Eastern Europe and to specify the limits of what it was willing to do to defend its interests in the region. In exchange, the United States would agree to not do anything to accelerate the changes, to use its influence to prevent such an acceleration, and to respect Soviet security interests.[11] Yakovlev, who saw in this proposal Kissinger's propensity to seek a management of an international equilibrium through concerted actions by the great powers,

10. See M. R. Beschloss and Strobe Talbott, *At the Highest Levels* (Boston: Little, Brown, 1993), p. 13.
11. Ibid., pp. 14–15.

declared that the USSR was ready to enter into such discussions. Gorbachev was also receptive, but more cautious, apparently believing that Kissinger was sounding him out to see what the Soviet Union was willing to abandon in Eastern Europe.[12] Gorbachev's preoccupation at the time, and in the weeks that followed, was to obtain a response to his arms reduction proposal from the new administration—a response that was, incidentally, quite slow in coming.

Even if Kissinger's idea was well received in Moscow, and by Bush and some of his advisers, no formal proposals were ever developed. A *New York Times* article of March 28, 1989 revealed that U.S. Secretary of State James Baker was preparing to take up Kissinger's project of negotiations; the article provoked negative reactions in the United States and in Europe. The idea was denounced as a new Yalta that would again be played out on the backs of the peoples of Eastern Europe.

Nonetheless, even if there was no formal accord, various signals coming from Washington and Bush's behavior during his visit to Eastern Europe in the summer of 1989 (to which we shall return) confirmed the Soviet leaders' belief that a tacit agreement, along the general lines sketched out by Kissinger's proposal, did exist between the United States and the Soviet Union.[13]

For the Soviet leadership, therefore, its support for—plus the progress of—reforms in Eastern Europe could bring several mutually reinforcing benefits. It would favor an amelioration of relations with Washington and advance the development of a "common European home." Better relations with the United States would also help to ensure that the development of a new European order would take place through a relatively controlled process. It should not be surprising, given these expectations, that by 1989 the Soviet leaders had definitively accepted the idea that the United States had an important place and role to play in the "common European home."

As we shall see, if there was an illusion on the part of the Soviet leadership, it was not with respect to President Bush's preferences concerning Eastern Europe but about his capacity to exercise decisive influence in the region. The two superpowers would, in fact, both prove remarkably impotent in the events which were to sweep Eastern Europe in the last months of 1989.

---

12. Ibid., p. 15.
13. All of the high Soviet officials with whom I spoke believed that a tacit agreement existed.

THE CENTRAL COMMITTEE:
A LESS PERMISSIVE APPROACH

If the Bogomolov institute's report can be described as radically reformist in the context of early 1989, then the report presented to Yakovlev by the Central Committee's International Department could be termed "cautiously reformist," perhaps "mildly conservative," or more simply, centrist. It reflected fairly closely the positions which the department's director, Valentin Fallin, had taken and would continue to hold.

First of all, while recognizing that Eastern Europe was in the midst of a difficult period, this report was clearly more confident than the Bogomolov institute's scenarios about the future of socialism in the region and about the Parties' chances of staying on top of the changes which were looming. In this connection, it gave its assessment that "*it is not appropriate to exaggerate the danger that one or another socialist state could simply switch to the capitalist road*"[14] because "the roots of socialism have penetrated too deeply." It asserted that such a rupture would lead to chaos and immense misery, and that even the capitalist countries would not encourage it, so as not to be obliged to assume the enormous costs that their support would entail. From this perspective, the consequences of a certain power sharing, which was considered inevitable and even beneficial in the Hungarian and Polish cases, seemed fairly limited.

The report partook in *perestroika*'s "initiativist" ideology. Of the three broad scenarios for the region's evolution that it foresaw, the first and most favorable grew out of this ideology. It contemplated "a societal movement, directed by the Parties in power, toward democratization and a new form of socialism." This did "not exclude certain important concessions on the question of power" or the necessity of coming to terms with "the growing importance of self-government" and "the participation of the constructive opposition in the administration of society, with the possibility of one of these forces being transformed into a rival for power."

The second scenario analyzed a "gun-to-the-head" evolution, where the regimes, faced with "mini-crises," would make concessions to avoid the worst outcome. The report saw this mode of action, frequently practiced in the past, as being very disadvantageous, since it would only

---

14. Emphasis present in the original text of the report, entitled *K strategii otnoshenii s evropeiskimi sotsialisticheskimi stranami* (*Towards a Strategy for Relations with European Socialist States*), pp. 11–12.

reinforce "the lack of confidence in the Party and the opposition's pretensions" and favor "a gradual societal evolution toward exiting the socialist framework." The author did not, incidentally, specify what he believed to be necessary for staying in the socialist framework. Implicitly, the preservation of a dominant, or at least pivotal, role for the Party seems to have been considered a necessary condition. Nowhere was an evolution toward social democracy mentioned as a positive alternative.

The third general scenario, considered the worst possible outcome from the Soviet standpoint, was immobilism on the part of the Parties in power, followed by social upheaval and repression.

The Central Committee's report contained very interesting and important policy recommendations for the USSR. First of all, the author deemed it necessary to recall Eastern Europe's importance for the Soviet Union. Perhaps basing his comments on complaints from Grosz and several others, he stated at the outset that "our friends have the impression we are abandoning them" and that relations with Europe's socialist states should absolutely "keep their priority nature for us."[15] In a rather prophetic manner, the report affirmed that "*our domestic stability and our influence in world affairs depend in great measure*" on these states.[16] It went on to remind its readers that Eastern Europe had, in the past, served as a "safety shield" for the "center of socialism," and that, even though international conditions had changed, they continued to partially exercise that role.

Countering an opinion that was doubtlessly gaining ground in Soviet political circles, the Central Committee report declared that "the stereotype according to which these countries are parasites living off of us must be decisively rejected." It further claimed, "despite petit-bourgeois conceptions," that trade between the USSR and other CMEA states was of great importance for the Soviet Union. The report cited a whole series of figures to demonstrate trade with CMEA countries was financially advantageous for the USSR.[17] It also pointed out that the Soviet Union itself was largely responsible for delaying the reform of CMEA and that it had only managed to establish 1 percent of its trade with Eastern Europe on the basis of direct links between enterprises. Success in reforming CMEA therefore depended to a great degree on the USSR's ability to

15. Ibid., pp. 1, 6.
16. Emphasis in the original text.
17. Among the numerous examples cited, it claimed that every ton of wheat imported by the USSR from the world market cost it between 1.45 and 1.5 tons of oil (sold for hard currency), compared to one ton of oil for the same quantity of wheat imported from the CMEA (pp. 8–9).

more forcefully implement economic change at home. In a veiled reference to the unilateral reduction of Soviet oil deliveries to Eastern Europe in the preceding months, the report insisted that the USSR needed to "remain a credible economic partner," if only to avoid causing additional problems for its reformist allies. Specifically, it demanded that the respective ministries respect their obligations and that oil deliveries be reestablished at the levels indicated in the Five-Year Plan.

Believing the economic integration of Europe as a whole to be inevitable and positive, the Central Committee report underscored the importance of "a rigorous fulfillment of obligations." This would enable integration to "take place in a balanced, coordinated fashion and *in association with a reinforcement of the integrative process among socialist states themselves.*"[18] We can clearly see the difference here between this report and the approach of the Bogomolov institute's account.

On an even more fundamental question, the report recommended "the joint elaboration of a new vision of socialism and capitalism," in order to establish "the limits of their interaction and interpenetration." This touches on a fundamental point. The author was asking for a more precise definition of the content of "reformed socialism," and what would be permissible and inadmissible in this regard. Evidently, there was no consensus on this point within the Soviet leadership. On the one hand, the question was the subject of continuous debates. On the other, for radical reformers, and notably for someone like Yakovlev, the quest for a new model of socialism was to be an open-ended process of research and experimentation which could not be entirely predetermined. Yegor Ligachev saw a great danger in this position, and Gorbachev himself, according to one of his principal advisers, "did not have a clear vision,"[19] and the limits he envisaged changed over time.

In accordance with the above recommendation, the report asked that "an inventory of our reactions" be prepared in case of "possible complications" or "abrupt changes" in the political orientation of the allied states. While it very explicitly excluded the use of force for the same reasons invoked by the reformists, it added a point which was totally absent in the Bogomolov institute's report. It stated that, even though the USSR was correct in affirming "the *principle* that freedom of choice is universal," it should, however, at the same time "maintain a certain indeterminacy with respect to concrete actions we might take in response to a

18. Emphasis added.
19. See Anatolii S. Cherniaev, *Shest' let s Gorbachevym: po dnevnikovym zapisiam (Six Years with Gorbachev: From Journal Notes)* (Moscow: Progress Kul'tura, 1993), p. 294.

given upheaval." This indeterminacy was deemed necessary in order "not to encourage anti-socialist forces to put the bases of socialism to the test in any given country."[20]

Simultaneously, the author reaffirmed that it was necessary to continue "dissipating the conservative regimes' expectations" about the role of an ultimate protector which the USSR might play for them. Furthermore, he suggested the Soviet Union take advantage of *perestroika* to reduce "the stereotypes about conservatism in Moscow" held in Eastern Europe and to "actively search for contacts with all those forces which could lay claim to power." The author believed that good relations between the USSR and these forces, as well as their participation in power sharing, would have a moderating effect on them, while simultaneously helping to solve the accumulated problems. In simple terms, one can say that the report recommended giving the opposition forces a "carrot," while also counting on the memory of the "big stick," which should not be eradicated altogether.

A nuance to this last part must immediately be pointed out. The report, which was somewhat ambiguous on this issue, also expressed a desire that the memory of previous Soviet actions be attenuated. To this end, the author recommended an important reform of the Warsaw Pact, so it would cease appearing to be an instrument of Soviet trusteeship and interference, possibly harming the credibility of reformist Communists. He therefore proposed a real "internationalization" of the Warsaw Pact's military mechanism, which had previously had the drawback of "being like a Soviet General Command, beside which the presence of other members is only a formality." The report also recommended that the reform take place on a more egalitarian basis and proposed the creation of joint forces without the participation of the Red Army. It also argued for a continued reduction of the Soviet presence in Eastern Europe through the framework of East-West negotiations; it even envisaged a complete withdrawal of Soviet forces from Hungary and Czechoslovakia, the two states which had already been subject to Soviet interventions. Such a withdrawal could also bring political dividends in broader East-West relations. The report did, however, also recommend that Soviet forces be replaced by a joint force made up of other members of the alliance.

Contrary to the Bogomolov institute's report, the Central Committee account recommended patience with the conservative regimes. In this

---

20. Ibid., p. 17; emphasis added.

regard, the recommendation is in contradiction to an earlier passage which considered immobilism to be a dangerous scenario. In the specific country analyses, the report indicated that Czechoslovakia's "1968 syndrome" was preventing the regime from orienting itself clearly toward democratization. At the same time, it observed that the regime was favorably disposed to embarking upon economic reform "while leaving changes in the area of democratization for later" and that Czechoslovakia's high standard of living would still play "a stabilizing role."

In the case of East Germany, the author interpreted its leaders' negative attitude toward *perestroika* as "objectively founded" on the fact that "the GDR came into being on an ideological and class basis, not one of nationality." He, too, believed that democratization could raise the problem of redefining relations between the two Germanys. Yet, the report did not make any particular recommendations concerning this sensitive subject.

THE FOREIGN MINISTRY: A BOTCHED REPORT

Despite a few contradictory elements, the reports by the Central Committee and Bogomolov's institute presented structured and relatively coherent views of the Soviet Union's interests in the future Eastern Europe. It is at this level that they are interesting, regardless of their prognoses' relation to reality. The report sent by the Ministry of Foreign Affairs (*Ministerstvo Inostrannykh Del*—MID) is very disappointing in this respect. The report's lack of coherence, both in terms of analyses and recommendations, is striking. Therefore, its importance lies elsewhere. Far shorter than the two other reports, and obviously written by a poorly prepared and supervised official, it reflects the fact that Eastern Europe was a low priority for Shevardnadze's ministry.[21] Occasionally borrowing elements of the conservative discourse and others from the camp of the radical reformers, the report does not, however, represent an articulate centrist position. Instead, it reflects the ideological and political confusion which had taken hold of numerous Party and state officials. Many of them sought to pay lip service to the new slogans of *perestroika* and "new thinking" in foreign policy without succeeding in truly integrating these concepts; their manner of perceiving things

21. While the Bogomolov institute's account was thirty pages in length, the MID's report totalled a mere ten pages.

remained marked by traditional approaches, resulting in contradictory statements.

In 1989, both radical reformers and conservatives dramatized the political situation in the Soviet Union and East Germany for purposes that were obviously very different, but using language that was sometimes similar. For the former, the purpose was to bring out clearly the urgency of the changes they were proposing. For the latter, the point was to emphasize the threat to the preservation of socialism resulting from the volatile situations.

The MID report was marked by a pronounced alarmist tone, in line with the second view above. It stated, for example, that "by gaining access to parliamentary and government institutions, the opposition can, either fully or partially, eject the Communist and Workers' Parties from power."[22] It added that "taking into account the mobilization of forces alien to socialism, this could have the gravest possible political consequences." At the same time, the report strangely took up one of the popular *perestroika* slogans of the time, stating that "the tendency toward political pluralism is becoming universal," without illustrating the benefits which East European Parties could derive from the process. The West's moderation was presented as being purely tactical and "its long-standing goals" were said to remain the same as before.

In the final analysis, was this report not more realistic than the other two, reflecting in its own way the impasse in which the East European regimes found themselves, regardless of what they endeavored to do? On the one hand, the report claimed that the policies of the four conservative countries were "in contradiction with the general tendency of the international community toward democratization" and that "their inevitable movement toward an authentic renewal of socialism, when it does come, will be accompanied [due to their tardiness] by profound political and social reverberations."[23] On the other hand, it only saw risks in the opposite approach taken by the Polish and Hungarian leaders.

If one is tempted to see this as an exercise in realism, the same cannot be said of the report's recommendations to the Soviet leadership. The first and "most important" of these was "not to permit the erosion of socialism in Eastern Europe and to keep all of the countries in the region

22. The MID report, dated 24 February 1989, was entitled *Politicheskie protsessy v evropeiskikh sotsialisticheskikh stranakh i predlozheniia o nashikhp prakticheskikh shagakh s uchetom skladyvaiushcheisia v nikh situatsii* (*The Political Process in the European Socialist States and Propositions Concerning Our Practical Measures toward the Situation Developing There*), p. 3.

23. Ibid., p. 4.

on the road to socialism." But how to achieve this, especially given that the MID author, too, explicitly and under all circumstances, rejected the use of force on the part of the USSR? On that point, the consensus among the three authors reflected a broader consensus in the Soviet leadership. Even Ligachev was, by now, in agreement.[24] It was on the question of whether stating it publicly was opportune that no consensus existed. The MID report, just like the one issued by the Central Committee, favored preserving an "indeterminacy concerning the possible role of our armed forces." At the same time, and in complete contradiction to the above, the author recommended that in the case of a use of force by any of the East European regimes, the USSR ought to refuse its support "for repressive actions which contradict international norms in the sphere of human rights." This reflects the fact that the international image of the USSR on this issue had become an important preoccupation of Shevardnadze's ministry.

In general, the MID report's recommendations were closer to those of the Central Committee than those of Bogomolov's institute, even if far less coherent.

What remains now is to show how all of these recommendations, expectations, and scenarios were able to influence the Soviet leaders' behavior and their understanding of the events which ensued.

24. See Yegor Ligachev, *Inside Gorbachev's Kremlin* (New York: Pantheon Books, 1993).

CHAPTER SIX

Poland

The Ideal Model

In January 1989, we—Kiszczak, Siwicki, Rakowski and I—
had to threaten resignation in order to have the necessity of
the "Roundtable" talks accepted. . . . At that moment, the
Party apparatus sensed that power was at risk of slipping
away. It was not mistaken: we, the architects of the "Roundtable," were the ones who misunderstood and were fooling
ourselves. We were sincerely convinced that we would win
the June elections.

Wojciech Jaruzelski (1992)[1]

The members of Solidarity should have known they were
going to win! Yet they didn't know at all. On that Sunday [of
the elections], I had a snack with Adam Michnik, who was
exhausted and dejected—and he had no idea. . . .

Timothy Garton Ash[2]

Even though things may appear quite different in retrospect, Jaruzelski's
words cited above illustrate that for him, just as for Gorbachev, the introduction of even such major reforms of the political system did not signify a desperate leap into the unknown. At least that was not the case at
the beginning of 1989, in any event.[3] If the eventual outcome proved
their conservative comrades right, it was only long after the final col-

---

1. Wojciech Jaruzelski, *Les chaînes et le refuge: Mémoires* (Paris: Jean-Claude Lat-
tès, 1992), p. 317; emphasis added.
2. Timothy Garton Ash, *La chaudière: Europe centrale, 1989–1990* (Paris: Gallimard, 1990), p. 334.
3. Rejecting the anachronism of certain ex post facto explanations, Martin David-
Blais has illustrated in a convincing way how the leadership of the Polish Party could have
had several solid reasons to believe that the Roundtable accords would benefit it. See his
excellent study, "Les communistes polonais et l'élection de juin 1989," *Revue d'études
comparatives Est-Ouest,* 21 December 1990, pp. 55–73.

lapse that reformers like Jaruzelski and Gorbachev apologized for having inadvertently misled them. But, for good reason, they refused to
admit that their opponents' prescriptions were a viable alternative.

General Jaruzelski had been considered a reformist leader for several
years, but his reform efforts, as they concerned the regime's relations
with Solidarity, had remained rather ambivalent until 1988. Certainly,
his advisers had spoken of the usefulness of dialogue, and even the necessity of establishing a new social contract with the union. In practice,
however, despite the government's relative tolerance and its liberalization in several areas, nothing very significant had been achieved. The
population's extreme apathy and an important, concomitant decline in
Solidarity's popularity and mobilizing potential in the years that followed the declaration of martial law in December 1981[4] had given the
authorities the impression that they had sufficient leverage to put in place
quite radical economic reforms without the union's direct participation.

A wave of strikes gripped Poland in August 1988, reaching a level not
seen since the 1980–1981 crisis. Lech Walesa used all of his influence in
order to put an end to the strikes, succeeding only with great difficulty.
In the aftermath, the government established direct relations with him.
Despite these developments and in spite of his reformist credentials,
Mieczyslaw Rakowski, who became prime minister in October 1988,
attempted what he saw as a subtle challenge to Solidarity: he unilaterally decreed the closing of the Gdansk shipyards, the birthplace of the
union, invoking economic profitability criteria recommended by Walesa's own economic advisers. Rakowski was to beat a hasty retreat on this
issue.

THE USSR AND THE ROUNDTABLE ACCORDS

Therefore, it was not until the end of 1988 that the Polish leadership
finally reached the conclusion that legalizing Solidarity and institution-
alizing its relations with the regime were inevitable and the only way of
stemming the continual decline of Poland's economy and social climate.

---

4. Some statistics reveal the change. Asked in July 1987, "Do the actions of Lech
Walesa and his entourage contribute to the collective well-being?" 18.3 percent answered
"No," while 57.8 percent were undecided, according to a fairly reliable opinion poll published in 1988. In August 1988, the same responses were 25.7 percent and 55.2 percent,
respectively. In November of the same year, however, following Lech Walesa's famous tele-
vised debate with the leader of the official union, the responses were 44.8 percent affirmative, 18.1 percent negative, and 37.2 percent were undecided (according to figures and
polls cited by David-Blais, "Les communistes polonais," pp. 55–73).

In this area, the Poles lagged behind the Soviet Union—not, of course, in terms of social pluralism, freedom of expression, or economic policy, but with respect to what Gorbachev and his entourage were willing to accept in Poland.

In July 1988, during Mikhail Gorbachev's visit to Poland, General Jaruzelski had told him of the possible legalization of Solidarity. Not only did Gorbachev not object, but he showed great interest in the issue and asked that he personally be sent a report on the question.[5] Even signs of Soviet support were openly given thereafter. For example, N. Shishlin, a high official of the Central Committee's Propaganda Department, told the French newspaper Le Monde in September 1988 that, from the Soviet point of view, "trade-union pluralism is not a heresy."[6]

Mikhail Gorbachev's support for General Jaruzelski was absolutely decisive. During the Polish United Workers' Party (PUWP) Central Committee meeting of January 1989, which sanctioned the opening of the Roundtable talks between the government and the opposition and the principle of Solidarity's legalization (which was the only precondition for the talks), Jaruzelski had to face majority opposition. As we have seen, he had to threaten resignation in order to carry the day. If his opponents had received a clear sign of encouragement from the Soviet hierarchy, they doubtlessly would have continued their opposition. Gorbachev ensured that the rule of noninterference, which in this case worked in his favor, was strictly respected on the Soviet side. (Support for the policy initiated by the leader of the Polish party could not be considered interference.) The leaders of the Polish conservatives, who had frequent contacts with Brovikov, the Soviet ambassador in Warsaw (one of those conservative ambassadors the Bogomolov institute recommended recalling), boasted of their support in Moscow during the Central Committee meeting. Called upon by those who believed this to be a "bluff" to name their supporters, the conservatives refused to do so.[7] They knew perfectly well the very close relationship that existed between Jaruzelski and Gorbachev, and it definitely helped the Polish leader to prevail.

The shadow of the Soviet Union and of the "Gorbachev enigma" was constantly looming over the Roundtable talks. In a conversation on the

5. Interview with Jozef Czyrek, who was a member of the Polish politburo at the time and its official responsible for international affairs, Warsaw, 6 May 1992.

6. Le Monde, 7 September 1988, cited by Georges Mink, La force ou la raison: histoire sociale et politique de la Pologne, 1980–1989 (Paris: La Découverte, 1989), p. 206.

7. Interview with Janusz Reykowski, who attended the Central Committee meeting and was the chief Party negotiator at the Roundtable, Warsaw, 8 May 1992.

sidelines of the talks, one of Solidarity's negotiators, Andrzej Stelma-chowski, who later became minister of education, asked General Jaruzel-ski: "What are the limits to the changes the Soviets are willing to accept in Poland?" Jaruzelski reportedly responded: "I don't know myself. Let's find them together."[8] Beyond the shrewdness of Jaruzelski's reply, there was good reason for him not to know, since even in Moscow, as we have seen, no clear policy had been formulated. At the time, both the leaders in Warsaw and Western analysts were convinced that Gorbachev had placed certain limits on how far change could go, both in Eastern Europe and in Soviet domestic politics. It was feared that these limits risked sur-facing very suddenly, even if they seemed to be constantly expanding. In that vein, a Polish author wrote at the time that "there would be no Roundtable among Poles if the Russians were not entitled to an 'empty chair' to which they could always invite themselves."[9]

We should be cautious on this point. Even if skepticism about the changes under way in the USSR was certainly too great, and although Gorbachev did not have very clear ideas about the limits of what he was willing to accept, that does not mean that "objective" limits to the tol-erance of Soviet power (as a whole) did not exist. They remain difficult to ascertain, even with hindsight and the information now available. The Soviet leaders, without resorting to military force themselves, could have pushed their Polish counterparts to change their policy and even to use solutions involving force.

Although the Russians' chair remained empty, the limits of their tol-erance, real or imagined, determined in large measure the orientation and results of the Roundtable negotiations. Above all, questions of for-eign policy, such as Poland's membership in the Warsaw Pact and the presence of Soviet troops on Polish soil, were entirely excluded from the talks, implicitly being considered nonnegotiable by both sides.

The question of the Party's leading role, which had always been untouchable and was effectively the keystone to the system, was not directly addressed—even if it was, in fact, at the very center of the talks between Solidarity and the government. Knowing full well traditional Soviet sensitivities on this subject, Lech Walesa sought to reassure them. In an interview given to a Soviet magazine (in itself a first) shortly before

---

8. Interview with Andrzej Stelmachowski, Warsaw, 7 May 1992. In my interview the next day, 8 May, with General Jaruzelski, he confirmed the accuracy of Stelmachowski's remark.

9. A. Drawicz, cited by Mink, *La force ou la raison*, p. 232.

the Roundtable talks opened, he declared that Solidarity wanted "autonomy and independence from the government, and not power. Let us leave power in the hands of the Communists."[10] Such statements helped convince Soviet reformers that the negotiations were effectively exercising a moderating influence on the "constructive opposition." They knew full well, however, that the real question of the day was the reduction of the Party's power. But how far?

On April 7, 1989, the Roundtable accords were signed. With varying degrees of precision, they touched on a broad spectrum of issues. Beyond Solidarity's legalization, they dealt with its access to the media, the principles of economic, administrative and judiciary reform, local government, and the framework and rules for the next national election. For Solidarity, its institutionalization and its freedom of social and political action were the most essential points. The most important element for the government side was Solidarity's agreement to participate in the elections, which would be governed by unique rules. In fact, the elections were to have the most decisive influence over the further course of events.

At first, the government had reason to be very satisfied. Under the new system, Parliament would be bicameral. It was agreed that in the Diet (the more important chamber), the opposition could hold 35 percent of the 460 seats, while the PUWP and its satellite parties would be conceded the other 65 percent. The new body, the Senate, would number 100 members, all of whom were to be elected in perfectly free elections, which practically guaranteed Solidarity and other opposition groups a dominant position in this chamber. It should be noted that the proposal for creating a freely elected Senate came from the government itself, as a reward to Solidarity and to facilitate the overall accords. By the terms of these accords, the Senate had the power to veto laws adopted by the Diet. To force the bill past the Senate, the Diet would have to readopt it with at least a two-thirds majority. Consequently, the Party might have to negotiate with the opposition on some of the government's major programs; this was one of the most politically significant elements of the April accords. The Polish president, who was to have considerable powers (nominating the prime minister, the right to veto certain legislation, the power to dissolve Parliament and even to decree a state of emergency), would be elected by the two houses of Parliament sitting in joint session. Given that the deputies of the Diet were far more numerous, this

10. "A Flexible Man of Iron," *Novoe Vremia* (in the English version, *New Times*), 7, February 1989, pp. 19–20.

formula ensured General Jaruzelski's election to a six-year term. A two-term limit was put on the presidency.

These measures reflect how the Party's power was to be fairly well protected. In addition, the government expected an election held with Solidarity's participation would reinforce its own legitimacy. In fact, it was a source of embarrassment for the leaders of Solidarity, and it was criticized on this count by its own supporters. The leaders defended themselves by stating that the accords merely represented a step toward democracy and claimed that they had only accepted these election rules for a five-year transitional period.

Soviet reactions to the results of the Roundtable were positive, even enthusiastic. *Izvestiia,* for example, stated that the accords had "dealt a death knell to the myth that socialism cannot be reformed."[11] The CPSU's theoretical journal, for its part, wrote that the PUWP had succeeded in "reestablishing its leadership in society and reinforcing its leading role in the state" by finding a way out of the crisis in which Poland had become trapped. It saw in the accords the emergence of a new system based "on a parliamentary socialist democracy and on a civil society."[12] While the process was certainly less advanced in the USSR itself, things were evolving in the same direction there, albeit with more genuine initiative from the Party in the Soviet case. In the March 1989 elections for the Congress of Peoples' Deputies, new electoral rules had permitted the victory of dissidents such as Andrei Sakharov and the unexpected defeat of a significant number of important Party officials. Unlike Poland, however, the opposition was not yet structured and organized.

From the Soviet reformers' point of view, the Roundtable accords represented the ideal model for Poland, and equally served as the most desirable and exemplary model for Eastern Europe in general. On the one hand, aside from the introduction of real institutional pluralism, it permitted the opposition to make an important entry into Parliament and possibly join a coalition government. Therefore, these were steps toward an authentic democratization. On the other hand, even if the Party's power had been limited, it still remained the master of the political game and held all the instruments necessary to stop the process from "spinning out of control." Hence, the Polish model held the promise of a controlled democratization process which would unfold step by step over

---

11. *Izvestiia,* 6 April 1989.

12. "Novyi etap v zhizni Pol'shi" (A New Stage in the Life of Poland), *Kommunist,* 7, May 1989, pp. 94–99.

time. If the model could have been maintained and extended to the other East European states, the advantages for the USSR would have been important on various levels. Above all, the democratization it entailed was credible enough that Western countries would feel obliged to support and encourage it, especially with economic assistance. In addition, since the process was not guaranteed to be irreversible at the onset, the incentive or obligation of Western nations to stimulate it would be all the greater. The USSR's tolerance and its participation in an East-West rapprochement that was becoming increasingly tangible and more anchored in the Eastern regimes themselves would have made Soviet calls for disarmament and the construction of a new European order more irresistible and imperative.

The Soviet leaders knew that the process upon which their Polish counterparts were embarking would necessarily have an effect on the other East European states.[13] In that sense, their open and apparently unreserved support of Jaruzelski during and after the Roundtable talks can be seen as a form of pressure or even an indirect offensive against the conservative regimes of the region. We asked General Jaruzelski if he had also seen things in this way. He responded affirmatively, but added that "at the same time, Gorbachev saw things in more positive terms." For the Soviet leader, Jaruzelski commented, the results of the Round-table "could reassure the other East European leaders by demonstrating that it was possible to cooperate with the opposition forces, without it leading to 'decommunization' or a White Terror."[14] He went on to say that "Gorbachev saw the Polish experience as a laboratory and a useful example, not only for East Europe but also for the USSR itself."

According to Gorbachev's advisers, he became increasingly concerned, as *perestroika* advanced, about the possible consequences of an East European conservative "front," representing the majority of regimes, which was hostile to his course.[15] But he always sought *indirect* means of weakening it. To cite but one example: when his advisers urged Gorbachev not to take up Fidel Castro's invitation to visit Cuba, the Soviet leader, in his decision to go, invoked precisely the need not to "broaden the front" of opponents to his policy in the Communist world.

---

13. *Kommunist,* for example, wrote that "the Polish Party's experience carries significance not only for Poland, but also for the other countries . . ." (ibid., pp. 94–99).

14. Interview with General Jaruzelski, 8 May 1992.

15. See Anatolii S. Cherniaev, *Shest' let s Gorbachevym—po dnevnikovym zapisiam* (*Six Years with Gorbachev—From Journal Notes*) (Moscow: Progress Kul'tura, 1993), pp. 268–269.

In the same way, his visit to China in May 1989, which sealed Sino-Soviet reconciliation and illustrated China's support for his reformist policies, served to enhance his base of legitimacy among socialist states.[16]

THE FIRST CONSEQUENCES
OF THE ELECTION RESULTS

Barely two months after the signing of the Roundtable accords, the scenario which they had sketched out began to crumble. The first round of parliamentary elections, held on June 4, took place according to the rules set out in the accords; as indicated above, however, they harbored an important surprise, both for the Polish leaders and for Solidarity.

In the Senate elections, Solidarity's Civic Committee won 92 of 100 seats in the first round. This was far more than predicted. But the gravest surprise was the performance of the Party and its allies in the competition for the Diet seats reserved for them. Solidarity was able to gain 160 of the 161 Diet seats that were open for competition, in all cases against real opponents. By contrast, only five candidates of the governing coalition (out of 299 seats reserved for them) managed to gather the 50 percent of votes necessary to win. It was the combination of the 50 percent requirement and the fact that voters were given the freedom of choosing between several Communist candidates in the districts reserved for them that explain the government's unexpected disaster. A segment of the population carefully crossed out the names of all Communist candidates on their ballots. Many others crossed out the names of the most famous Communists on their ballots, as well as of those most closely identified with the government. The result was that valid votes cast were often split more or less equally among lesser-known candidates, rendering it very difficult for them to gain the needed 50 percent.

Solidarity's triumph was directly proportional to the government's humiliation. Of course, given the rules of renunciation and nonopposition to which Solidarity had agreed, the governing coalition was able to win the 294 other seats guaranteed it in the second round of the elections, held on June 18. Voter turnout, however, was a mere 25 percent; for most voters, the real elections had already taken place. The government's delegitimization and Solidarity's legitimization were felt all the more strongly since their magnitude was totally unexpected. Solidarity

---

16. Following the repression of the Tienanmen Square demonstrations, which disrupted Gorbachev's visit and were partially stimulated by it, Chinese and Soviet reform policies began to diverge widely.

had not had any way of measuring its strength so concretely since 1981. It seemed even stronger than in 1981, even though all the signs had indicated that it had declined extensively since then. Within the Party apparatus, frustration was so widespread that General Jaruzelski decided to meet the Central Committee in two separate groups to analyze the election results, in order to avoid a vote of no confidence.

Despite all this, General Jaruzelski held to the formal election results, and designated the interior minister, General Czesław Kiszczak, as the next prime minister and made him responsible for forming a new government; Kiszczak had been the main government figure in the dialogue with Solidarity. The political atmosphere had, however, changed radically. One of the unexpected consequences, which eventually played a major role, was the defection of the PUWP's satellite parties. They took advantage of the Party's weakness to escape its tutelage. The old government coalition of Communists and satellites had 65 percent of the seats in the Diet, but the PUWP alone had only 38 percent. The small parties soon made it known that they would refuse to participate in a coalition government with the Communists alone, insisting on Solidarity's participation; Solidarity itself initially refused. During the course of the next several weeks, the shape of Poland's new government was uncertain.

It was in this context—in fact, despite it and against advice given him in Moscow which we have indicated above—that Gorbachev chose to go further than he had ever gone before in publicly rejecting the Brezhnev Doctrine.[17] It was especially significant since the remarks were made in the context of an important speech before the Council of Europe in Strasbourg, which was one of the highlights of his swing through Western Europe. His first stop had been Bonn, where he received a triumphant welcome from the German population. That visit also heralded a new and important convergence of views, not only with the German Social Democrats, but also with Chancellor Kohl, on a series of political and economic questions, notably on disarmament in Europe. Incidentally, the United States, after an initial period of hesitation, had just responded to the Soviets with a bold proposition of its own on troop reductions in Europe by both superpowers. We shall return to this point.

17. The declaration was much more significant than previous ones, as it made specific reference not only to sovereign states in general, but to allied nations. Gorbachev specifically declared: "The political and social order in one country or another has changed in the past and can also change in the future. Still, it is exclusively up to the peoples themselves. It is their choice. All interference, whatever its nature, in the internal affairs of a state to limit its sovereignty of a state, even from a friend or ally, is inadmissible" (*Pravda,* 7 July 1989).

Suffice it to note that Gorbachev had almost reached the summit of his international glory and that his project of changing the European order seemed, in the summer of 1989, increasingly realistic.

Benefitting from the democratization already begun in Poland (and simultaneously in Hungary—as we shall see below) and giving proof of Soviet "good behavior," Gorbachev expected to put many bricks into the building of the "common European home." This underscores that, from the Soviet perspective, its European policy had a higher priority than its East European one. In fact, Gorbachev's declaration came at a critical moment in Poland, where it contributed to a change in Solidarity's perception of its freedom of action.

Gorbachev made an interesting profession of his socialist faith during his visit to Paris—not in response to Communist conservatives, but to a skeptical French journalist. As if a raw nerve had been struck, he declared: "If anyone believes that we are renouncing our values or that we are renouncing the power of the people, that is an illusion. . . . Through democratization and *glasnost'*, through the return of the people into the political and economic process, what we desire is to breathe new life into socialism."[18] In the Soviet reality itself, the concept of renovated socialism became increasingly elastic. But it remained a crucial and operative carrier for reform, to the extent that it was the essential motivation and justification for the risks that Gorbachev was taking. His international project and the successes he had achieved played a similar role.

THE GROWING POLARIZATION
WITHIN THE WARSAW PACT

Immediately after his trip to Western Europe, Gorbachev went to Bucharest for a meeting of Warsaw Pact heads of state and Party leaders, which took place on July 7 and 8, 1989. The events in Poland had strongly accentuated the polarization within the Pact and greatly contributed to the climate of tension that dominated the closed-door meetings, pitting the USSR, Poland, and Hungary against Romania, the GDR, Czechoslovakia, and Bulgaria.

One month later, Nicolae Ceausescu sent a letter to his Warsaw Pact counterparts, demanding that collective action be taken to put an end to the "counterrevolutionary" process taking place in Poland. The PUWP

18. *Pravda*, 7 July 1989.

Politburo decided to make Ceausescu's letter public.[19] Betting on the international discredit of Ceausescu, the Polish leaders intended to neutralize him and make it more difficult for other conservative Pact leaders to take a position similar to his. In short, it was a move to divide the conservative majority. The action was all the more useful since Zhivkov, more cautiously, had sent his Polish counterparts a message of support, pledging to aid them in any way they deemed necessary to redress the situation and to help mobilize support for them in other socialist states.[20]

During the July meeting, the Polish situation had already been the source of profound divisions. Even if Poland was not the subject of any official criticism, the transcript of the closed-door meeting of heads of state and of Communist Parties on July 8, to which this author was granted access,[21] reveals direct confrontations on the general situation of the Communist world. The altercations took the form of an exchange of information concerning the situation in each country, with Gorbachev taking the initiative. "We are receiving letters of panic from everywhere, written by those who believe that socialism is seriously threatened," he declared. "These fears are not founded and those who are afraid had better hold on, because *perestroika* has only just begun. Our transformations are not of a cosmetic nature, and there must not be any illusions about that. . . . We are going from one international order to another." Looking directly at Ceausescu, his self-proclaimed black sheep, he added: "The need to deal with changes and new challenges affects all of us." He even went so far as to speak of "intrigues against the Soviet government, encouraged from abroad, by those who support fractious activities."

As always, Ceausescu was the most direct and virulent in his attack on Gorbachev, whom he accused of destroying all of socialism's conquests through his policies. More surprisingly, Milos Jakes, whom Gorbachev had generally given the benefit of the doubt and who usually paid lip service to *perestroika,* was particularly aggressive. Remarking upon the reawakening of nationalisms within the USSR, he asked whether it was "evidence that *perestroika* can be the wrong road." He denounced

19. Interview with Jozef Czyrek, the Politburo member responsible for international affairs, Warsaw, 6 May 1992.

20. Interview with Andrei Lukanov, a member of the Bulgarian Politburo in 1989 and prime minister in 1990, Sofia, 14 November 1994.

21. I would like to particularly thank Col. Gornicki, aide-de-camp of General Jaruzelski. During a long interview on 7 May 1992 in Warsaw, he shared with me his transcript of the conversations and allowed me to take notes from it.

"the activism of rightist forces in his country," adding that "the old leaders are demanding their rehabilitation and reintegration into the Party, without uttering a word of self-criticism." "We reject and will continue to reject these demands," he said, "and we will preserve our control over the means of information." Having suffered a mild stroke that was certainly not due solely to the meeting, as some argued afterward, Honecker had to make an emergency return to East Berlin, well before the meeting ended.

The tensions which occurred behind closed doors did not leak out to the public. The Soviet Union's leadership in the Warsaw Pact was still too strong and the international position of its conservative members too weak to allow the conservative critics to voice their opposition in public. The long final common communiqué endorsed Gorbachev's European policy in detail, even in those aspects most unacceptable to the conservative regimes, notably concerning the respect for human rights "by all countries."[22] Evidently targeting Ceausescu's opposition to the Polish course, one passage of the communiqué stipulated that "no country should seek to dictate the course of events in another country or arrogate to itself the role of judge. . . ."

GEORGE BUSH'S "POSITIVE ROLE"

While the Warsaw Pact meeting was unfolding in Bucharest with General Jaruzelski's participation, the political situation in Poland was becoming more complicated—even as far as the immediate future of the president himself was concerned. In the context of the PUWP satellite parties' political emancipation, several of their members announced that they intended to vote against General Jaruzelski's candidacy at the joint session of the two houses of Parliament planned for electing a president. The Roundtable accords had been designed in such a way as to "permit" the Solidarity deputies to vote against Jaruzelski, without affecting the anticipated outcome. Especially in view of the new postelectoral political context, they had no intention of supporting him. As a result, the general's election to the presidency, which had been one of the central implicit elements of the Roundtable agreements, became uncertain and was at risk of being compromised.

22. *Pravda*, 9 July 1989. One passage in the communiqué deserves to be underlined in this context: "One of the basic conditions for assuring peace and cooperation in Europe is the application, *in every country,* of the entire gamut of freedoms and fundamental human rights, as they were formulated in the Universal Declaration of Human Rights and the international accords on human rights in the last act of Helsinki. . . ." Emphasis added.

It was in this context, and just one day after the end of the Bucharest Warsaw Pact summit, July 10, that George Bush arrived in Warsaw for a long-planned official visit.

Much later, Andrei Grachev, a high official in the CPSU's International Department in 1989 and later Gorbachev's official spokesman, granted this author an interview. When asked if Gorbachev and his advisers had not begun, during the summer of 1989 and the acceleration of events in Hungary and Poland, to fear a disaster for the socialist camp, he responded: "No, because we believed that the USSR had the political means to circumscribe the processes at work in those two states, and we also counted on the cooperation of the United States in that regard."[23] As indicated above, that expectation was not unfounded.

As is often the custom before trips abroad, George Bush received journalists from the Solidarity newspaper, *Gazeta Wyborcza,* at the White House on the eve of his departure for Poland. Speaking of his upcoming visit, he told them: "We're going in a constructive vein, not in some critical vein or not in some mode of trying to complicate things for somebody else . . . I will not be trying to inflame things. . . . I'm not going to deliberately do anything that is going to cause a crisis."[24] Of course, the American president wanted to encourage changes and democratization in East Europe—that was, in fact, the aim of his trip—but, just like Gorbachev, he wanted a controlled process to achieve those changes. He even declared in private, to members of his entourage, that a sudden collapse of the Polish regime might be "more than the market can bear."[25] According to their account, he found Walesa more unpredictable than Jaruzelski. As two American analysts have noted, Bush (like many other statesmen, for that matter) had "an instinctive preference for reassuring, gradual processes, for change in the framework of order."[26] In addition, by this time, Bush was sufficiently convinced of Gorbachev's reformist intentions (of which the evolution in Poland was proof), even if he remained cautious and reticent about the latter's disarmament proposals. In any case, he was willing to count on Gorbachev staying in power.

Before the Polish parliament, Bush warmly praised this evolution and announced that he would ask Congress for a $100 million fund to assist the development of private enterprises, and promised U.S. support in the

23. Interview with Andrei Grachev, Paris, 2 March 1993.
24. See M. R. Beschloss and Strobe Talbott, *At the Highest Levels* (Boston: Little, Brown, 1993), p. 85.
25. Ibid., p. 87.
26. Ibid.

World Bank for the rescheduling of Poland's debt. That was much less than Walesa hoped for—he had suggested that the United States provide $10 billion over three years. At the G-7 summit which took place some days later, it was decided that the EEC would organize an international conference on economic aid to Poland and Hungary. During a two-hour meeting with Jaruzelski, Bush congratulated him on the role he was playing in Polish political affairs and implicitly voiced his desire that this role continue.[27]

In his memoirs, General Jaruzelski writes that President Bush's behavior in general, and toward himself more specifically, played a crucial role in his election to the presidency several days later, on July 18.[28] That outcome was made possible by the abstention of several Solidarity members and the voluntary absence of several others, for which both groups were harshly criticized by some of their supporters.

Whether or not George Bush's behavior was somehow determinate on this precise issue, his visit to Warsaw and Budapest was judged by Moscow to have been positive, and the Soviet press presented it the same way. In a rather arrogant, presumptuous manner, an *Izvestiia* commentator even wrote that Bush "is essentially just approving the changes that Moscow has already approved or initiated in practice."[29]

EVENTS BEGIN TO SPIN OUT OF CONTROL

Neither President Bush's visit nor General Jaruzelski's election to the presidency could put an end to the political impasse and uncertainty burdening Poland. The prime minister-designate, General Kiszczak, was still not able to form a government, despite extensive negotiations. He was proposing a grand coalition of all parties, which Solidarity refused to join; meanwhile, the former PUWP satellites continued to insist that they would not join the Communists alone to form a coalition.

On August 7, Lech Walesa raised the stakes. Taking up a slogan introduced by Adam Michnik the previous month—"your President, our Prime Minister"—Walesa claimed not just the position of prime minister for his political alliance, but also demanded a government without Communists. The PUWP Politburo rapidly reacted with hostility, accusing Walesa of violating the Roundtable accords and pushing the country toward crisis and destabilization.

27. Ibid., pp. 88–89.
28. Jaruzelski, *Les chaînes et le refuge*, p. 337.
29. *Izvestiia*, 16 July 1989.

The Soviet press, which had remained very cautious up to this point, took up the PUWP's arguments, even accusing Walesa of wanting to carry out a "coup d'etat."[30] While Gorbachev and Shevardnadze refrained from publicly intervening, A. L. Adamishin, deputy minister of Foreign Affairs, commented on the situation in a radio interview. He warned that Solidarity's policy was a break from the "national concord" and expressed the "wish" that it would not push things "all the way to a destabilization of the situation in Poland, which inevitably would have serious consequences for the situation in Europe as a whole."[31]

These Soviet warnings did have an effect. On August 15, Walesa announced that his political movement would accept forming a government that included Communists. He also added that a Solidarity-led government would do nothing to interfere with the smooth functioning of the Warsaw Pact. To this end, and in order to reassure the Soviets, he suggested that the defense minister be a Communist. Walesa, in a move to appease the PUWP at least somewhat, further proposed that the interior minister also be a Communist. Immediately, Soviet commentators changed their tune. The newspaper *Izvestiia* highlighted a statement Walesa had made on West German television, according to which "Poland cannot forget its geographic location and its obligations" and that "Solidarity will fulfill its Warsaw Pact commitments."[32] Tadeusz Mazowiecki, the Solidarity adviser who was designated by President Jaruzelski on August 20 to form the new government, repeated Walesa's commitments; they were again noted and emphasized in Moscow.

For the Polish Communists, the political battle was not yet over. They did not intend to settle for the two ministries promised by Walesa, insisting on a number at least commensurate with their "representation" in Parliament. In the end, they were only able to obtain four ministries, the two others being Transportation (closely linked to Warsaw Pact logistics) and Foreign Trade (very important for CMEA). The important Foreign Affairs Ministry was given to K. Skubichevski, an independent and respected expert who had been a member of Jaruzelski's Consultative Council.

On August 22, shortly before giving his final blessing to the Mazowiecki government's composition, Mieczyslaw Rakowski, who had replaced Jaruzelski as PUWP general secretary, had a forty-minute

---

30. See *Izvestiia*, 12 August 1989; *Pravda*, 14 August 1989.
31. Foreign Broadcast Information Service, Soviet Union, 14 August 1989, p. 8.
32. *Izvestiia*, 19 August 1989.

telephone conversation with his CPSU counterpart, Mikhail Gorbachev. He reportedly asked for Gorbachev's support in order to obtain a more favorable distribution of portfolios in the new government.[33] In this author's interview with him, Rakowski did not confirm having made such a request. Asked if Gorbachev had expressed any anxiety about the turn of events in Poland or reservations about the composition of the government as it was shaping up, he answered, "Not the least objection, nor the least reservations."[34] On the contrary: Rakowski says that he expressed the desire to go to Moscow for consultations with Gorbachev, but the latter refused. He preferred putting off the meeting. According to Rakowski, Gorbachev said that an immediate meeting would be inopportune because it could be interpreted as a sign of Soviet opposition or interference. So, at this point, the Soviet leadership had decided that the USSR needed to appear not only as the power which authorized the process, but also as the one accompanying it. Mazowiecki was congratulated and invited to Moscow. His government was described as an "important factor of stability" for Poland and Europe. This "benevolent" attitude initially appeared to bear fruit, as the new prime minister declared that the new Soviet-Polish relations, based on partnership, not domination, would only reinforce the stability of Poland's international obligations. His words were duly noted in the Soviet press.[35]

It should be pointed out that the guarantees which the USSR, and even the Polish Communists, had received were not negligible. In addition to the preservation of Soviet military presence in Poland, the main instrument of its European policy, the Warsaw Pact, did not appear to be threatened. Even if they no longer had a hegemonic hold on the government, the Communists' influence remained far greater than the number of ministries under their control. Jaruzelski continued to be commander-in-chief of the armed forces and had the constitutional power to

33. See, in particular, Anna Swidlicka, "The 14th PUWP Plenum and its Aftermath," *Situation Report, Poland* (Radio Free Europe), 12 September 1989.

34. Interview with M. Rakowski, Warsaw, 3 March 1993.

35. "The new prime minister has declared: 'All foreign observers of the transformations taking place in Poland must convince themselves that the Polish events do not threaten or undermine international stability. On the contrary, international relations based on sovereignty and partnership are more stable than an order founded on domination and force. Our opening toward all of Europe does not signify the denial of our old links and obligations. If we repeat today that the new government will respect its obligations to its allies, this is not a tactical excuse designed to tranquilize. It flows out of our understanding of Poland's interests and our analysis of the international situation." L. Krasutskii, "Pol'sha i PORP v period perestroiki" (Poland and the PUWP in the *perestroika* period), *Kommunist*, 15, October 1989, pp. 96–106.

declare a state of emergency and dissolve Parliament. All the institutions and instruments of repression remained in the hands of Communists. The Mazowiecki government could have been considered, at the time, as a government under strict surveillance.

In Moscow, the leadership undoubtedly believed that, under the circumstances, this would be the best solution it could expect for the Party of the socialist country which had known the largest number of sociopolitical crises since its creation.

Even if a fundamental political change had taken place in Poland in early autumn 1989, nothing was irreversible yet, particularly in the event of a political change in Moscow, as Adam Michnik himself acknowledges.[36] It is only after the Berlin Wall and the East German regime fell that the change became truly irreversible.[37]

The Polish Communists' position in the government hierarchy in early autumn 1989, and the emerging coexistence of private and public sectors in the economy, evoked the general situation in Eastern Europe in 1946 and 1947—a model mentioned explicitly, as indicated above, by Soviet reformers. After World War II, it was the Communist Parties that were on the offensive, pushed by Moscow in a context of increasing East-West confrontation.

In these conditions, could Moscow still believe that reformed socialism would have a chance in Poland? Certain Soviet reformers were already almost openly grieving over the loss of Poland, characterizing the situation there as a "Finlandization." That Finlandization, they said, was perfectly acceptable—as long as "the necessary guarantees" were given that "Soviet interests would not be endangered during the period of transition toward a world-wide restructuring of East-West relations."[38] The preservation of Polish engagements in the Warsaw Pact was the most essential "necessary guarantee."

Apparently, Gorbachev was one of the last to reconcile himself to the idea that the PUWP had essentially lost power, and that socialism,

36. Interview with Adam Michnik, Warsaw, 4 March 1993.
37. One observer of Polish affairs wrote: "Mazowiecki's time in power is divided by a psychological split. Before the fall of the Berlin Wall, everything seemed bold and fired up by a revolutionary flame, to the point that one wondered if the limits of Soviet tolerance were not being passed." See Georges Mink, "Pologne: le paradoxe du compromis historique," pp. 51–66, in Pierre Kende and Aleksander Smolar, eds., *La grande secousse: Europe de l'Est, 1989–1990* (Paris: Presses du CNRS, 1990).
38. Migranian, "An Epitaph to the Brezhnev Doctrine: The USSR and the other Socialist States in the Context of East-West Relations," *Novoe Vremia*, 34, September 1989.

even "renovated," was doomed in Poland. Even after the opening of the Berlin Wall when, in the aftermath of the Malta summit, he called a meeting of the Warsaw Pact heads of state and leaders of Communist Parties in power, Gorbachev invited Rakowski, as well as Jaruzelski and Mazowiecki. Mazowiecki was so upset by Gorbachev's invitation to the general secretary of the PUWP (which could no longer be considered a leading party) that he refused to travel to Moscow on the same plane.[39] In a book about the Soviet leader, Rakowski relates the following incident during that December meeting: "From my stay in Moscow, one scene comes to mind. During a break, Gorbachev approached the Polish delegation, greeted its members and asked me how things were going. He added: 'Mieczyslaw, don't forget that our socialist ideas have a future.'—'The ideas do, but we don't have one'—He had heard my response. He did not say anything. For me, it was clear that Gorbachev knew the system born after the October Revolution found itself in an impasse. Did he believe we could still change things? I think he did."[40]

Whatever the case may be, before the fall of the Berlin Wall, Gorbachev was convinced that the future chances of his European policy were better than ever, due notably to the "stabilization" in Poland and Soviet behavior—and despite what he considered a grave setback for the "fraternal Polish reformist party." Neither he, nor practically anyone else, foresaw the debacle that was soon to follow.

In 1987 and 1988, the USSR's domestic economic situation had not improved. Even worse, it began to seriously deteriorate in 1989, despite attempts at economic reform; in addition, the nationalist fever was rising in the Baltic republics, penetrating the Communist Parties which ruled them. That is why, in early autumn 1989, even before the opening of the Berlin Wall, Gorbachev's East European policy and the pursuit of the panacea which the construction of the new European order was to be, began to resemble a desperate attempt to catch up, or at least a race against the clock.

39. Interview with M. Rakowski, Warsaw 3 March 1993.
40. Mieczyslaw Rakowski, *Gorbaczow: Pierwszy i Ostatny* (Warsaw: Polska Oficyna Wydawnicza BWG, 1992), p. 114; passages translated from Polish for this book by Jan Grabowski.

CHAPTER SEVEN

Hungary

An Acceptable (and Accepted) Evolution

A coalition government as the result of an election (not later
than June 1990) appears to be a real possibility, with the
(now reformed) Communist Party exerting a kind of leading
role, in virtue of its better performance in the elections.

Radio Free Europe (Summer 1989)[1]

Gorbachev shares our own fears and preoccupations, which
are: that the road to reforms not end in anarchy; that the
HSWP [Hungarian Socialist Workers' Party] remain *one of
the essential forces* in the renewal of society; and that Hungary not abandon its friendship with the Soviet Union in a
unilateral movement toward the West.

Rezso Nyers (September 1989)[2]

In Hungary, the replacement of Janos Kadar in May 1988 had shifted
the balance of forces within the Hungarian leadership decisively in favor
of the reformers. Very quickly, however, the victorious alliance of 1988
began to split up over the rapidity and depth of political change that the
Hungarian Socialist Workers' Party (HSWP) should initiate—given a
social and economic situation that was to become particularly strained
in the first months of 1989.

TOWARD A MULTIPARTY SYSTEM

At the beginning of 1989, Imre Pozsgay (who had been elected to the
Politburo the previous year) was clearly identified as the most resolutely

1. Vladimir Kuzin, "The Changing Parties," *Background Report* (Radio Free
Europe), 138, 4 August 1989.
2. Rezso Nyers, President of the HSWP, *Corriere della Sera,* 9 September 1989;
emphasis added.

reformist leader. He maintained continual contacts and excellent relations with the movement which was to become the main opposition group, the Hungarian Democratic Forum (HDF). So excellent were the ties that the HDF was often accused of being manipulated by the regime.

On January 28, 1989, Pozsgay made a move that was both bold and risky. He believed that the Party could never really hope to create a new legitimacy and establish the credibility of its break with the past, without revising its position on the most tragic moment of the Party's history, namely the 1956 uprising and its suppression.[3] He led a commission charged with reexamining the "events of 1956" and, without waiting for a decision from the superior organs of the Party, declared in a radio interview on January 28 that the events had not been a counterrevolution but rather "a popular insurrection against an oligarchical power." He further announced that the commission's report would be published immediately.[4]

Obviously, Pozsgay's public declaration was a sensation. It was printed by the major Budapest newspapers on Monday, January 30. "That day, [Imre Szokai, an official of the HSWP's International Department close to Pozsgay, told us] we gathered in his office, to await with him, and with apprehension, Moscow's reaction."[5] Far more than Grosz's reaction, which they assumed would be negative, it was the Soviets' response they feared. The USSR was, after all, implicitly being accused by Poszgay's declaration of having bloodily crushed a legitimate popular insurrection. "After two days without any Soviet reaction," Szokai continued, "we telephoned our friends in Moscow ourselves. They reassured us by saying that there would not be any Soviet reaction." This was enormous encouragement for Poszgay and his ensuing actions.

The absence of a Soviet reaction was not the result of any kind of negligence. In fact, Valentin Falin, then director of the CPSU Central Committee's International Department, prepared a memorandum to the Hungarian leadership immediately after Pozsgay's statement, in which he reminded them of the Soviet position and of the counterrevolutionary character of the events in Hungary.[6] Falin's initiative is not surprising. Moscow still made a clear differentiation between the Prague Spring

3. By moving unilaterally, he was doubtlessly also pursuing personal ambitions, for which he was later reproached; subsequent events confirmed the charges.

4. See *Situation Report, Hungary* (Radio Free Europe), 3, 28 February 1989.

5. Interview with Imre Szokai, Budapest, 2 May 1992.

6. According to his deputy director for socialist countries. Second interview with Valerii L. Musatov, Moscow, 26 April 1993.

and the Hungarian Uprising, during the course of which Communists (in fact, members of the secret police) were hanged by the mobs. However, because of a specific interdiction from Gorbachev himself, who invoked noninterference, the memorandum was not sent to Budapest.[7] His decision had an immediate effect on the course of events in the Hungarian capital, as we shall see.

If Pozsgay took a risk in making his January 28 declaration, it was because he could not know what to expect from Moscow. If General Jaruzelski himself, who had excellent personal relations with Gorbachev, did not know very well where the limits of Soviet tolerance lay, then radical Hungarian reformers who stood in the second ranks of the hierarchy were obviously in the dark. According to their own testimony, they knew that there were struggles over political direction within the Soviet leadership, and they sensed a "positive" evolution. On the other hand, they had great difficulty estimating not only the balance of forces at different moments in time, but also Gorbachev's ultimate intentions. At the end of 1988, Pozsgay met Aleksandr Yakovlev and asked him for support, but Yakovlev was cautious and reserved. He did not want to seem to be supporting a fractious move against Grosz, to whom Gorbachev had demonstrated his support just a few months earlier.[8] So, the Hungarians observed the mixed signals coming from Moscow carefully, hoping to correctly decipher them. If Yakovlev's reserve could not be interpreted as very encouraging, the absence of a Soviet reaction to Pozsgay's statement was perceived by him and his supporters as an opposite, stronger signal.[9]

During the spring and summer of 1989, at each step of the HSWP's political evolution, Karoly Grosz and other more conservative leaders invoked the negative reactions that would come from the USSR.[10] Each time, those reactions did not materialize, and hence the conservatives'

7. Ibid.

8. We learned that, in 1988, Gorbachev and his entourage distrusted Pozsgay to some extent. He was seen as being a nationalist since, through his ties with the HDF, he took an aggressive stance on the question of the Hungarians in Transylvania and because he ostensibly refused to have contacts with the Soviets. At the end of 1988 and the spring of 1989, however, he actively sought higher-level contacts with Soviet officials. Interview with Andrei Grachev (deputy director, CPSU Central Committee's International Department in 1989 and Gorbachev's official spokesman in 1991), Paris, 2 March 1993.

9. Interview with Imre Szokai, Budapest, 2 May 1992.

10. Interview with Laszlo Kovacs (deputy minister of Foreign Affairs and Gyula Horn's first assistant in 1989; currently minister of Foreign Affairs, after the return to power of the reformed Communists), Budapest, 2 May 1992.

position kept weakening. Here again, the lack of a response was deliberate, and even more significant because, as we learned from informed sources in Moscow, Grosz repeatedly asked Gorbachev and other Soviet leaders to intervene on his behalf in the ongoing Hungarian debates.[11] They consistently and knowingly refused to do so.[12] In this sense, it is not surprising that Grosz felt "deserted" by Gorbachev and subsequently concluded that the Soviet leader had decided to abandon Hungary and Eastern Europe to their fate.[13]

But we should not get ahead of our story. In the first months of 1989, Grosz's position in the Hungarian political apparatus was still very strong. Nonetheless, during an extraordinary meeting of the Party Central Committee which took place on February 10 and 11 and was called to debate Pozsgay's famous declaration made several days earlier, the latter was able to score some points. While Pozsgay was criticized for the "unilateral and premature" character of his declaration, he was not punished, as some had wished. On the contrary: the Central Committee renewed its confidence in him.[14]

Additionally, the Central Committee, in affirming the necessity of important political changes, formally endorsed the principle of introducing a multiparty system in Hungary. This gave a more specific definition to the notion of "political pluralism" which had already been accepted. Nothing was decided, though, about the exact framework or conditions of the multiparty system, nor, more importantly, about electoral rules. Immediately after the meeting, Grosz sought to limit the potential breadth of the decisions by specifying that pluralism would function within the socialist framework; that the political parties ought to operate "on a socialist basis"; and that the introduction of the new system should happen gradually and would take time.[15]

Ten days later, the Central Committee approved the major outlines of a new draft constitution to be submitted to the National Assembly. The

---

11. Interview with Vadim Zagladin (Gorbachev's presidential adviser in 1989), Moscow, 29 April 1993.

12. Grosz was, however, satisfied on one point. On the occasion of a trip by Pozsgay to Moscow in May 1989, Gorbachev decided not to meet him personally, on Grosz's direct request. Second interview with Valerii L. Musatov, Moscow, 26 April 1993.

13. See chapter 4.

14. On the question of the 1956 events, the Central Committee confirmed that there had been an "authentic popular insurrection," but that it was subsequently accompanied by "counterrevolutionary acts." See *Situation Report, Hungary* (Radio Free Europe), 4, 22 March 1994.

15. See the summary of his remarks in *Izvestiia*, 14 February 1989.

HSWP's leading role no longer appeared in the draft. This was a very important step. The Party was confirming its commitment to preserve its leading role through persuasion and the use of political instruments, not constitutional ones. At the same time, the draft constitution defined Hungary as a "socialist state," and, of course, political parties were to act in conformity with the constitution.[16] Several days later, on March 17, the Central Committee (which met ever more frequently, a reflection of the rapidity of change in the political situation) approved a new program of action, which supported the principle of free elections. In the absence of an electoral framework and law, and given strong divisions within the Party leadership on this point, the opposition forces did not take the Central Committee's decision seriously.

Karoly Grosz himself confirmed to this writer that he was opposed to holding free elections, at least given Hungary's state of economic, political, and social instability at the time.[17] At that moment, and subsequently, there were persistent rumors in Hungary that Grosz had planned, at the beginning of 1989, to use the control of the armed forces and security apparatus he still had then, to decree a state of emergency, expecting the Central Committee to go with the tide and endorse a fait accompli. The objective would not, of course, have been to establish a permanent political-military dictatorship but to realign the balance of forces in favor of the Party, in order to negotiate the conditions of a return to normalcy and the gradual introduction of pluralist elements with the opposition, as General Jaruzelski seemed to have succeeded in doing in Poland.

We asked Grosz if these rumors had any basis in fact. "Only partially," he responded. "It was a state of economic, not military, emergency, that I had envisaged." He told us that after having asked for, and been refused, emergency economic aid from the USSR, he prepared a program of exceptional measures. He enumerated several of them for our benefit: a freeze on salaries; the closure of a series of nonprofitable plants; a return of all foreign currency to central control, to deal with the foreign debt crisis; and the privatization of enterprises, open only to Hungarians (to the exclusion of foreign capital). We asked him if, given the already strained social and political context in Hungary at the time, measures such as freezing salaries and closing factories would not have nec-

16. Ibid.
17. Interview with Karoly Grosz, Gödöllö, 1 May 1992.

essarily led to confrontation and a general state of emergency. He simply answered: "Maybe."

Apparently believing that we knew more than we were telling him, Grosz proceeded to make the following, astonishing remarks: "At that time, our relations with Romania were very strained, due to the problems of the Hungarians in Transylvania. Having received nuclear (sic) threats from Ceausescu,[18] I had troops along the Austrian border transferred to the border with Romania. That troop movement may have been perceived by Western intelligence services as preparation for military action."

We asked him why, given that he opposed free elections and believed that they risked leading the Party and the country into disaster, he did not use force to stop this evolution, when he still had the means to do so. "Not only would we have been condemned by Western countries and subjected to sanctions, but, above all, such an action would have collided head-on with the whole thrust of Soviet foreign policy, and we would have been isolated in our own camp, as well. I therefore decided that the best I could do was to offer resistance, using political means, for as long as I could."

It is clear that Grosz had understood the highest priorities of Soviet foreign policy. In the absence of Soviet support, however, his resistance through political means would not last long. Contrary to his assessment, Soviet reformers, like their Hungarian counterparts, believed that Hungary and the HSWP had a very good chance of success.

TOWARD THE ELECTIONS AND A SOCIAL-DEMOCRATIZATION OF THE HSWP

At the beginning of the summer, an event of major symbolic importance was to significantly change the political atmosphere in Hungary. The event was the solemn reburial, on June 16, of Imre Nagy, marking the thirty-first anniversary of his execution. Two hundred thousand people took to the streets to participate in the ceremony. It also epitomized the

---

18. Surprisingly enough, this remark is apparently not unfounded. Ceausescu supposedly made it known to Hungary, as of August 1988, that Romania could produce nuclear weapons, and it appears that it had begun to develop a medium-range missile capable of carrying a nuclear or chemical charge. See Jonathan Eyal, "Looking for Weapons of Mass Destruction?", *Jane's Soviet Intelligence Review*, 1 (8), August 1989, pp. 378–382, cited by James F. Burke, "Romanian and Soviet Intelligence in the December Revolution," *Intelligence and National Security*, 8, (4), October 1993, pp. 26–58.

end of the Kadar regime. The former Party chief had been removed a month earlier, on May 6, from his last functions as president and member of the HSWP's Central Committee, and died shortly after Nagy's funeral. Officially, the funeral was organized by Imre Nagy's family, but it was, in fact, the opposition that was the major force behind it. Some of the most important Party reformers—Pozsgay, Prime Minister Miklos Nemeth, and the new president of Parliament, Matyas Szuros—were granted permission to join the guard around Nagy's casket, symbolizing the willingness of the opposition and the reformist Communists to compromise and overcome the differences of the past. Some of the more radical (and pessimistic) elements of the opposition even asserted that the reformed Communists had succeeded in co-opting Nagy, who himself had been a Communist reformer during the 1956 uprising.

Less than ten days after Imre Nagy's reburial, on June 25, Karoly Grosz's powers were drastically reduced. While he nominally remained general secretary, effective leadership of the Party was handed over to a quadrumvirate, in which Grosz was surrounded by Pozsgay, Miklos Nemeth, and Rezso Nyers, who was the father of economic reform and now became president of the Party.

On May 25, Pozsgay declared that the elections to be held would be "entirely free." Also, when the Hungarian Roundtable finally began its arduous discussions at the end of June, it was already practically accepted, given the changes that had taken place in the HSWP leadership, that the elections scheduled for 1990 would be truly free and open. The two main groups to face the HSWP at the Roundtable were the Democratic Forum (the most important group) and the Union of Democrats, which represented a more clearly anti-Communist platform.

With a view to creating the best possible conditions for itself in the upcoming elections, the Party's Central Committee (which had been responsible for the changes in the Party leadership) called an early, extraordinary Party congress for early October 1989. The goal was nothing less than to transform the HSWP into a social-democratic party. Throughout the summer, while the Roundtable negotiations were concentrating on the new constitution and on electoral laws and mechanisms, the leading bodies in the Party were developing a specific program for its new orientation.

At the risk of stating the obvious, it should be underscored that, just like their Soviet and Polish counterparts, the Hungarian Communist reformers did not have any sense, in the summer of 1989, that they were leading their Party toward disaster—though they were, of course, conscious of the fact that they were involved in a difficult and close strug-gle. Their calculations were founded on a certain number of objective considerations. Because of its reformist legacy and of the political cred-it of its new leaders, the Hungarian Party was better prepared for elec-tions than its Polish counterpart.

In the summer of 1989, for example, opinion polls, considered by Western specialists to be reliable, gave the changing HSWP the support of 36 percent to 40 percent of intended Hungarian voters. Given the number of other political groupings and the divisions among intended voters, the HSWP's closest competitor did not even surpass 20 percent, according to the same polls. In these conditions, and even without an absolute majority, the reformed Communists would have remained, if not the masters, then at least the inevitable arbiters of the political game for the next four years. The political cleavages among various opposi-tion groups and parties were larger than those which separated the future socialist party from some of them. As such, its chances of becoming the dominant force in a coalition government were excellent. It was on the basis of opinion polls such as these that the prognosis of Radio Free Europe's research director, cited at the beginning of the chapter, was founded.

In addition, somewhat following the example of the Polish Round-table negotiations, there was a tacit understanding with the Hungarian Democratic Forum that Imre Pozsgay would become the next president of Hungary. This was an additional, and very important, guarantee of the future socialist party's preeminence. Even in totally free presidential elections, Pozsgay seemed certain to win against any candidate the oppo-sition could field. It was essentially the radical change of the interna-tional context, following the fall of the Berlin Wall, that put an end to these favorable scenarios. The perception of the Soviet Union's power and international influence had been a fundamental component of the situation up to that time.

CONSISTENCIES AND INCONSISTENCIES WITH THE SOVIET EVOLUTION

In the summer of 1989, the HSWP's positions were, in appearance, a marked contrast to those of its Soviet counterpart. Even if Gorbachev had been speaking for over a year about political pluralism for the USSR, the CPSU was still far from admitting the principle of a multiparty sys-tem. Such a system was still officially rejected, not to mention the idea of free elections. Also, Western observers continued to debate the new limits of Soviet tolerance.

Beyond the officially expressed positions, things were quite different, and, even externally, numerous signs to that effect were visible. Specifically concerning Hungary, it was not only the absence of a reaction to Hungarian revisionism about the 1956 events. Even the most official Soviet media's reactions and accounts of the transformations in Budapest during the summer were far less equivocal.

In fact, these reactions were remarkably favorable. Shortly after the HSWP Central Committee plenum at the end of June, *Pravda* presented its new objectives as being those "of democratic socialism, a law-based State, a multiparty parliamentary system, and a market economy based on the decisive role of social property."[19] Even more interestingly, the CPSU Central Committee's paper wrote that the HSWP, still considered a fraternal party, was "dedicated to Marxist values and to the humanist ideas of left socialism." No reference was made to Leninism, and *Pravda* described the HSWP's ambitions as those of "a renovated party which seeks to become a force striving for a new synthesis of Communist and social-democratic values."[20]

We have seen in chapter 5 how, from the beginning of 1989, internal documents circulating within the CPSU leadership considered social-democratization to be one desirable alternative for Eastern Europe. This was, in fact, the Bogomolov institute's clearly expressed position at the time. By the summer of 1989, even if it was not very apparent then, this idea had made considerable headway within leading Soviet circles, not only with regard to Eastern Europe, but also with respect to the USSR's own future.

Within Gorbachev's entourage, there were discussions at the time about the appropriateness of some form of a Soviet-style multiparty system.[21] One idea, in particular, was for the top of the CPSU itself to initiate a split of the Party, in order to establish true, organized political

19. *Pravda*, 27 June 1989.

20. Ibid. See also the very favorable Soviet reactions to the founding congress of the new Hungarian Socialist Party at the beginning of October 1989. The congress was described as being, in large measure, a product of Soviet *perestroika*, in S. Kolesnikov and E. Shahkov, "Vengriia: prioritet reformy" (Hungary: The Priority of Reform), *Kommunist*, 16, November 1989, pp. 94–105.

21. Interview with Andrei Grachev (deputy director of the Central Committee's International Department in 1989, and Gorbachev's official spokesman in 1991), Paris, 2 March 1993.

competition between its conservative and reformist wings. In this way, party pluralism could be circumscribed within the socialist framework, a notion that was still not open for debate. In tandem with this, and even if Gorbachev was still personally very hesitant about it,[22] the possibility of removing the *constitutional obligation* of the Party's leading role was discussed.[23] Such a measure would have given more tangible meaning to Yakovlev's slogan that the Party should preserve and deserve its leading role through political means.

If a gradual estrangement from Leninism was already very visible and pronounced in the Soviet view of the world and of the international system, it was much slower and more ambiguous in the sphere of domestic politics. As is now clear, by the summer of 1989, in the process of elaborating the transitional ideology that accompanied *perestroika,* it was the most central tenet of the Leninist legacy which began to be addressed. That tenet was the preservation, at any price, of the Communist Party's leading role. The fact that this debate was not yet apparent fed the skepticism which still existed concerning the depth of changes taking place in Soviet politics.

Undoubtedly, it was on the basis of this change taking place in the CPSU that Karoly Grosz, still a faithful Leninist, later told this writer: "It is not the collapse of the East European regimes that led to the collapse of the USSR, as you seem to believe. It is the opposite which took place. It is because, in its essence, the Soviet regime had already collapsed that the East European regimes fell."[24]

For the reformers among Gorbachev's circle, the Hungarian process was seen as a very favorable development.[25] Since the Hungarian Party's quest to regain its leading role through political means, universally recognized as democratic, had a very strong chance of succeeding, it seemed to confirm their expectations and the appropriateness of their political gamble. That is why they saw the Hungarian developments as a testing ground for the Soviet Union itself.[26]

---

22. At the beginning of December 1989, in a private conversation with Petar Mladenov, the new head of the Bulgarian Party, Gorbachev was still expressing reservations about abolishing Article 6 of the Soviet constitution, which defined the Party's leading role. Mikhail Gorbachev, *Avant Mémoires* (Paris: Odile Jacob, 1993), p. 142.

23. Interview with Vadim Zagladin (Gorbachev's presidential adviser in 1989), Moscow, 29 April 1993.

24. Interview with Karoly Grosz, Gödöllö, 1 May 1992.

25. Interviews with Aleksandr Yakovlev, Moscow, 8 November 1994; Vadim Medvedev, Moscow, 10 November 1994; and Vadim Zagladin, Moscow, 29 April 1993.

26. Ibid.

From a centrist perspective, such as Gorbachev's, the Polish model, as it was established at the Roundtable, was doubtlessly more satisfying. It was acceptable both for some of the conservatives and for the reformers, since it was supposed to combine democratization with a guarantee of the Party's leading role. It could be the future model for the region's conservative regimes. As for the Hungarian model, which was tacitly accepted by Gorbachev, and more enthusiastically so by his associates, it might represent the Soviet Union's own future path.

On the international level, the Hungarian process, given its greater degree of democratization, served Soviet interests even better. President Bush was personally impressed by the changes, and, here again, wishing to see them consolidated, he did not want to do anything to accelerate them. Paradoxically, even among the Hungarian reformist leaders, he preferred the most moderate. After his visit to Warsaw, Bush went immediately to Hungary. On July 12, he met simultaneously with Grosz, Nyers, and Nemeth in the morning, and with Pozsgay in the afternoon. He came away with a markedly more favorable impression of the first three. According to comments from Bush's advisers, he was "disconcerted" by the iconoclastic statements of Pozsgay—which the latter had probably made thinking that they would please him. He wondered whether the new leaders had "the tactical skill to manage their delicate relationship with Moscow."[27] When he later met with leaders of the non-Communist opposition, he told them: "Your leaders are moving in the right direction." Embarrassed by their impatience, he said, in private, after having met them: "These really aren't the right guys to be running this place. At least not yet."[28]

Apart from his aversion to unpredictability, Bush's prudence and reticence stemmed from two complementary preoccupations, which can be easily deduced: to avoid destabilizing Gorbachev's position in Moscow and to preserve the gains that democratization had made in Eastern Europe.

Bush was so impressed by what he observed in Hungary, after Poland, that he decided, in the days following his visit to Budapest and invoking precisely what was happening there, that his next meeting with Gorbachev should not wait until the summit planned for the following year.

---

27. See M. R. Beschloss and Strobe Talbott, *At the Highest Levels* (Boston: Little, Brown, 1993), p. 91.
28. Ibid., p. 92.

Instead, he decided to organize at least an informal, early meeting to reinforce Soviet-American confidence.[29]

Thus, the benefits which Moscow expected from "controlled" democratization in Eastern Europe seemed to have been well calculated and were taking shape. It favored accelerating and deepening East-West rapprochement. At the same time, the relaxation of tensions also seemed to facilitate the control and limitation of the evolution in these countries.

THE SOVIETS' NEW "LIMITS OF TOLERANCE"

During a visit to Budapest in July 1989, Eduard Shevardnadze told the Hungarian leaders in private: "Do what you think is best to preserve the positions of the Party."[30] His Hungarian audience considered it to be especially important that he spoke of "positions," rather than "the position," or the Party's leading role. This understanding of things is reflected in Rezso Nyers' comments cited at the beginning of the chapter; they express Gorbachev's "preoccupation" that the HSWP remain "one of the essential forces" in Hungary. This implicit lowering of Soviet requirements helps us understand how Moscow was able to resign itself to the sudden slide in "the position" of the Polish Party in August. If the change was not openly expressed, it was because there was no consensus on the issue within the Soviet leadership. Only on the "freedom of choice and action of each Party" was there consensus.

In Budapest, however, the "socialist orientation" (irrespective of its content) was considered to be one of the limits of tolerance for Gorbachev and his entourage. Rezso Nyers pleaded with the opposition during their negotiations in the summer, invoking precisely the boundaries of Soviet tolerance, so that the reference to socialism finally was preserved in the preamble to the new Hungarian constitution.[31] Within his own party, Nyers had to use the same arguments so the platform to be presented to the Party congress in October would speak of a "change of models" rather than of "systems." On August 19, he finally succeeded in having the document refer to the "socialist character of the system."[32]

---

29. Ibid., p. 93.
30. Interview with Imre Szokai, Budapest, 2 May 1992.
31. See Pierre Kende, "Hongrie: du réformisme communiste à la démocratie consolidée," in Pierre Kende and Aleksander Smolar, eds., *La grande secousse: Europe de l'Est, 1989–1990* (Paris: Presses du CNRS, 1990), p. 80.
32. See François Fejtö, *La fin des démocraties populaires* (Paris: Le Seuil, 1992), pp. 268–269.

The laxity of Gorbachev and other Soviet reformers concerning the Parties' leading role and the content of socialism did not extend to all aspects of relations between the USSR and Eastern Europe. On the contrary: fearing that their permissiveness on these questions might lead to an erosion of multilateral institutions in the East, they formulated very explicit and pressing demands on this issue. During his July 1989 visit to Budapest, Shevardnadze asked the Hungarian leaders to formally commit themselves that Hungary, due to its alliance obligations, would not conclude any accords with Western "integrative institutions" unless it received previous agreement from the USSR. It was as much the European Community as NATO which the Soviet leaders had in mind.[33] The Hungarian leaders interpreted these demands, which were made insistently during the negotiation of a new, bilateral Hungarian-Soviet treaty throughout the second half of 1989, as reflecting a Soviet desire to take affairs in Eastern Europe back into their own hands, after a period of neglect.

What the Soviets feared, to restate Nyers' quote cited above, was "a unilateral movement" by Hungary toward the West, which could leave the Soviet Union behind and deprive it of the benefits it intended to gain from the organized overall rapprochement negotiated under its leadership. Nyers was obliged to give Moscow assurances, not only concerning his Party's intentions, but also with respect to those of the main opposition groups. In an interview with *Pravda,* he declared that "they accept and respect our participation in the Warsaw Pact and CMEA."[34]

Matyas Szuros, president of the Hungarian Parliament, described the situation accurately when he told Radio Free Europe in July: "In my opinion, the Soviet Union considers the question of what type of socialism exists in a given country to be of secondary importance. Its priority is to maintain the present alliance system for as long as NATO exists."[35]

The importance which the Soviet leaders gave to the Warsaw Pact again reflects the high priority which their pan-European policy held. It should be remembered that it was the Warsaw Pact which institutionalized the USSR's place in Europe and acted as the main instrument of its European policy. It conferred upon the Soviet Union a certain parity with

33. Interview with Peter Hardi (director of the Hungarian Institute of International Affairs in 1989), Budapest, 4 May 1992.

34. *Pravda,* 4 October 1989, cited by François Fejtö, *La fin des démocraties populaires,* p. 271.

35. *Background Report* (Radio Free Europe), 127, 20 July 1989.

the United States in negotiations on disarmament and the future of Europe.

In early autumn 1989, the domestic evolution in Poland and Hungary began to surpass the pace of the construction of a new European security structure. The Vienna negotiations on a dramatic reduction of armaments in Europe, which was to be the basis for the process, were advancing slowly—despite Gorbachev's impatience and a clear American willingness to move ahead. In a memorandum sent to Gorbachev in October (that is, before the fall of the Berlin Wall), Shakhnazarov urged him to prepare a calendar to accelerate the creation of a new European security system. He recommended that Gorbachev propose the end of the century as the target date for a simultaneous dissolution of NATO and the Warsaw Pact. As an intermediate goal, he suggested that the military organizations of both alliances be dissolved in 1995, on the occasion of the fiftieth anniversary of the end of World War II.[36] "It is important," he stressed, "that we hold the initiative on this matter." Detailing an idea initially expressed one year earlier, he recommended that the USSR announce a unilateral withdrawal of its troops from Poland, Hungary, and Czechoslovakia. He argued that, despite their assurances to the contrary, the governments of Poland and Hungary might very soon demand such a retreat; if they were the ones to do it, the Soviet negotiating position with NATO would be weakened. Therefore, Moscow needed to take the initiative in order to achieve benefits which would initially translate into "a colossal gain in confidence." With regard to Germany, he proposed that Moscow put a separate declaration on the table, in addition to the general propositions on parallel Soviet and American reductions. In it, the USSR would state its willingness to withdraw all of its troops from the GDR, if the United States were ready to do the same from the Federal Republic.[37]

As one can see, if the Soviets strove so ardently, after the summer of 1989, to obtain new guarantees from their allies about the preservation of the Warsaw Pact, it was in order to extract maximum benefit from the exchange and dissolution—and, of course, to limit the centrifugal forces which were surfacing. In the meantime, to accommodate them, a

36. Memorandum of 14 October 1989, reprinted in Georgii Shakhnazarov, *Tsena svobody: reformatsiia Gorbacheva glazami ego pomoshchnika (The Price of Liberty: Gorbachev's Reformist Enterprise through the Eyes of His Assistant)* (Moscow: Rossika Zevs, 1993), pp. 423–424.
37. Ibid.

reform of the Pact was becoming more urgent, as had been discussed in the Soviet leadership since the beginning of the year, and the intention of which was announced at the Bucharest summit in July. The debate on this question (just like the issue of urgently reforming CMEA) became broader, without giving rise to concrete measures which would have necessitated the more immediate and sustained attention of the leaders of all interested parties.[38]

After the fall of the Berlin Wall on November 10, and the incredible acceleration of events which followed, this lag became much greater and proved impossible to make up. Hungary, as we shall see, was to play a central role in the events which led to the dismantling of the Wall.

38. See M. E. Bezrukov and A. V. Kortunov, "What Kind of an Alliance Do We Need?" *New Times (Novoe Vremia),* 41, October 1989.

CHAPTER EIGHT

East Germany

The Fatal Acceleration

Was another model, that of social democracy, possible on
German soil? I believe it was.

Vadim A. Medvedev (1994)[1]

Like everyone else, we were surprised by the rapidity of what
happened in East Europe. The difference is that much of the
rest of the world did not believe we were serious about the
right of each country to choose its own road.

Valentin Falin (1990)[2]

Even though Eduard Shevardnadze claimed, after the fact, that he and
other Soviet leaders had foreseen the necessity of German reunification
as early as 1986,[3] nothing—in either their actions or their remarks—has
come to light to this day that would corroborate his claim. Gorbachev
himself does not pretend to have been this clairvoyant. He writes in his
memoirs: "I would be lying if I were to suggest that I foresaw this evolution and the consequences it would have for us."[4]

Until 1989, he and the rest of the Soviet leadership essentially held
fast to the German Social Democrats' position; in other words, a change
in inter-German relations (with no mention even of reunification) should
come from acceptance of the status quo, in order to reassure the parties
concerned, and it should happen toward the end, as a result of an

1. Vadim A. Medvedev, *Raspad: kak on nazreval v "mirovoi sisteme sotsializma"* *(The Collapse: How It Happened in the "World Socialist System")* (Moscow: Mezh-dunarodnye Otnosheniia, 1994), pp. 164–170.
2. Valentin Falin, "The New World Disorder?" *New Perspectives Quarterly,* 7 (2), 1990, pp. 22–26.
3. Eduard Shevardnadze [Edouard Chevardnadze], *L'avenir s'écrit liberté* (Paris: Odile Jacob, 1991), p. 241.
4. Mikhail Gorbachev [Michail Gorbatschow], *Erinnerungen (Memoirs)* (Berlin: Siedler Verlag, 1995), p. 700; translated from German for this book by Laure Castin.

inter-European process of reconciliation, rather than at the beginning. The question was, hence, to be put off into the distant future. One can perhaps interpret this to have been the meaning of Gorbachev's remarks to West Germany's president, Richard von Weizecker, in 1987, that history would address the question of German reunification in a hundred years' time.[5]

For Erich Honecker, who believed that the existence of the GDR had become an unalterable historical fact, talk of reunification, even after such a long and uncertain delay, was unpalatable. In fact, Honecker seems to have understood much more quickly than Gorbachev that the Soviet conception and policies concerning a "common European home" risked putting the German question on the agenda far sooner. He avoided referring to these Soviet concepts, and research in the GDR archives after its collapse has shown that Honecker's opposition to Gorbachev's undertaking was as much aimed against the direction he saw the latter's European policy taking as to his desire to democratize socialism, and perhaps even more so.[6]

In 1989, it was the conjuncture of several factors which led the Soviet leaders to the conclusion that Honecker and his team were becoming an increasingly awkward obstacle to their policy. These factors included the growing polarization in the region, due to the changes taking place in Hungary and Poland; the dynamic created by the very success of Gorbachev's European initiative, notably in Soviet relations with the Federal Republic; and, to a limited extent, the USSR's worsening economic situation. Top Soviet officials began to show increasingly explicit signs of their dissatisfaction with Honecker, and to act accordingly. As long as Honecker was in power, however, Gorbachev did not bring himself to officially propose a new policy on relations between the two Germanys.

Vyacheslav Dashichev of the Institute of the Economy of the World Socialist System had, as we have seen, been the first intellectual close to the circles of power to recommend, in 1987, putting the inter-German

---

5. Remark cited by Gorbachev himself in *Perestroika: Vues neuves sur notre pays et le monde* (Paris: Flammarion, 1987).

6. "The reasons for the SED [*Sozialistische Einheitspartei Deutschland*] leadership's rejection of *perestroika* were related, to a far greater extent than has been assumed until now, to the concept of a European home and a redefinition of the Soviets' German policy which could result from it." D. Küchenmeister, "Wann begann das Zerwürfnis zwischen Honecker und Gorbatschow? Erste Bemerkungen zu den Protokollen der Vier-Augen-Gespräche" (When Did the Discord between Honecker and Gorbachev Begin? First Reflections on the Protocols of the One-on-One Meetings), *Deutschland-Archiv*, 1, 1993, pp. 30–40; translated from German for this book by Laure Castin.

status quo up for debate, as the most effective and logical instrument of the Soviets' new European policy. In April 1989, he again took up this approach, and directed his message to the highest levels. He sent a long memorandum entitled "The Concept of the 'Common European Home' and the German Question"[7] to Gorbachev and Shevardnadze. This report was markedly less radical than the one he had prepared for the Ministry of Foreign Affairs in 1987. At the time, he had suggested that, of all the various alternatives to the status quo which he analyzed, German reunification and neutrality were the most advantageous for the USSR. In his 1989 memorandum, he recommended a more gradualist approach, in tune with the general spirit of Gorbachev's enterprise, which included the preservation of the GDR. For the purposes of his argument, he endeavored to show the GDR's nonviability in the framework of its economic and political regime at the time. Dashichev underscored that East Germany was falling further behind the Federal Republic and that public discontent was growing in a context in which the USSR was determined not to use force to come to the regime's rescue. He added, "The only alternative for the GDR is to put in place radical reforms, like those in the USSR, China or Hungary." Conditions for the success of these reforms were better in the GDR than for other socialist states, he argued, because they would receive significant support from West Germany. At the same time, assistance would be forthcoming from other Western powers not favorably disposed to German reunification and "not interested in seeing Europe destabilized." He was promising the best of both worlds: change in the context of stability, and the possibility of winning on all levels at the same time. In those conditions: "A progressive and controlled reform in the GDR would lead to a rapprochement between the two German states and their political and economic structures, hence reducing the acuteness of the German question and permitting the opening of a road to confederation of the two states or to other forms of cooperation."[8]

Once such a process had been initiated, Dashichev went on to write, the foundations of Europe's militarization would be called into question. A reformed East Germany could become the principal agent for bringing the two Europes closer together. In short, the real key to the end of

7. "Poniatie 'Obshchego Evropeiskogo Doma' i germanskii vopros." A copy of the original text was given to me by V. Dashichev in November 1991. An abridged version was published in German in *Der Spiegel*, 5 February 1990.
    8. Ibid.

Cold War (and all its potential advantages for the USSR) was to be found in Berlin, and reconsidering the German question was "the *sine qua non* condition for the construction of the common European home." Dashichev's proposals were all the more appealing since they reproduced the official pan-European model on an inter-German scale. That model foresaw the preservation of the two blocs, but also their "disantagonization" and progressive demilitarization with the construction of a pan-European superstructure. Dashichev was proposing the same for Germany, and it was difficult to argue with his logic.

He never received any response to his memorandum from Gorbachev or Shevardnadze. The rapid evolution of events, however, was to put his ideas on the Soviet leaders' agenda very soon. But the initiative, so often reclaimed and recommended, would be missing.

THE CONSEQUENCES OF CLOSER RELATIONS WITH WEST GERMANY

As indicated above, the improvement of East-West relations in general, and of European relations in particular, went through an exceptional phase early in the summer of 1989. Within Europe, it was precisely on the intensification of Soviet relations with West Germany, and the new perspectives arising from it, that Soviet hopes were focused.

One could say that a certain cumulative dialectic of acceleration was developing between the events in Eastern Europe and the improvement of East-West relations. Soviet permissiveness regarding Poland and Hungary considerably enhanced the credibility of Moscow's foreign policy and its reception in the West—just as the Soviet leaders desired. In turn, these successes encouraged them to go further and faster in Eastern Europe and to demonstrate their increasing impatience with the recalcitrant conservative regimes of the region.

When Gorbachev arrived in West Germany on an official visit in June 1989, his popularity there had reached unparalleled heights. If it was higher in the Federal Republic than in other Western countries, the reason was precisely the diffuse and imprecise, but tangible, expectations and hopes that his foreign policy was raising about the future of inter-German relations. Some innovation or movement concerning the "German question" was expected as a logical consequence of his policy. In a more specific and immediate way, Gorbachev's popularity was due to his dramatic disarmament proposals, and to the special sensitivity of this issue in Germany, given that the largest quantities of both alliances' weapons were on German soil. On the eve of his visit to Bonn, opinion polls showed that 47 percent of Germans considered the USSR to be the "principal force" working for world peace, while only 22 percent gave that role to the United States.[9] It was that state of affairs which put the United States on the defensive and led President Bush, in early May, to propose important American and Soviet troop reductions in Europe as a way of regaining the initiative. Gorbachev's immense popularity and the spectacular welcome he received in West Germany in 1989 gave the impression that he himself held the future of Europe in his hands—and, to a great extent, hid the general weakness of the USSR's position. In fact, that was one of the main functions performed by his new foreign policy.

Chancellor Kohl, who had compared Gorbachev to Goebbels in 1986, had to adjust and deal with the popularity of the Soviet leader's policies. Between his visit to Moscow in October 1988 (during which a DM 3 billion credit line was opened for the Soviet Union) and Gorbachev's 1989 trip to Bonn, a significant change had taken place in Kohl's Atlantic policy. It was a consequence of the impact of the unilateral reductions of Soviet conventional forces in Europe, announced before the United Nations in December 1988. At the beginning of 1989, against American and British policy (which feared a denuclearization of the European theater), the West German government announced objections to NATO's plans for modernizing short-range nuclear missiles and proposed negotiations with the USSR on reducing their number. Moscow, for its part, had proposed their complete elimination. That plan was widely welcomed in West Germany, since these tactical weapons, given their range, were essentially targeting German soil, be it from East or West. As a new incentive for Kohl, the USSR announced, in May, the unilateral removal of 500 nuclear warheads from the GDR (out of a total of at least 10,000). There were also other military issues where Soviet and German interests converged. The Bonn summit, for example, underscored the importance both sides attached to respecting the ABM treaty. That treaty represented a considerable obstacle to carrying out the "Star Wars" program, and the USSR was fearful that the United States would withdraw from it.

In the context of 1989, therefore, the Soviet leaders had every reason to count on West Germany's political leadership within the Western world in order to advance their project of a "common European

---

9. *Washington Post,* 30 May 1989; cited by Michael Sodaro, *Moscow, Germany and the West: From Khrushchev to Gorbachev* (New York: Cornell University Press, 1990), p. 353.

home."[10] In an eloquent fashion, the joint Soviet-German declaration signed at the end of Gorbachev's visit to the Federal Republic emphasized that the two governments "consider it their supreme duty to contribute to overcoming the division of Europe."[11]

During the visit, eleven agreements on economic cooperation and other matters were signed, including the establishment of a "hotline" between Moscow and Bonn. In practice, Chancellor Kohl's position on the "German question" had become quite similar to that of the Social Democrats. But only in practice. He did not condition his improved relations with the USSR on a resolution of the question. At the same time, though, he was not willing to put aside the idea and the principle of reunification (The leaders of the SPD, during that period, even wanted the explicit mention of it removed from the Federal Republic's constitution.) It was on Kohl's direct request that the joint declaration made mention of both parties' "unconditional respect for the norms and principles of international law, and particularly the people's right to self-determination." In the context of his visit, it would have been difficult for Gorbachev to refuse this reaffirmation of "freedom of choice," even if the legal terms of the declaration repeated the exact terms traditionally used by West Germany to demand free elections in the GDR[12] Of course, the declaration also spoke of the "unconditional respect for the integrity and security of each state." East Germany's leaders, however, immediately understood the potential dangers hidden in the terms of the declaration, and avoided reporting them.[13]

10. Commenting on the joint declaration signed at the end of Gorbachev's visit to Bonn, and on the state of Soviet-German relations at the time, Timothy Garton Ash wrote: "In 1945, the United States and the Soviet Union had decided what ought to become of Germany. Now, West Germany and the Soviet Union were signing a joint declaration on what the United States ought to do! The implicit change in Bonn's relations with the United States were as dramatic as the explicit change in its relations with the Soviet Union. In fact, President Bush had already acknowledged the (re-)emergence of (West) Germany as the leading power in Europe (and not only West Europe)." Timothy Garton Ash, *In Europe's Name: Germany and the Divided Continent* (London: Jonathan Cape, 1993), p. 114.

11. *Izvestiia*, 15 June 1989.

12. See Hannes Adomeit, "Gorbachev and German Reunification: Revision of Thinking, Realignment of Power," *Problems of Communism,* 39, July-August 1990, pp. 1–23.

13. See Sodaro, *Moscow, Germany and the West,* p. 375.

While these types of ex post facto reconstructions must be treated with caution, Anatolii Cherniaev, who was then Gorbachev's assistant for international affairs, describes the consequences of the June 1989 Soviet-German summit in his memoirs as follows: "The most important thing was that in the GDR, both at the top and at the base, it became understood that West Germany had become the higher priority for the USSR in its relations with the two Germanys, and would be its principal partner in the construction of a new Europe. All of a sudden, the 'conclusion' for the East Germans was: the Soviet Union no longer represents an obstacle to reunification. . . ." Anatolii Cherniaev, *Shest' let s Gor-*

Helmut Kohl counted on the dynamic inherent in the new Soviet-German relations and on what was happening in Poland and Hungary in order to obtain a gradual change in the Soviet position on the "German question." During a long, private conversation with Gorbachev, Kohl told him that, even if the Soviet Union could still obstruct the process for a number of years, in which case Kohl would not see German unity during his lifetime, it was both natural and inevitable. Gorbachev made no objections and, after a moment of silence, told Kohl about the USSR's economic difficulties, inquiring whether the Federal Republic would be willing to help him in case of an emergency. Kohl responded in the affirmative. He later declared he had felt, at the time, that he had just experienced a "decisive moment" on the road to German unity.[14]

There is nothing which would lead us to believe that, at the time, Gorbachev envisaged German reunification in the foreseeable future—on the contrary, as we shall see. When this author asked him about that, he did, however, say: "My trip to the FRG in the summer of 1989 convinced me that changes were becoming inevitable. But when and how? No one could predict it. Incidentally, it seemed to me that the rapprochement of the German states was inevitable, but that the process leading to it would take a long time. . . . In any case, it was a task which did not yet require concrete practical solutions."[15]

During the weeks that followed his visit to Bonn, though, various signs illustrate with certainty that, within his immediate circle, there was a realization that movement on the "German question" had become desirable and necessary. Furthermore, Gorbachev's aides saw that Honecker had become an obstacle whose removal needed to be more actively sought, albeit through cautious and indirect measures, as was characteristic of the Gorbachev leadership style and relations with Eastern Europe.

THE SUMMER OF 1989: THE FIRST OPENING OF THE BERLIN WALL—IN BUDAPEST

Honecker was not only becoming an obstacle on the level of inter-German relations. In the context of the increasing polarization taking

---

bachevym—po dnevnikovym zapisiam (Six Years with Gorbachev—From Journal Notes) (Moscow: Progress Kul'tura, 1993), p. 291.

14. From a Timothy Garton Ash interview with Helmut Kohl, Bonn, 1 October 1991, in Ash, In Europe's Name, p. 118.

15. M. S. Gorbachev, Otvety na voprosy professora Zh. Leveka (Responses to Questions from Professor Jacques Lévesque), Moscow, 12 July 1995.

place in Eastern Europe, CMEA's future was becoming more problematic—and just at a time when the Soviet leaders had new reasons to insist
on preserving the two multilateral international institutions tying the
region to the USSR. Certainly, the Warsaw Pact was considered more
important than CMEA, but the state of the latter, after much neglect,
was becoming more worrisome. A CMEA summit meeting planned for
June 1989 had to be cancelled and put off until the fall. The meeting was
cancelled because of the deadlock which existed with regard to reforming the organization. This reform, as mentioned above, presupposed, in
particular, direct relations between enterprises in the various states and
their autonomy in negotiating trade and the types of products and prices;
all these collided head-on with the mechanisms in place in the entirely
centrally planned economies. Apart from Romania, which had always
played a marginal role in CMEA, and considering that Czechoslovakia
and Bulgaria were making some pretenses of economic reform, the GDR
was seen by Moscow as being the central locus of rigidity and incompatibility with the direction it wanted to give the organization.[16] At a
time when Western Europe's economic integration and the improvement
of East-West relations were accelerating, this represented an additional
motive for the Soviets' impatience with Honecker and his regime.

In July 1989, a very influential citizen of the GDR was, himself, in a
position to see the depth of that impatience and to understand the meaning it was developing. The person in question is Markus Wolf, the
famous chief of the East German secret service, who had left that position in 1986. Influenced by the example of the transformations in
the USSR, he had subsequently begun a struggle (a relatively solitary
one, according to his own testimony, which is contested by other
sources)[17] for a democratization of socialism in the GDR. The term
"semi-dissidence," which one might use to characterize his situation, is
perhaps a bit exaggerated; given the importance of the services he had
rendered the GDR and his high-level connections in the USSR (of which

16. See, notably, the comments of the former head of the Central Committee's department for relations with socialist states, Vadim A. Medvedev, in his *Raspad*, pp. 188–189.
17. In a book with a very explicit title, Pierre de Villemarest claims that Markus Wolf
used his network of important contacts in the USSR and GDR to organize a vast plot which
ended in Honecker's ouster in October 1989. See Pierre de Villemarest, *Le coup d'État de
Markus Wolf* (Paris: Stock, 1991). For his part, Wolf says that he played a more limited
role. See Markus Wolf, *In Eigenem Auftrag: Bekenntnisse und Einsichten (My Own Mission: Confessions and Reflections)* (Munich: Schneekluth Verlag, 1991); excerpts translated for this book by Laure Castin. Even if Wolf surely does not disclose everything in his
book, Pierre de Villemarest's assertion rests too much on speculation and nonverifiable
information for it to be accepted, given what one can currently ascertain.

he was still a citizen in the early 1980s), he enjoyed solid immunity. In fact, in early 1989 he was still able to meet with Honecker personally, trying to convince him of the need to reform the GDR and put it on the same wavelength as the Soviet Union. In March, he had published—in West Germany—a novel (translated in the USSR) with strong pro-Gorbachev overtones. The story, entitled *Die Troika,* follows the life and political formation of three adolescents educated in the Soviet Union.

Invited to Moscow to introduce his book, he met on July 20, at the CPSU Central Committee headquarters, with Valentin Falin, director of the International Department. "To my great surprise," he writes, Falin, as well as several of his KGB friends, asked his opinion about the possible prospects of an opening of the Berlin Wall and of German unity. Until then, Wolf claims, he had been interested in the introduction of reforms in the GDR, without really thinking about their extension to the level of inter-German relations. He was also surprised to learn that Soviet experts on German affairs, like Falin, "had already expressed their support for a process of controlled reforms in the GDR, articulated with a parallel process of drawing nearer the two German states, which could end in the formation of a confederation. . . ."[18] He even adds that "additionally, for the Soviets, the historic opportunity of a rapprochement between the two great workers' parties [the SPD and the SED] was emerging. . . ." In short, the "Euro-Left" dream which the Italian Communist Party had held so dear, was back.

Knowing very well the Soviets' bureaucratic customs, he wrote: "Falin was not saying these things without a reason. He apparently had me pass on a message."[19] This does not mean that Gorbachev was already personally committed in favor of any very specific project. But given Falin's position in the Party hierarchy, he would not have allowed himself to transmit such a "hypothesis" to a person of Wolf's stature without at least Gorbachev's implicit agreement. Gorbachev himself told this author that he, for his part, did not have "any concrete idea of a confederation or anything of the kind in the summer of 1989."[20] But, he added, "observing the course of events in the GDR and seeing that the country's leadership was proving incapable of embarking on the road of transformations, we were forced to think about the future, about possible shifts in events."

18. Wolf, *In Eigenem Auftrag.* The same remarks are repeated, word for word, in Markus Wolf, *L'oeil de Berlin* (Paris: Balland, 1992), p. 234.
    19. Ibid., p. 234.
    20. Gorbachev, *Otvety na voprosy.*

As this quote indicates, Gorbachev has remained, to this day, quite discreet about what he precisely did and authorized. Referring to the anxiety he was then experiencing due to the GDR's political immobilism, he wrote in his memoirs: "I would be lying if I were to say that we stood by with our arms crossed."[21] Without saying anything more, what he actually did was probably sufficiently indirect to allow him to immediately add: "But I must, just as expressly, deny the idea that our contacts with the GDR during this critical period were only attempts to put pressure on East Germany, for imposing change on it." When asked to specify what he meant by indicating that he had not remained "arms crossed," his response remained evasive.[22]

As for Markus Wolf, he returned to the GDR and continued, more or less in the background, to try to support the promotion of Hans Modrow, who had the confidence of Gorbachev's team.[23] Markus Wolf was not the only foreigner to whom Falin passed on a similar message. But another type of message was soon to be directed to the GDR.

Toward the end of the summer of 1989, Hungary's political evolution was to have a decisive impact on the GDR's own political future. In a gesture fraught with symbolism, Budapest had decided in May to "lift the Iron Curtain," by opening its western border with Austria. Many will recall the images of hundreds, and then thousands, of East German tourists descending on Hungary in late July and August in order to use the new situation as an exit to the West, and to West Germany. The same agreements between the GDR and other East European states which allowed East German citizens to go to Hungary also, though, forbade the governments of those countries from allowing them to leave to nonauthorized destinations. Since a small number of East Germans had nonetheless succeeded in crossing into Austria, thousands of others gathered in Hungary, with some of them occupying the West German embassy in Budapest. Their growing numbers, which at one point reached 65,000, put considerable pressure on the Hungarian gov-

---

21. Gorbachev, *Erinnerungen,* p. 711.

22. "We could not be indifferent to the events as they were unfolding in the two Germanys and in the relations between them. And certainly, we had to be ready for any possible change of events. That is what I had in mind when I said that we could not observe what was happening with our arms crossed" (Gorbachev, *Otvety na voprosy.*

23. He recalls, "On October 2, fifteen thousand people demonstrated in Leipzig. That was the determining moment for me: I had to convince the greatest possible number of Central Committee members to do something! *Stern* [a West German magazine—author's note] helped me by publishing a photomontage: on one side, Honecker, Mielke, Krenz, and Stalin; on the other, Wolf, Modrow, Höpcke, and Gorbachev. The two camps were somehow becoming official!" Wolf, *L'oeil de Berlin,* p. 239.

ernment, which was soon asked by Bonn to give them the right to leave. On the opposite side, East Berlin was pressing the Hungarian authorities to respect their commitments to the GDR. The rest of the story is common knowledge. On September 10, Hungary finally opened its western borders for East Germans; that immediately led to a dramatic rise in departures from the GDR and extended the problem to Czechoslovakia.

At the time, as well as afterward, the Hungarian government stated that its decision was taken "fully independently." Two "nuances" should be added to that statement. The first, and less important, concerns the role of the FRG. Some days before the Hungarian decision, Gyula Horn, then foreign minister, was secretly sent to Bonn, where he met with Chancellor Kohl to discuss the possibility of opening the border for East Germans. In exchange, he obtained a promise from the Chancellor for DM1 billion in loans. It was the Hungarians who suggested allowing a "decent" delay after the border opening, before announcing the granting of credits; they were made public in October.[24]

The second "nuance" relates to the supposedly nonexistent role of the USSR. In an interview he granted us in 1992, Laszlo Kovacs (deputy foreign minister under Gyula Horn in 1989, and foreign minister since the 1994 return to power of the reformed Communists) gave us very important details about that role. "We were very worried about possible Soviet reactions to a decision on our part to let the East Germans leave for Austria. We knew that the East German reactions would be virulent. We expected economic reprisals, and we had made contingency plans to that end. But we were considerably more troubled about the possible response from Moscow."[25] Here again, the East European actors found it difficult to gauge the Soviet position, evaluating it rather conservatively. In formally keeping to the thesis of this being an independent Hungarian decision, and without using the actual term "consultation," Kovacs told us that, several days before notifying the main concerned parties, "we sent a note to Shevardnadze to inform the USSR about the probable direction we were intending to take." Shevardnadze's answer was terse: "This is an affair that concerns Hungary, the GDR and the FRG."[26] Quite simply, the USSR was declaring itself disinterested. The Soviet note was immediately interpreted in Budapest as a green light.

24. Ash, *In Europe's Name*, p. 371.
25. Interview with Laszlo Kovacs, Budapest, 2 May 1992.
26. Ibid.

"Of course," Laszlo Kovacs continued, "we couldn't foresee that our decision would lead, two months later, to the fall of the Berlin Wall, and shortly thereafter to that of the East German regime, but we knew it would be a tough blow for Honecker and his power." Moscow knew it as well. The Soviet decision to exercise "neutrality" was all the less innocent, given that the GDR was insisting that the USSR pressure Hungary to respect its commitments to other Warsaw Pact members. Since some minimum of solidarity with the GDR regime had to be shown, it was the Federal Republic, not Hungary, which was blamed in Moscow for the East Germans' exodus. Ironically or cynically, it was Yegor Ligachev who was sent to East Berlin to affirm Moscow's solidarity and to explain the Soviets' positions.

One cannot overestimate the importance of Soviet behavior in this affair. In fact, if Moscow had strongly insisted that Hungary uphold its obligations to the GDR, its decision would very probably have been different.

THE FALL OF HONECKER

Less than a month after the opening of the Hungarian-Austrian border to its citizens, the GDR celebrated the fortieth anniversary of its existence. While many people continued to leave for Czechoslovakia, demonstrations within the country had been increasing rapidly throughout the month of September, despite the constant threat of repression. The organizers of this challenge and of the demonstrations, whose influence had seemed marginal only a few months earlier, now seemed to be gaining clout rapidly. They had emerged from small groups of disgruntled Communist intellectuals who had become dissenters, and from the progressive Christian movement. As François Fejtö notes, they were all persuaded that the GDR could survive as a democratic and socialist state. They invited their compatriots to join them in the struggle toward this end, rather than emigrating, which they criticized.[27] Their claim to a "third road," which had been absent from the discourse of the main opposition groups in Poland and Hungary, could be somewhat comforting for the Soviet reformers.[28]

---

27. See François Fejtö, *La fin des démocraties populaires* (Paris: El Seuil, 1992), p. 281.

28. Referring to the GDR at the time, Gorbachev wrote in 1995: "The society, however, expected changes. It seemed altogether willing to leave the initiative to the country's leaders, simply provided that the changes correspond to their expectations . . ." (Gorbachev, *Erinnerungen*, p. 934).

"According to a poll published in the West German weekly *Quick* in November 1989, 67 percent of East Germans stated that they were in favor of "socialism with a human

Invited to attend the fortieth anniversary celebrations, Gorbachev hesitated about going. He did not want to be seen as sanctioning Honecker's leadership. The opportunity he was offered to meet and discuss with the entire political leadership, and not just with his East German counterpart, finally convinced him to go.[29] On October 6, he was welcomed like a liberator by huge crowds in East Berlin. In his main public speech that day, Gorbachev not only avoided expressing solidarity with, but even confidence in, the SED leadership—contrary to what was customary in such situations. He instead expressed confidence in the SED itself, in terms that constituted an implicit invitation to change its leaders and policies. "We have no doubt," he declared, "that the SED, given its vast intellectual potential . . . will be able to find, in cooperation with all social forces, answers to the questions which are on the agenda of the Republic and which preoccupy its citizens."[30] In a move fraught with symbolism, he spoke of the "process of the drawing together of East and West, through which *all the walls* of hostility, alienation and distrust between Europeans will fall."[31]

The next day, in his private meeting, first with Honecker and then with the entire East German Politburo, Gorbachev made his famous warning that "life punishes those who come too late," which was immediately made public by the Soviet side.[32] The complete transcript of his remarks, published two years later, is very interesting. Gorbachev explained to his interlocutors that the SED was much better placed than

---

face," while only 33 percent supported adopting the West German economic and social model" (*Quick*, 47, 16 November 1989; cited by Anne-Marie Le Gloannec, "RDA, la révolution aux deux visages," in Pierre Kende and Aleksander Smolar, eds., *La grande secousse: Europe de l'Est, 1989–1990*. Paris: Presses du CNRS, 1990, p. 95).

29. Valentin Falin, *Politische Erinnerungen (Political Memoirs)* (Munich: Droemer Knaur, 1993), p. 484; translated for this book by Laure Castin.

30. *Pravda*, 7 October 1989.

31. Emphasis added.

32. R. F. Laird, *The Soviets, Germany and the New Europe* (Boulder: Westview Press, 1991), p. 167.

Hannes Adomeit argues that the meaning and the intent of this sentence has been widely exaggerated. He relies for this on a comment made by Gorbachev to Krenz during their meeting of November 1, found in the East German archives. Gorbachev told Krenz that in making this statement, he "had really talked about himself" (see Hannes Adomeit, "Gorbachev, German Unification and the Collapse of Empire," *Post-Soviet Affairs*, July-September 1994, pp. 197–230).

However, Alexander Dallin is perfectly right when he writes: "The explanation that Gorbachev's remark about history punishing the laggards referred to himself, rather than to the East Germans, may well have been more revealing of his diplomatic skills than of his true feelings" (Alexander Dallin, "The Broader Context: A Comment on Adomeit," *Post-Soviet Affairs*, July-September 1994, pp. 231–233.

its Polish and Hungarian counterparts to undertake reforms, and with less risks. "I believe that the CPSU and the SED are the most solid Parties," he declared.[33] His remarks were not just prepared for the occasion, and were not his conviction alone. Valentin Falin, the most important specialist for German affairs within the CPSU hierarchy, shared his view.[34]

In the context of the regime's increasing crisis, and with specific orders having been given to Soviet troops to keep totally removed from any possible repression, Gorbachev's visit and remarks had a decisive effect for finally ending the East German Politburo's support of Honecker. After the meeting with Gorbachev, Egon Krenz said to Falin: "Your man said all he needed to say. Ours didn't understand anything." Falin responded in clear, but still cautious, terms: "The Soviet guest has done more than one can expect from an invitee. The rest depends only on you."[35] Ten days later, on October 17, the Politburo demanded and received Honecker's resignation, and Egon Krenz took over as leader of the Party and state.[36] Gorbachev confirms that he saw it as a favorable evolution in all respects.[37]

33. A stenographic transcript was published in Günter Mittag, *Um jeden Preis: im Spannungsfeld zweier Systeme (At Any Price: At the Heart of Tensions between Two Systems)* (Berlin: Aufbau Verlag, 1991), pp. 359–384; translated for this book by Laure Castin.

Speaking of the Soviet experience, Gorbachev says: "There do exist, of course, groups that are contesting, but they are not organized into social movements or currents. Certain of them even demand a return to the monarchy and to tsarism. . . . But these reactions are insignificant, because the principal forces of society have declared themselves in favor of reform. . . . I will say a word about the strike of the Kuzbass workers: no one there was against the reforms or the Soviet government and its leaders. On the contrary, they confirmed their attachment to socialism. . . . We are the ones who now have the initiative."

34. He writes in his memoirs: "Shakhnazarov and I supposed that the Honecker regime's days were numbered. We had expected rather naively up to then that, unlike the Polish and Hungarian Parties, the SED had significant support from low- and mid-level officials, and that it had good organizers who supported reforms" (Falin, *Politische Erinnerungen.*

35. Ibid., p. 487.

36. Honecker later recounted the developments in the Politburo leading to his dismissal. He reports that he was violently attacked before by Hans Modrow (who was not a Politburo member) during a meeting with regional first secretaries. The dismissal proposal was introduced by Willi Stoph, who stated that the question of confidence had been put forth by the regional first secretaries (which, according to Honecker, is incorrect). See Andeert Reinhold and Wolfgang Herzberg, *Der Sturz: Honecker im Kreuzverhör (The Fall: Honecker Answers)* (Berlin: Aufbau Verlag, 1991), pp. 22–36; translated for this book by Laure Castin.

37. "As far as I was concerned, I must admit in all honesty that I hoped the new leadership would succeed in directing events in the GDR toward the establishment of new relations between the two German states by introducing major domestic reforms" (Gorbachev, *Erinnerungen,* p. 712).

. . . AND OF THE BERLIN WALL ON NOVEMBER 9

From the Soviet leaders' gradualist perspective, Honecker's divestiture should have opened a period of making reforms and breaking important new ground for the improvement of East-West relations. This aborted stage of development, which was to precipitate another, would last less than a month, giving neither the GDR nor the USSR the time to gain any tangible benefit from it.

The situation in the GDR after Honecker's departure would have been difficult to master, no matter who succeeded him. In any case, though, Egon Krenz was definitely not the man of the hour, nor, as we have seen, was he the Soviet reformers' first choice. He was much too closely linked to Honecker (seeming to have been groomed as his designated successor) to have any credibility as a representative of significant change. In addition, besides Honecker, only two other Politburo members were dismissed at that time, and it was only under duress, shortly before the opening of the Berlin Wall, that Modrow was appointed to it.

While promising reforms, Krenz did not immediately undertake anything decisive. He put off legalizing *Neues Forum* (the New Forum), the principal opposition movement, and continued to insist on the Party's leading role; yet, enormous pressures on the government were encroaching from all sides. Four sources should be mentioned. First, the number of demonstrations and participants in them was multiplying, and their focus widened. The number of demonstrators in the weekly demonstrations went from 140,000 to 540,000, and then to 1,350,000 in the three weeks following Honecker's removal.[38] At the same time, the number of people wanting to emigrate showed no signs of decreasing, soon creating a new problem with another East European ally, a conservative one this time. Since exit permits to Hungary had stopped being issued, those seeking to emigrate had been massing in Czechoslovakia. Only at the beginning of November did East Germany consent to allowing them to leave from Czechoslovakia directly for the Federal Republic, rather than having to return to the GDR, for specific authorization. As of that moment, three hundred East German cars an hour entered Czechoslovakia.[39] The influx reached such proportions that, fearing its possible

38. See Le Gloannec, "RDA," p. 89.
39. See Vincent Jauvert, "Les seize jours qui ont changé le monde," *Le Nouvel Observateur*, November 1994, pp. 50–51.

"contaminating" effects for themselves, the Czech leaders were soon threatening to close their border with the GDR, which would have made the situation there even more explosive.

On October 31, the East German Politburo became aware, for the first time, of a most disastrous report on the GDR's economic situation. The country risked being insolvent from one week to the next, unless it were able to obtain significant new credits or implement rapid austerity measures, which would have led to a draconian reduction in the population's standard of living. Taking this situation into account, Krenz authorized secret negotiations with West Germany to obtain emergency loans in exchange for a certain liberalization concerning the movement of individuals between the two Germanys.

This was the context in which Krenz went to Moscow, where he met Gorbachev on November 1. The Soviet leader was speechless on learning of the GDR's dire economic situation and its request for loans on the order of DM12 billion.[40] Given the problems which the USSR itself was facing, he refused to promise any specific assistance. Egon Krenz informed Gorbachev of his intention to "half open" the GDR's western borders. Not surprisingly, the latter did not make any objections and encouraged his East German counterpart to obtain the greatest possible compensation from West Germany.

It should be noted that there was no question then of a dismantlement of the Berlin Wall, but only of a regulated liberalization of exit permits from the GDR. As incredible as it may seem, the USSR—clearly a concerned party in the opening of the Wall, which took place eight days later—was never consulted on this issue.

Incidentally, the East German leaders never made a decision, as such, to open the Wall. We now know that it was under the combined pressure of the factors enumerated above, and in great haste (without even being able to wait for a confirmation of the West German financial guarantees demanded in exchange), that the decisions were taken simultaneously on November 9 to renounce the Party's leading role; to accept free elections; and to authorize trips abroad on request. The immediate announcement of this last measure, the details of which were supposed to be announced only the next day, led to the formation of vast crowds, which began moving toward the Wall. In an attempt to avoid riots, it

---

40. According to East German archival material reviewed by Jauvert, "Les seize jours qui ont changé le monde."

was in these circumstances of panic and confusion that all the borders were opened.[41]

As everyone remembers, it was an extraordinary historical moment. For two or three days, but not more, Egon Krenz seemed to have won the bet which he had not really made himself. The vast majority of people going to West Berlin returned home afterward, and the mood was one of overwhelming, universal joy.

In Moscow, where the leadership was faced with a fait accompli, the head of the Central Committee's International Department protested the fact that the USSR had not been consulted on a question of such importance for it.[42] Soviet officials found that the GDR's leaders were dangerously telescoping steps together, and they worried about the East Germans' inept control of the situation.[43] Yet, Gorbachev had a message sent to Krenz that was replete with serenity and confidence: "All has been accomplished in the correct fashion, continue energetically and resolutely in the same direction."[44] That was also the tenor of public reactions. In the spirit of *perestroika*, the leadership wanted to show it was in step with events, in order to gain the maximum possible benefits from them. Quickly and elegantly, Shevardnadze's spokesman declared: "These are changes in the right direction. We are evolving from a divided post-war Europe toward the common European home."[45] The fall of the Berlin Wall and the USSR's attitude marked the defining moment of glory for Gorbachev. After all the other signals, these events proved in an even more striking way Soviet willingness to transcend Europe's division and to move toward a new international order. From the outside, the opening of the Wall seemed to be in direct continuity with Gorbachev's other spectacular initiatives (albeit certainly much more climactic this time); and there were good reasons to believe that it had been decided in concert with Moscow.

41. See the account of the confusion which reigned in the GDR's ruling circles and the conditions in which the Berlin Wall was opened, given much later by the counsellor of the Soviet embassy in Germany, Igor' Maksimychev, "End of the Berlin Wall," *International Affairs*, March 1991, pp. 100–108.

42. See Falin, *Politische Erinnerungen*, p. 488.

43. Interviews with Aleksandr Yakovlev and Vadim Medvedev, Moscow, 8 and 10 November 1994.

44. Cited by A. A. Akhtamazian, *Ob'edinenie Germanii, ili Anshlius GDR k FRG (The Unification of Germany, or the FRG's "Anschluss" of the GDR)*, vol. 2 (Moscow: MGIMO, 1994), p. 13.

45. See the chronology detailed by Charles Van Der Donckt, *Six mois qui ébranlèrent le monde* (Québec: CQRI, 1990), p. 148.

In fact, Soviet officials hinted to their Western counterparts that the move had been suggested to Krenz by Gorbachev.[46]

On November 11, just a bit more than one day after the opening of the Wall, Gorbachev had a telephone conversation with Kohl. Through the calm and farsightedness he was displaying, glimpses of his anxiety were showing. He spoke to his German counterpart in these terms: "I believe that at the present moment, a historical turn is happening toward new relations and toward a new world. It would be unpropitious to prejudice such a turn through some maladroit gesture. And even more so to force the course of events and to push its development in an unpredictable direction, toward chaos. . . . I hope that you will use all of your authority, your political weight and your influence so that they are kept in an appropriate framework and rhythm."[47]

Helmut Kohl responded that he had just come out of a cabinet meeting, and "if you had been present at it, you would have been surprised to see how our views coincide."

This happy coincidence of views lasted but a very short time. In the first days following the fall of the Wall, no one in the governments of East or West planned to put German reunification on the agenda. It would have been, to use President Bush's expression, "more than the market could bear."[48] But it was in the streets of East Berlin and other East German cities that the question rapidly came up. The extraordinary way in which the popular movement removed itself from the political control of its founders, and how the slogans about the unity of the German people spontaneously surfaced from within it, have been adequately described and analyzed elsewhere.[49] At the same time, the flood of immigration to the FRG continued at a worrisome pace. Another 130,000 people emigrated in November. The program of important reforms, introduced by the new coalition government of Hans Modrow on November 17, was not sufficient to calm the course of events.

46. See M. R. Beschloss and Strobe Talbott, *At the Highest Levels* (Boston: Little, Brown, 1993), p. 134.

47. Transcript in Anatolii S. Cherniaev, *Shest' let s Gorbachevym: po dnevnikovym zapisiam (Six Years with Gorbachev: From Journal Notes)* (Moscow: Progress Kul'tura, 1993), p. 305.

48. See chapter 6.

49. See, in particular, the description of the movement by one of the heads of the Soviet intelligence service in Berlin, I. N. Kuz'min, *Krushenie GDR, zametki ochevidtsa (The Downfall of the GDR, Notes from an Eyewitness)* (Moscow: n.p., 1993), pp. 44–45.

To a certain extent, it was in order to try to slow down the exodus from the GDR, which was causing increasingly serious problems in West Germany, that Kohl decided to put forth the question, thinking that the prospect of reunification could calm emotions in the East. This obviously was not his only consideration for intervening. According to Horst Telschik, Kohl's advisor and one of the main negotiators of reunification, the USSR's remarkable behavior in the aftermath of the opening of the Berlin Wall, which considerably surprised the West German chancellor, convinced him that the "new thinking" was irreversible and that reunification was becoming a realistic possibility.[50]

On November 28, to everyone's surprise, Helmut Kohl presented a ten-point plan before the Bundestag designed to lead to reunification. No precise end date was set. The plan anticipated several intermediate steps. Undoubtedly in order to reassure Soviet leaders, he proposed, as a first step, a "contractual community" between the two German states; this was a term which had already been used by the Soviets and Hans Modrow. The following step was to be a confederation. The international aspects of the process were entirely left out of Kohl's proposal.

Despite the gradualist character of Kohl's plan, and his use of an acceptable concept during the first phase, the plan was received very negatively in Moscow. Several days after it was presented in Bonn, Hans-Dietrich Genscher, the West German foreign minister, was seen by Gorbachev in Moscow and subjected to a full dressing-down. The Soviet leader complained about the "totally unexpected" nature of the plan, calling its ten points "demands that resemble an ultimatum."[51] Claiming to have been duped, he stated: "Kohl assured me that he did not want to destabilize the situation in the GDR and that he would act with even-handedness. The Chancellor's actual position, however, contradicts those assurances."

At the same time, as if there were suddenly no longer any question of transcending the division of Europe, Shevardnadze and the entire Soviet diplomatic hierarchy stated that it was necessary "to respect the postwar realities in Europe" and that "the existence of two German states is part of those realities."

---

50. H. Telschik, 329 Tage, Innenansichten der Einigung (329 Days, Unification Seen from Inside) (Berlin: Siedler Verlag, 1991), p. 381; cited by Laure Castin, "L'URSS et la question allemande de 1985 à 1991" (DEA essay in international relations, Université Paris 1, 1992), p. 100.
51. Transcript in Cherniaev, Shest' let s Gorbachevym, p. 306.

Of course, the Soviet leaders had not abandoned the project of a "common European home", but the turn which relations between the two Germanys were taking suddenly threatened the spirit and the substance, if not the goals, that they attributed to the project. The construction of the "common home" and the rapprochement between the two Germanys, which became its most central and delicate point, was supposed to occur not only gradually, but, as we have indicated before, on the basis of trade-offs. The projected process was designed so that each East German and Soviet concession would be accompanied by West German and Western concessions—in the economic sphere, on the level of the balance of military forces, and with respect to the creation of a new European security framework. With the East German leaders' loss of control and the precipitous crumbling of their regime, the USSR risked losing the principal trump card in its European game, without any German or Western compensation. That central preoccupation was echoed clearly in Gorbachev's reproaches of Kohl, as he expressed them to Genscher. The German foreign minister was told that Kohl was trying to impose "his music and the pace of the march" and was reminded that the improvement of relations between the two German states ought to be accomplished "through stability" and "through mutual respect."[52]

Therefore, it was not so much the possibility of reunification that worried Gorbachev, but rather the way it risked coming about, and its consequences for his European policy. For a time, he believed he could slow events down by categorically refusing to speak, not only of reunification, but even of confederation which, given the context of a loss of control, seemed to him to be premature and dangerous. Here again, the reproaches Gorbachev made to Genscher on December 5 are illuminating: "What does confederation signify? Obviously, a confederation presupposes a unified defense, a unified foreign policy. Where will the Federal Republic then be? In NATO? In the Warsaw Pact? Or maybe it will become neutral? What would NATO mean without West Germany? And, in general, what would happen afterward? Have you thought about all of this?"[53]

After November 28, Soviet initiatives in Soviet-German relations came to an end. The USSR did not seek any more to encourage change and accompany events, but rather tried to slow them down. This spelled the end of the triumphant phase of Gorbachev's foreign policy. The disappointments were accumulating faster than the benefits. The crumbling

52. Ibid., p. 307.
53. Ibid.

of the GDR, which proved to be the keystone of the entire East European system, gave a formidable push to the events throughout the region.
The fragile political equilibria achieved in Poland and Hungary were bat-
tered, and it was Eastern Europe, in its entirety, that finally hurled itself
through the Berlin Wall.

Before going on, it may be useful to summarize the Soviet leaders'
behavior and their balance sheet in Eastern Europe through November
28. We have seen how they adapted themselves and even stimulated the
events in Poland, Hungary, and East Germany, despite the risks. This led
U.S. Secretary of State James Baker to say at one point of Gorbachev:
"He not only rides a tiger, but he even spurs him on." The risks were, of
course, constantly underestimated in regard to the importance of the
domestic and foreign policy project of which they were a part. The risks
were not only accepted, but integrated and put to use for the project. In
this way, Gorbachev played his weaknesses and succeeded, for a certain
period, in transforming them into strengths. That was true until November 28, 1989.

The project, of which Soviet behavior and its rationalization were a
part, was itself evolving and had its own dynamic. We have seen this in
the case of Germany. It was the logic and the dynamic of the project
which, in the summer of 1989, led the leaders to consider a movement,
but only a *movement,* toward German unification to be desirable. This
explains why, despite the anxieties it could entail, an event such as the
fall of the Berlin Wall was received calmly and without any sign of panic.
Several days later, when the events became precipitous and began to
seriously threaten the viability of the European project, one can say
that Gorbachev and his team had already burned all their bridges and
could no longer go back. Helmut Kohl's calculation proved to be well-
founded. But this argument needs to be treated with caution. Political
behavior is never completely inevitable. There is always the choice of
making mistakes and going down dead-end roads, and politics allows us
to observe that frequently. This leads us to the great issue of the use of
force.

An essential part of Gorbachev's political capital accrued from the
absence of a recourse to force. The value of that capital rested on the conviction from the outside that he had the option to use it; hence the credit
of not exercising it, a credit that needed to be nurtured. Another part of
his political capital was based on what he had to offer very concretely.

With regard to both of these questions, the fall of the Berlin Wall was
a crucial turning point, on top of being a great moment in history. In the
weeks that followed, Gorbachev's partners became convinced, or were

willing to wager, that he could no longer use force, and simultaneously recognized that what he had to offer was slipping out of his hands.

To use force is one thing. Threatening to use it is another. In 1991, when the USSR itself was going in the direction of disintegration, Gorbachev threatened to use force to stop the process on several occasions. But he never brought himself to do so in a decisive manner. That was both his great historical merit and his political tragedy. As for what interests us here directly, it is remarkable that even the threat of using force, or simply a show of force, was never used to slow down an evolution deemed to be harmful.

One small fact is very revelatory in this regard. Only a few days after Kohl's speech to the Bundestag on November 28, the Malta summit between President Bush and Gorbachev took place. Just the same as on the Western side, a meeting had been planned between Gorbachev and the other Warsaw Pact leaders after the summit, so that he could report on its results. By confidential, diplomatic channels, Krenz and Modrow proposed holding the meeting in Berlin. In a note to Gorbachev, Shakhnazarov advised him to decline the invitation, claiming that, under the circumstances of events in Berlin, a Warsaw Pact summit there "would be seen as a type of show of force."[54] The meeting took place in Moscow.

Soviet behavior, given the nature and importance of the stakes and the objectives it was pursuing in Europe, did, in fact, make the use of force very difficult in the autumn of 1989. But for the Soviet leaders to avoid even indirect shows of force indicates that the "taboo," or the active ideological role of the nonuse of force as a political instrument, had acquired considerable importance. This has yet to be explained satisfactorily.

As we shall see, the grand international and European design, though in great trouble after November 1989, was pursued with obstinacy and doggedness. This time, however, it was done by trying to slow down rather than trying to accelerate the course of events, and with declining means. The Soviet leaders invested less and less enthusiasm and means into it. Gorbachev still counted on the importance of the USSR's power and international role, as he thought it was appreciated by his Western interlocutors. He relied on their goodwill and the proofs of good behavior he was giving them. They did make some efforts to assist him, but they could hardly put the ground that was slipping away, back under his feet.

---

54. See the text of the note in Georgii Shakhnazarov, *Tsena svobody: reformatsiia Gorbacheva glazami ego pomoshchnika (The Price of Liberty: Gorbachev's Reformist Enterprise through the Eyes of His Assistant)* (Moscow: Rossika Zevs, 1993), p. 440.

CHAPTER NINE

Bulgaria

The Most Faithful Ally until the Very End

The Communist Party Central Committee plenum on
November 10, 1989, which deposed Todor Zhivkov, came
somewhat out of nowhere, without any open public pressure.
The democratic opposition was hence deprived of a victory
and the Communist Party could glorify itself as having been
the initiator of democratic changes in the country.

Vladimir Kostov[1]

TODOR ZHIVKOV:
HIS REGIME AND HIS *PERESTROIKA*

From the beginning of the socialist camp's existence, Bulgaria had been
its only member that had never caused the USSR any problems, either
through domestic sociopolitical unrest or through any kind of challenge
or contestation from its leaders to Soviet policy. As a result, it enjoyed
privileged treatment, certainly not with respect to its formal status, but
in economic terms. Since it was also the smallest of its European allies,
the USSR could better afford to extend such "largesse" to it. In per capita terms, Bulgaria was by far the most subsidized nation in Eastern
Europe. The need to redress the Soviet economy soon led the Gorbachev
government to end a number of the advantages Bulgaria had previously
enjoyed.[2]

The character and leadership style of its supreme ruler constituted one
of Bulgaria's most peculiar attributes, and strongly influenced its political life. When Gorbachev came to power in 1985, Todor Zhivkov was
the oldest Communist leader in the region. He had been the leader of his

---

1. Vladimir Kostov, "Bulgarie, les changements manquent de souffle," in Pierre
Kende and Aleksander Smolar, eds., *La grande secousse: Europe de l'Est, 1989–1990.*
(Paris: Presses du CNRS, 1990), pp. 124–126.
2. See V. V. Kuzin, "Gorbachev and Eastern Europe," *Problems of Communism,* Jan-
uary-February 1986.

Party for thirty years. With the exception of Ceausescu, who outlasted him by less than two months, he was the last of the Party chiefs of 1985 to be carried off by the effects of *perestroika*. This says a lot about his abilities to hold on to power. In Moscow, the last head of the Department for Liaison with Ruling Communist Parties described his power as "colored by Oriental despotism."[3]

As one of the principal players in his removal remarked, Todor Zhivkov was possessed by two potentially contradictory "obsessions": to keep power and to innovate.[4] He had a predilection for fashionable ideas and liked organizing (and sometimes even presiding over) seminars of intellectuals; he notably invited, among Soviets, several of the stars of *perestroika*. He also enjoyed having various theoretical analyses of social and political questions prepared, which he would send to Moscow as advice. They were received in the Soviet capital with disdain by one of his main addressees, who obviously considered himself more sophisticated than Zhivkov and wrote that "all of this carried the mark of provincialism, of theoretical emptiness and primitiveness."[5]

Long accustomed to adapting himself to the political impulses emanating from Moscow and of adding to them some elements of "originality," he had much less difficulty than the other conservative leaders of the region in adopting the slogans of *perestroika* and policies flowing from it. During the first phase, when the Soviet catchwords were acceleration and the improvement of productivity through technology, he launched an important program (on the basis of initial Western transfers) to produce microelectronic equipment. He expected to make an entry into the world market in this area and transform Bulgaria into Eastern Europe's "little Japan." After the failure of his attempt, he turned to the USSR and CMEA, where he was rather badly received.

In early 1987, after the January Soviet plenum which emphasized democratization and political transformations, Zhivkov seems to have had a brief phase of perplexity and hesitation. It was, though, rapidly overcome with the vast program which he had the Party adopt in July.

---

3. Vadim A. Medvedev, *Raspad: kak on nazreval v "mirovoi sisteme sotsializma" (The Collapse: How It Happened in the "World Socialist System")* (Moscow: Mezhdunarodnye Otnosheniia, 1994), p. 45.

4. Interview with Andrei Lukanov (member of the Bulgarian Politburo from November 1989 and prime minister of Bulgaria in 1990), Sofia, 14 November 1994.

5. Medvedev, *Raspad*, p. 47.

Inspired by the aforementioned themes of the Soviet plenum, he pretended to go further and faster. He announced the introduction of a new model of socialism, based on a fundamental revision of the Party's role in society. The Party was only to act as a source of inspiration and to cede a growing amount of political space to social organizations. Even if the relationship of reality to these objectives was not always obvious, they were not simply words. A genuine attack was launched against the Party and state apparatuses. Over 30,000 officials were dismissed from their positions, which for a country the size of Bulgaria was a considerable number. The twenty-eight administrative divisions of the country were reduced to eight, the number of ancient Bulgarian provinces. Entire ministries were eliminated, while others were totally reorganized. New laws on employment and the powers of enterprises and cooperatives were rapidly adopted, giving them greater autonomy and guaranteeing the election of managers. A new constitution that would confirm and structure all of these changes was to be introduced.

Petar Mladenov, who was to succeed Zhivkov in November 1989 and was the minister of foreign affairs at the time, affirms that he found the program (which he did not help prepare) "bold and interesting," and he was convinced of its merits until early 1988.[6]

Inspired by the political survival tactics of the Stalinist period, when it was necessary to understand the dictator's new whims in time, and to anticipate them a bit in order to act as their most zealous promotor, Zhivkov intended to position himself as the avant-garde of *perestroika* through his new program. Given that Gorbachev was not another Stalin, Zhivkov, with his predilection for innovation, even planned to prove to the Soviet leader that he could surpass him. None of the changes that Zhivkov introduced, however, called into question the most direct levers of his personal power nor his capacity to intervene.

If Mladenov was impressed by Zhivkov's new program, the Soviet authors and implementers of *perestroika* were not. During a visit to Sofia in September 1987 to prepare a Soviet-Bulgarian summit scheduled for the following month, Vadim Medvedev put several remonstrances and warnings to Zhivkov. In a paternalistic and condescending tone, he expressed concern about the rapidity and improvisation of the measures which had been introduced, stating that they would possibly lead to "economic ruptures," "social tensions," and to "discrediting *perestroika*

---

6. Interview with Petar Mladenov, Sofia, 12 November 1994.

itself."[7] In a more subtle tone that was clearly less schoolmasterly, Gorbachev expressed similar reservations in his meetings with the Bulgarian leader, albeit in the form of questions and doubts.[8]

Despite his readiness to effect a considerable number of changes, Zhivkov never succeeded in gaining the new Soviet leaders' confidence. In March 1988, the Soviet ambassador, Grekov, was called back and replaced by Viktor Sharapov, who had been in Andropov's circle and had Gorbachev's trust. Zhivkov took Grekov's recall as a personal rebuff.[9]

He did not, however, intend to step aside. Since 1986, he had been promoting the career of a relatively young and particularly dynamic leader, Shudomir Alexandrov, by giving him numerous important responsibilities. At the beginning of 1988, he seemed ever more to be the second person in the regime and Zhivkov's possible successor, all with the latter's apparent support. By the summer, though, Zhivkov decided to get rid of him. It was not the first time that he had relegated a presumed heir. But, in the atmosphere of uncertainty which hung over his relations with the new Soviet leaders, he judged it even more prudent and opportune to do so since they had shown particular affection for Alexandrov.[10] He was, in fact, relegated in July 1988, shortly after the 19th CPSU Party Conference which reinforced Gorbachev's authority. His dismissal was justified on the basis of a report from the Bulgarian intelligence service, according to which his father-in-law had given information on Partisan activities to the collaborationist government during the war. Sent to Moscow, on Zhivkov's request, but with a negative note from Sharapov, the report was received with incredulity and increased the contempt in the Soviet capital for the Bulgarian leader.[11]

7. As if his remarks couldn't be applied in equal measure to the USSR, he told Zhivkov: "History has taught us that important measures in the life of society, and even more so ones which are oriented toward a deepening of democracy, cannot be ensured by decree from above." See the transcript of the conversation in Medvedev, *Raspad*, pp. 60–76.

8. See the transcript of their meeting on 15 October 1987 in Moscow, in ibid., pp. 76–79.

9. According to Andrei Lukanov, Grekov was totally devoted to Zhivkov for reasons that he advised us not to publish, telling us that they were not worthy of a university publication; but let us give them anyway, hoping that Lukanov will pardon us. Grekov's son, a "hooligan," according to Lukanov, was caught by the Bulgarian police in an "extremely unpleasant situation." It was unpleasant and serious enough that it could have seriously damaged his father's career. Zhivkov supposedly intervened personally to make the affair disappear, correctly calculating that the ambassador would be indebted to him.

10. According to Lukanov, Zhivkov being the way he was, the Soviets made a mistake by making comments about Alexandrov that were too positive.

11. On July 28, Shakhnazarov sent a note to Gorbachev, reporting on the information sent by Zhivkov and Sharapov's opinion that the information had been "fabricated" (quotations in the text) by the intelligence service, on Zhivkov's request. Text of the note in Georgii Shakhnazarov, *Tsena svobody: reformatsiia Gorbacheva glazami ego pomoshch-*

After this, Zhivkov would avoid promoting anyone else from the circle of his assistants. Shortly after Alexandrov's dismissal, during a Politburo meeting, he proposed resigning from his offices. All those who wanted it to happen understood that it was a trap, designed to identify potential rivals. His proposition was unanimously rejected.[12] The control he exercised over his assistants and the fear he inspired in them were such that it would take another year before they would begin to act, timidly, in a conjuncture that pushed them more into action.

In fact, during that time, the Zhivkov regime's problems worsened. As his Soviet partners had feared, his massive and inappropriate reorganizations brought about economic dislocations. In order to palliate the declining growth rate (which had already reached zero, though that was not publicly known at the time) and the elimination of several Soviet subsidies, the government borrowed massively from Western markets. Those loans soon tripled its foreign debt, which reached $10 billion.[13] Nonetheless, they were not sufficient to stop the decline in the population's standard of living. If Zhivkov did somewhat heed Soviet advice, slowing down his structural changes, that did not put an end to his innovative plans. In 1989, for example, seeming still very much ahead of the USSR in this area, he announced his intention to transform most state enterprises into mixed, semiprivate ones. Nothing, however, was to come of it.

The effects of *glasnost'* and democratization in the USSR added to the deterioration of living standards, extending and deepening discontent with the regime. The Bulgarian language being very similar to Russian, a large part of the population could closely follow what was happening in the Soviet Union. It was on the basis of the Soviet example that the first opposition movements, such as the Club for the Support of *Glasnost'* and *Perestroika,* developed. Though the regime used all sorts of intimidation tactics against these opposition movements, it did not dare suppress them directly, given its official intention to imitate the USSR.

Growing Bulgarian difficulties contributed, apparently in an attempt to divert attention, to an accentuation of the coercive measures against Bulgaria's Turkish minority. Shortly before Gorbachev came to power,

nika (The Price of Liberty: Gorbachev's Reformist Enterprise through the Eyes of His Assistant) (Moscow: Rossika Zevs, 1993), p. 358.

12. Interview with Dimitar Stanichev (Politburo member, secretary of the Central Committee and head of the Bulgarian Party's International Department in 1989), Sofia, 16 November 1994.

13. See François Fejtö, La fin des démocraties populaires (Paris: Le Seuil, 1992), p. 220.

Zhivkov had led a policy of "Bulgarianization" of the important Turkish minority, which was estimated to number 1.5 million and represented
20 percent of the population. Bulgarians of Turkish origin were first
forced to adopt Bulgarian names. Measures were also taken to forbid
them from using their language. The "Bulgarianization" campaign
became particularly intensive in the summer of 1989. Increasingly strong
pressure, intimidation, and extortion caused more than 200,000 people
to "emigrate" to Turkey. These were, in fact, expulsions. In May, Turkey
had agreed to open its borders to them, but faced with a growing flood
of refugees, it closed them again in July.

In launching this campaign in 1984, Zhivkov had wanted to assure
his place in history as the unifier of the nation. In pushing it to its
extremes, in the context of his difficulties in the summer of 1989, he
planned to stimulate and bring into play in his favor nationalism and
memories of Turkish domination among the population. To his Soviet
counterparts, who were unhappy about the policy, he claimed that it
helped reinforce the southern flank of the Warsaw Pact against Turkey.[14]

The advantages he gained from this initiative were more than coun-
terbalanced by the difficulties he reaped. Bulgaria was condemned by
several international institutions and organizations for human rights
violation and was the subject of accusations and pressure from numerous Western governments. The domestic opposition groups took up the
issue in the name of "traditional national tolerance of Bulgarians" and
received wide international acclaim.[15] At the same time, Bulgaria found
itself increasingly isolated from the USSR, which is, of course, what
Zhivkov had sought to avoid.

THE PLOT FOR CHANGE
AND THE ROLE OF THE USSR

Zhivkov's removal in November 1989 was organized, according to their
own statements and those of Zhivkov himself, by a group of three individuals: Petar Mladenov, the foreign minister; Andrei Lukanov, deputy
prime minister responsible for CMEA affairs; and Dobri Zhurov, the
defense minister. Dimitar Stanichev, secretary of the Central Committee
and head of the International Department, also joined this group.[16]

14. Medvedev, *Raspad,* p. 49.
15. See *Situation Report, Bulgaria* (Radio Free Europe), 8, 1 September 1989.
16. See Dimitar Tsanov, *Smianata: kaki zashcho se stigna do 10 noemvri (The Change:
How and Why It Happened on November 10)* (Sofia: Universitetsko izd., 1995); translated from Bulgarian for this book by Bronislav Nicolov.

These leaders, and most others, knew at least by the beginning of 1988 that Gorbachev and his entourage did not have any confidence in Zhivkov at all. Incidentally, they all say so. Moscow had let them know quite directly, through various criticisms and on several occasions. But for them to take the initiative and risks for deposing him before 1989, an explicit invitation from the Soviets to do so would have been necessary, as well as a promise of support. Such a course of action, however, would have been contrary to the rules of behavior which the Soviet leadership had imposed on itself, as we have seen; it must also be said that Bulgaria had very little importance in the Soviet Union's foreign policy.

In these conditions, one had to await the accumulation of problems described above and Zhivkov's total discreditation for them to take the initiative to do something. Even then, one of their first moves was to sound out the top echelons of power in Moscow. What we can reconstruct from the "plot," as well as several details which Mladenov and Lukanov gave us, is all entirely characteristic, not only of the Soviet approach, but also of the fears, hesitations, expectations—in short, the behavior—of the East European states' second echelon of leaders. This holds not only for Bulgaria, but equally for the GDR and Czechoslovakia.[17] For that reason, it is useful to give some details of the "plot," which may resemble a detective story.

At the Warsaw Pact summit in Bucharest on July 7 and 8, 1989, Zhivkov was, of course, accompanied by his foreign and defense ministers. Because of the absence of "clear instructions" from the Soviet officials he generally met, Mladenov sought to speak to Gorbachev personally. But, he says, "to ask for a meeting with Gorbachev would have immediately aroused Zhivkov's suspicion."[18] That is why he decided to speak to Gorbachev with Zhivkov's knowledge and within his view. He had brought with him a copy of Gorbachev's book *Perestroika*. During a conversation between Gorbachev and the Bulgarian delegation, he asked the Soviet leader to be so kind as to dedicate the book to his niece. In this way, he could get Gorbachev two or three meters away in order to use the window sill for writing a few lines. So, in full view of Zhivkov, but without him being able to hear, Mladenov told the Soviet leader, "We are determined to carry out a change in Bulgaria," while the latter was writing. Gorbachev reportedly responded: "We sympathize with you,

---

17. Romania is somewhat an exception to this, to the extent that it was considerably detached from the USSR.

18. Interview with Petar Mladenov, Sofia, 12 November 1994. The details which follow were provided to us by Mladenov during this interview.

but it's your business."[19] He had fully understood the meaning of Mladenov's message; as Mladenov learned much later, Gorbachev reported the content of their brief conversation to his ambassador in Sofia, Sharapov.

Though he did not say this to us directly, Mladenov was somewhat disappointed by Gorbachev's response. He had wished for more solid encouragement and support. But, quite clearly, Gorbachev did not want to be a part of the plot and take responsibility for it. That is probably the main reason why it took another four months before Mladenov finally decided to make his move.

It was actually made on October 23. The context at the time was encouraging. Five days had passed since the removal of Honecker, which had "gone well" thanks to indirect pressure from Gorbachev. That day, Mladenov received a telephone call from Zhivkov, in which the latter insulted him and accused him of complacency with respect to the U.S. ambassador, whom he deemed guilty of meddling in Bulgaria's internal affairs because the United States was intervening in favor of the Turkish minority. For Mladenov, the call was precisely the "pretext"[20] he needed to act. He wrote a long and virulent letter of resignation which he directed to the members of the Politburo and the Central Committee of the Party. The letter was particularly harsh about Zhivkov. Mladenov wrote in it: "In analyzing my experience, I have come to the conclusion that the real reason for his irritation and his brutal behavior toward me is due to the fact that he realizes he has led the country into a profound economic, financial and political crisis. He knows that his political program only consists of maneuvers and intrigues to stay in power with his family, at any price and for as long as possible. He has 'succeeded' in isolating Bulgaria from the rest of the world and even from the Soviet Union. We are at the point of being in the same boat as the dictatorial and corrupt regime of the Ceausescus. . . . I believe that it is time for the Politburo, the Central Committee and the whole Party to deal with these questions."[21]

As one can see, the letter was intended as a call to action to those who were already mobilized and to rally the undecideds and potential sympathizers. Before sending the letter, Mladenov gave a copy to Lukanov,

---

19. Ibid.

20. It was Mladenov himself who used this term to explain the circumstances around the sending of his letter. See Petar Mladenov, "Bulgarie: percée vers le renouveau," *La Vie internationale,* 5, May 1990, pp. 3–8.

21. Text in Petar Mladenov, *Jivot't: pliusove i minusy (Life: Pluses and Minuses)* (Sofia: Peteks, 1992), p. 322; translated from Bulgarian for this book by Bronislav Nicolov.

so that he could take it to Moscow, where he was going the next day.[22] Terhaps in order to dramatize things a bit, Mladenov told us that, after having sent the letter and preparing for the worst, he made it known that he had left his dacha where his family was staying (so they would not run any risk) and that he had taken refuge alone, with a revolver, in his downtown apartment. It should be said that if the old general Zhurov, a former Partisan, controlled the armed forces, Zhivkov still had full power over the intelligence services, which stayed faithful to him to the end.[23]

As has been noted by D. Tsanov, a researcher in the Bulgarian Academy of Sciences who analyzed the circumstances of Zhivkov's ouster, it is surprising that his removal came more than fifteen days after Mladenov sent his letter.[24] He attributes this delay to bad organization and the fear or lack of courage of Mladenov's accomplices. Zhivkov tried to obtain Mladenov's dismissal from the Politburo, and the latter limited himself to resisting this demand.[25] Three Politburo members were sent to Mladenov's home, in order to demand he retract his letter, which he refused to do.[26] He did, however, retract or ignore his resignation as foreign minister, since he left on an official visit to China on November 4, returning to Sofia on the evening of November 8. Contrary to what has been claimed by various sources, he categorically denies having stopped in Moscow during his trip.[27]

On November 8, Dimitar Stanichev and Dobri Zhurov, accompanied by a third veteran from the Partisan movement, met Zhivkov to ask him formally, for the first time, to tender his resignation and put the issue of

22. Lukanov confirmed the accuracy of Mladenov's claim to us. He did not, however, want to tell us to whom, precisely, he had given the letter in Moscow, simply indicating that it had reached the top. Interview with Andrei Lukanov, Sofia,14 November 1994.

23. On the other hand, Lukanov believes that, at this stage, given the situation prevailing in other socialist countries, Zhivkov could no longer allow himself to use "criminal means" to keep himself in power. But perhaps it is easier to say that after the events.

24. Tsanov, *Smianata*.

25. Interview with Andrei Lukanov, Sofia, 14 November 1994.

26. Interview with Petar Mladenov, Sofia, 12 November 1994.

27. Charles Gati claims that Mladenov stopped in Moscow on his way back. His information is dubious, as he notes that Mladenov learned there of the Soviet leaders' complacent attitude concerning the opening of the Berlin Wall, which is factually impossible. Charles Gati, *The Bloc That Failed: Soviet-East European Relations in Transition* (Bloomington: Indiana University Press, 1990), p. 182. Inversely, British sources say that it was on his way to Peking that he made a stopover in Moscow. *Situation Report, Bulgaria* (Radio Free Europe), 11, 15 December 1989.

Mladenov denies these reports, suggesting that the impossibility of the corresponding flights matching his known departure and arrival times to and from Sofia and Peking be verified.

a replacement on the agenda of a Central Committee plenum on agriculture already planned for November 10. Surprised and somewhat upset by such a direct demand, Zhivkov refused to submit.[28]

In the meantime, Zhivkov was in constant contact with the Soviet ambassador. In his study of these events, D. Tsanov attributes a key role to the ambassador, especially in the mobilization of the main protagonists against Zhivkov. To do so, however, he only invokes indirect evidence, such as meetings (which, in any case, were frequent and normal) between the ambassador and several leaders during this period. It is, in fact, possible that the ambassador played a more direct and active role than Gorbachev, but that remains difficult to determine. We know from Gorbachev himself that Zhivkov asked at the time, via the Soviet embassy, to come to Moscow for "consultations" with his Soviet counterpart on the situation in his country. Knowing that Zhivkov wanted to use the visit to put an end to the pressures being exerted on him, by showing himself as still being Moscow's interlocutor, Gorbachev immediately refused the visit.[29] Zhivkov, having well understood the refusal's significance, tried to divide his opponents and gain time by asking the ambassador for his and Gorbachev's opinion on the possible designation of Alexander Lilov as his successor.[30] Lilov was a former heir apparent to Zhivkov whom the Bulgarian leader had removed from the Politburo several years earlier. Sharapov indicated to him that the Soviets had no opinion to give on the issue and that it was up to the "Bulgarian comrades" to settle these matters.

On November 9, at a Politburo meeting several hours before the fall of the Berlin Wall, on the eve of the Central Committee plenum, Zhivkov was still resisting and attempting diversions. Seeing that a large majority of the Politburo wanted his resignation, he sought to gain time and divide Mladenov's supporters and the rest of the Politburo. His proposal to designate Lilov (who was in London) as his successor was rejected. He then proposed G. Atanassov, the prime minister, who was present at the meeting.[31] The latter refused and supported Mladenov's candidacy. Zhivkov had to give in and accept that the agenda of the Central Committee meeting the next day be changed to settle his succession as desired by the Politburo. He even tried during the Central Committee meeting

28. Interview with Dimitar Stanichev, Sofia, 16 November 1994.

29. Mikhail Gorbachev, *Avant Mémoires* (Paris: Odile Jacob, 1993), p. 130.

30. According to Andrei Lukanov, who says that he received the information from Sharapov himself. The information is indirectly corroborated by Gorbachev, as we shall see below.

31. Interview with Petar Mladenov, Sofia, 12 November 1994.

itself to keep his functions as head of state, under the pretext that the question had not been explicitly resolved by the Politburo the day before. It was a lost cause, and the Central Committee confirmed his replacement as head of the Party and state by Mladenov. The political atmosphere in the country was changed radically through the event, even if the most substantial changes, such as the renunciation of the Party's leading role and the acceptance of free elections, would only come later.

The first official and private meeting between Gorbachev and Mladenov after the latter's assumption of power took place on December 5 in Moscow, following the Malta summit. The transcript of the private meeting, published several years later, is quite interesting. On the one hand, Gorbachev claims some credit for Mladenov's victory. But, on the other hand, the facts that he lists for his Bulgarian counterpart to support his claim are very minor indeed. At a certain point, in fact, he gives the impression of implicitly apologizing for not having done much. His comments merit being reprinted word for word.

> We here in Moscow immediately appreciated Piotr [Petar] Mladenov's courage; we know what it cost him to write his letter of resignation that everyone interpreted as a bold protest. From our side, we showed him unreserved support. We declined Zhivkov's request to come to Moscow under the pretext of "consultations." Our irrevocable attitude was to consider that Bulgaria's affairs should be settled by the Bulgarian comrades, by the Bulgarian Communists. That does not in the least signify that Bulgaria's affairs left us indifferent. Not at all. Bulgaria was, of course, very close to us, we know our friends well, but we cannot interfere in its domestic affairs nor create obstacles to the domestic development of the situation. . . . Your former leader manifestly wanted to implicate us in his maneuvers. We understood from the beginning that he had asked to come here in order to, as that had often been the case before, pretend that Moscow supported him, that Gorbachev supported him. But we have always expressed our sympathy and support for the Bulgarian people, for the Communist Party of Bulgaria. That does not mean we can decide here about the manner in which the Bulgarian people should live or behave in their country. We have firmly resolved, whatever the circumstances, to end such practices.[32]

Speaking again about the October 23 letter, Gorbachev stated that the "Mladenov spark" had "shown that the situation was objectively ripe, *even too ripe*."[33] As if he felt that the last comment had been directed at him, Mladenov responded in a way that can be understood as

---

32. Transcript reproduced in Gorbachev, *Avant Mémoires*, pp. 130–131. Mladenov told us that it was only during his meeting with Gorbachev that he learned Zhivkov had sought to come to Moscow in November.
33. Ibid.; emphasis added.

much as a confession as an implicit reproach of Gorbachev: "You are perfectly correct to say that our situation was ripe, but it was very important for us to know your point of view and to know that you were with us morally."

Gorbachev, however, did not seem to understand these words as a reproach, since a bit later in the course of the conversation he added, "If in the GDR and Czechoslovakia they had been attentive to the march of time and the advice of their comrades, if adequate decisions had been taken as little as a year ago, they would not have been forced to make them in an atmosphere of rallies and over the din of the crowds."

It was as if his refusal to act more directly and with greater determination had not played any role, there, too, in delaying the changes. And as if his cautious, philosophically couched advice could have sufficed under the circumstances. We have seen the nature of his advice in the case of the GDR. We shall see it again in the case of Czechoslovakia.

As for Bulgaria, despite the lag in removing Zhivkov and in introducing a truly reformist course, the events took a positive turn for the Bulgarian Communist Party and for the USSR. They even evolved in the direction of the most optimistic Soviet expectations. Though the non-Communist opposition developed rapidly after November 10, the reformed Communist Party, transformed into a socialist party, was to win the first free elections in June 1990.[34]

Unfortunately for Gorbachev, however, Bulgaria did not hold great importance for the future of the international order in Europe.

---

34. Shortly thereafter, though, Mladenov resigned from the presidency of the republic, giving in to pressure from student demonstrations. Parliament named the principal figure of the democratic opposition before November 1989 to replace him. That concession, despite the electoral victory of his party, is largely explained by the context of what was happening elsewhere in Eastern Europe.

CHAPTER TEN

Czechoslovakia

From Neglect to Paralysis

November 24, 1989

But when he appeared on the balcony in the freezing evening
air, illuminated by the television spotlights, the crowd let out
a cry the likes of which I have never heard: "DUBCEK!
DUBCEK!" It echoed off of the tall buildings which surround
the long, narrow square. . . . He still believes in socialism—in
other words, in a reformed Communism—with a human
face. At least in Prague, Havel is the true leader of the movement, not Dubcek. But for the moment, that is not very
important. For the moment, it only matters that the leg-
endary hero is really present to address the immense crowd
assembled in Wenceslas Square, while the emergency meeting
of the Central Committee has been moved, we are told, to a
distant suburb. "Dubcek to the Castle!" the crowd chants,
that is: Dubcek for President!

Timothy Garton Ash[1]

Czechoslovakia was the second to last East European country to jump
on the train of 1989. Apart from Romania, where the dictatorship's
brutality was particularly terrible, the Czechoslovak population, traditionally and perhaps unjustly known for its resignation, did in fact show
the greatest patience. In parallel, it was also there that the timid Communist Party reformers were slowest to act under popular pressure.

Their timidity is above all explained by their particular weakness. The
real reformers had been excluded by the tens of thousands from the Party
following the military invasion and repression of the Prague Spring in

---

1. Timothy Garton Ash, *La chaudière: Europe centrale, 1989–1990* (Paris: Gallimard, 1990), p. 392.

1968.[2] No form of reconciliation had taken place thereafter, and the leaders of the Prague Spring, as well as those who had participated in it at all levels, were systematically kept out of the Party. Of course, in any ruling Communist Party, the accumulation of problems always generates a certain number of reformers, and there were a few in the CCP (Czechoslovak Communist Party) who gave some resonance to *perestroika*. Nonetheless, there was not really a reformist current in this Party, as it existed elsewhere, even in the GDR. The Communist reformers were on the outside. A change toward reform, albeit only on the psychological level, necessitated at first some kind of political opening in the direction of the Prague Spring veterans, who had, incidentally, regrouped themselves into an organization in early 1989. In 1987, Prime Minister Lubomir Strugal, in his unsuccessful quest for power, had tried, cautiously, to trace out such an opening. His successor, Ladislav Adamec, on whom Gorbachev's reformist circle was counting,[3] was considerably more timid on this question. On the Soviet side, certain leaders knew very well that any reform process in this country had to pass through a reassessment of the Prague Spring. That is why it was recommended to Gorbachev that he make a declaration in this direction during his trip to Prague in April 1987. As we have seen, he did not want to do so unilaterally, but he allowed the lieutenants of his camp to "invite" their Czechoslovak counterparts to make such a statement.

GORBACHEV'S CONTRADICTIONS

In Czechoslovakia, as elsewhere in Eastern Europe, Gorbachev waited for the reforms to come, initially at least, from within the existing power apparatus. All of his exhortations went in that direction; for him, this was a guarantee of "stability in change." No other conservative leader in the region was the recipient of as much patience, and even personal complaisance, on the part of Gorbachev as Milos Jakes, who had been one of the principal officials responsible at the beginning of the 1970s for the campaign to exclude Prague Spring veterans. At least until the summer of 1989, Jakes found himself constantly given the benefit of the doubt by the Soviet leader. Can this attitude be explained through per-

---

2. See Jacques Rupnik, *Histoire du Parti communiste tchécoslovaque. Des origines à la prise de pouvoir* (Paris: Presses de Sciences Po, 1981), p. 288.

3. This information is confirmed by both Shakhnazarov and Yakovlev.

sonal reasons, Jakes having been an old acquaintance? Aleksandr Yakovlev also says that it relates to a certain ambivalence on the part of Jakes concerning the implementation of reforms.[4] And yet, concretely, he had done less than Zhivkov.

It is important to take a moment here to analyze the particular traits of Gorbachev's character and behavior, as it is without a doubt in Czechoslovakia that they had the clearest consequences for the failure of his own East European policy. Due to their effects, which are easily identifiable here, it is the Czechoslovak case which may best justify the claim that he did not have a real policy for Eastern Europe.

On April 18, 1989, approximately two months after his meeting with the Italian Communist Party leader, Achille Occhetto, during which Czechoslovakia was discussed (see above, p. 84), Gorbachev met Jakes in Moscow and had a long private conversation with him, of which we now possess long excerpts. "I hope you have not lost interest in the transformations?"[5] he asked his Czech interlocutor. Jakes responded in a tone that started off on a humorous note: "Not yet. . . . We are greeting the refreshing wind that is coming to us from the USSR. But the people fear that the course of events at home might take the same turn as in Poland and Hungary.[6] Our people do not want a shock, they do not wish a repetition of 1968. . . . We agree with the idea of pan-European forces of the Left, but we cannot agree with the Italians [Communists] who link it to Dubcek's rehabilitation."

He then added with some apprehension: "I know that they are putting pressure on you so that you will advise us to change our appreciation of the 1968 events." Gorbachev responded that "such questions cannot be resolved through interference" and that they were "the Czechoslovak leadership's matter." And, as incredible as that may seem considering that this was already April 1989, he continued: "You know our position. I always repeat that in January [1968], the problems were correctly posed. But, in the summer, things went toward counterrevolution. When I went to Czechoslovakia, someone may have been expecting other declarations from me, but I heard nothing about it [This is an allusion to

4. Interview with Aleksandr Yakovlev, Moscow, 8 November 1994.
5. See the transcript of the conversation in Georgii Shakhnazarov, *Tsena svobody: reformatsiia Gorbacheva glazami ego pomoshchnika (The Price of Liberty: Gorbachev's Reformist Enterprise through the Eyes of His Assistant)* (Moscow: Rossika Zevs, 1993), p. 109; excerpts from this conversation also occur in the following paragraph.
6. It should be noted that in Poland, the Roundtable accords had just been signed, but the elections had not yet taken place.

Strugal, clearly—author's note]."[7] Immediately after these words, as if to echo what he had previously said to Occhetto,[8] Gorbachev sought to make his guest understand that it was dangerous to continue to hold to the old positions, and that Czechoslovakia, which had a good standard of living and low foreign debt, could undertake reforms more easily than the others and "even put itself in the avant-garde of the reconstruction processes and give an example to the others."

We see here very clearly all of Gorbachev's ambivalence and, in this case, his inconsistency. Handing back to the Czechoslovak leadership the initiative for a revision of the Prague Spring is one thing. But was it necessary to tell Jakes that, as far as he was concerned, until a reinterpretation, he was holding fast to exactly what had been the Brezhnev-era interpretation of events, even using the term "counterrevolution"? His words are surprising. Not only was he in total contradiction with everything his reformist entourage had been thinking and telling him for more than two years but, above all, the domestic evolution in the USSR, by April 1989, was already further along than Czechoslovakia had gone in 1968.

Andrei Grachev, who was Gorbachev's official spokesman and who was present during several of his meetings with state leaders, sees in these words a personality trait of the Soviet leader: to never directly confront his interlocutor, to cede some terrain to him in order to better pull him over to his own side.[9] Georgii Shakhnazarov, who witnessed the conversation with Jakes, goes in the same direction and sees Gorbachev's comments as a way to "tranquilize."[10]

If Gorbachev's objective was to convince Jakes not to hold fast to old positions, the result was exactly the opposite. Questioned by Western journalists after his meeting with Gorbachev, Jakes declared that "no revision of the Party's policy on the subject of the events of 1968, no rehabilitation of Dubcek and his friends was envisaged." He even added that "the support that the CPSU is giving the CCP in this regard allows us to pursue our policy more firmly."[11]

The next month, an emissary from Prime Minister Adamec, the head of his press service, came to Moscow to seek support. In all his official

---

7. See chapter 3. Here again, Gorbachev seems to want to put the ball back in the court of the Czech leaders.

8. See chapter 4.

9. Second interview with Andrei Grachev, Paris, 27 February 1995.

10. Shakhnazarov, *Tsena svobody.*

11. Cited by François Fejtö, *La fin des démocraties populaires* (Paris: Le Seuil, 1992), pp. 292–293.

meetings, M. Pavel was accompanied by representatives of his country's embassy. That is why the meetings which he truly considered important often took place late in the evening, in a semiclandestine setting.[12] To the Soviet reformers he met, he told them of Adamec's reformist intentions and asked them for their support and that of the CPSU leadership. His hosts listened with sympathy, and they underscored that Gorbachev and the CPSU leadership were clearly in favor of political reforms in Czechoslovakia. But, as for concrete measures of support, his Soviet interlocutors could not take the initiative to promise anything. In order to better bring across his point of view, Adamec's emissary dared to tell Oleg Bogomolov that the USSR had intervened to put the current regime in power in Czechoslovakia, that it was therefore directly responsible for the existing situation, and that it should do something to induce change. Bogomolov, who paradoxically had himself pressed Gorbachev to intervene more actively, could only hide behind the official political line and respond with an quip: "Maybe you would be happiest if we brought change in again with tanks."[13]

On a certain level, Gorbachev's behavior can be deemed coherent. He recommended and supported reforms but not any specific individual. But the practical strength of his support for reforms in Eastern Europe necessarily suffered as a consequence. Other than the complacency toward Jakes, we can distinguish two other reasons for his behavior regarding Czechoslovakia. First, he did not see any particular urgency there. The summer of 1989 is very close to the final collapse, but it must be remembered that no one could then predict it, as we now tend to overlook. Second, according to Andrei Grachev, Gorbachev saw himself at the time as a figure busy taking care of the international system's future with the most important Western heads of state. For him, Czechoslovakia, Bulgaria, and Romania were secondary problems. Given what was happening on the level of East-West relations and elsewhere in Eastern Europe, he considered that these countries would at some point have no choice but to take the road of reforms. Therefore, it was not for him to get involved in their leadership quarrels when, even during the repudiated Brezhnev period, it happened only in rather exceptional circumstances.[14]

12. See the work by one of Adamec's principal assistants, Oskar Krejci, *Proc to prasklo? (Why Did It Blow Up?)* (Prague: n.p., 1993), p. 26; translated for this book by Viktor Obst.

13. Ibid., p. 26.

14. Second interview with Andrei Grachev, Paris, 27 February 1995.

ADMONITIONS AND INDIRECT PRESSURES

If the Soviet leadership held back from intervening directly in the delicate problems of the fights for power in Eastern Europe, that is not to say that it didn't interfere in their internal affairs on other, less compromising, questions, notably when it saw a particular interest for its European policy in doing so.

In November 1988, for example, in anticipation of a meeting of the thirty-five member states of the CSCE to control and ensure the continuation of the Helsinki process, which was to take place in Vienna in January 1989, Aleksandr Yakovlev went to Prague in order to press the Czechoslovak leaders to stop jamming the broadcasts of, among others, Radio Free Europe.[15] Since the USSR was championing the Helsinki process, in which it saw an especially important framework and tool for attenuating the division of Europe, it wanted the Warsaw Pact to be able to show results regarding the free flow of ideas. Of course, this interference in the domestic affairs of Czechoslovakia was presented as an international question arising out of the Warsaw Pact's collective responsibilities. Yakovlev had enormous difficulties "convincing" his Czech hosts, and Gorbachev was obliged to intervene personally to obtain results.[16] Jamming of Radio Free Europe did, in fact, cease on January 1, 1989. In the same way, the Soviet leaders interceded with their Czechoslovak counterparts on several occasions in a timely manner to get exit visas issued to dissidents.

At the beginning of July, Ladislav Adamec, who might have wished to do more, presented to Parliament the government's intention to introduce a certain number of cautious changes, essentially of an economic nature. Without pronouncing the name "Prague Spring" or mentioning the year 1968, several themes from the economic reform of that period were reintroduced.

Several days later, as a result of the Soviet pressures, the Czechs and Slovaks could listen to a speech by Vaclav Havel, broadcast by Radio Free Europe. In it, he stated that the process of change in his country would be slower and more tortuous than in Hungary. Speaking of the emergence of "a new, more democratic system," he added: "I don't know what type of system it will be. . . . But, from all indications, it will be dif-

---

15. Jaromir Sedlak (adviser in the office of Prime Minister Strugal), "The Road to the Velvet Revolution" (research report prepared for this writer), vol. 2 (1993), p. 19.
    16. Ibid.

ferent from a normal parliamentary democracy."[17] In short, what he envisaged in the summer of 1989 was a formula very compatible with Gorbachev's philosophy and as vague as that philosophy could be at the time.

On August 21, to mark the twenty-first anniversary of the 1968 invasion, and despite preventative arrests and all the measures taken to stop them, tens of thousands of persons demonstrated in Prague. At the same time, indirect pressure from the Soviet side was increasing. In early September, a former Soviet Politburo member, Kirill Mazurov, who commanded the Warsaw Pact invasion force in Czechoslovakia (under the code name "General Trofymov," as he revealed), began to give interviews to the media, which were reported by *Izvestiia*; in them, he regretted the role that he himself and the Soviet Union had played then. He even added that the Czech leadership team ought to "leave the stage."[18] In mid-September, *Izvestiia* published a letter from Jiri Hajek, the foreign minister during the Prague Spring and one of the main organizers of Charter 77, the oldest dissident group, in which he justified Dubcek's policies and compared them to those of Gorbachev.[19] Still in September, a Soviet television team working in Czechoslovakia obtained an interview with Alexander Dubcek himself.

Need we point out that *Izvestiia* was an official government newspaper and not some particularly avant-garde publication like *Ogoniok* or *Moscow Times,* and that the government controlled television more strictly than the print media? Undoubtedly, such articles were not printed on Gorbachev's behest. But, with the polarization between socialist states that had been increasing since the summer of 1989, all of that was a part of the indirect pressures which were being intensified against all the conservative regimes of the region, orchestrated by Gorbachev's circle, with at least his tacit consent. The Czechoslovak leaders, who protested to the Soviet Party leadership against these "demonstrations of hostility," did not receive any response.[20]

It was only a bit later, in a context of increasing urgency, that Gorbachev intervened personally, and in a fashion that is characteristic for him. It happened just after the fall of Honecker but before the opening of the Berlin Wall. On November 7, during a Kremlin reception for the

17. Cited by Fejtö, *La fin des démocraties populaires,* p. 295.
18. Cited by Charles Gati, *The Bloc That Failed: Soviet-East European Relations in Transition* (Bloomington: Indiana University Press, 1990), p. 179.
19. *Izvestiia,* 17 September 1989.
20. Sedlak, "Road to the Velvet Revolution," p. 22.

anniversary of the October Revolution, Gorbachev, accompanied by Prime Minister Ryzhkov, took the Czechoslovak ambassador aside, asking him to inform his Party's leadership of his comments. Believing certainly that his remarks to the East German politburo a month earlier had had a decisive effect, he repeated essentially the same things to the ambassador, namely that "those who arrive late are punished by history." He also made reference to Honecker's fate and to the difficulties his successor was having in reestablishing control over the situation.[21] The message was, indeed, received in Prague by all the interested parties, including Adamec. However, it was not followed by any immediate consequences. Shortly after the fall of the Berlin Wall and its immense psychological and political impact, it was the crowds in Prague that intervened in a decisive way, beginning with the large demonstration on November 17.

That very day in Moscow, after a meeting with the director of an institute of the Czechoslovak Academy of Sciences, Shakhnazarov sent a note to Gorbachev, written in a tone of relative urgency. He indicated to the Soviet leader that "the [Czechoslovak] leadership's obstinate unwillingness to adopt 'corrective' measures is leading to the accumulation of explosive material." He added that it was consequently "particularly absurd that no steps have been taken toward the rehabilitation of several tens of thousands of those excluded and deleted from the CCP who, independently of their positions in 1968, define themselves as supporters of socialism."[22] Without such a move, he said, they risked to be "pushed into the camp of the Right." Apparently knowing Gorbachev's point of view well, Shakhnazarov said that he had reminded his Czechoslovak interlocutor that "the solution of the country's problems depends on the Czechoslovak comrades themselves," but he immediately added that he was of the opinion that "if it becomes known that Moscow is moving toward a reevaluation of the 1968 events, it would exert a stimulating influence on the process of revising the CCP's policy and accelerate the adoption of indispensable measures."

As we have seen, this was not the first time that such advice was given to Gorbachev. Shakhnazarov hoped that, in the context in which it was

21. See Krejci, *Proc to prasklo?*; Sedlak, "Road to the Velvet Revolution." Through leaks in Prague, information about Gorbachev's message made its way a bit later to the *New York Times* (16 November 1989).

22. Complete text of the note in the documents annexed to Shakhnazarov's work, *Tsena svobody*, p. 434. The somewhat strange formulation "independently of their positions in 1968" may be aimed at dissipating Gorbachev's prejudices about certain Prague Spring protagonists.

renewed, it would be followed by action. It was very late for the recommended course of action to possibly give the expected results. Whatever the case may be, Gorbachev remained faithful to his promise to the Czech leaders and it was only after their Party, or rather what remained of it, had revised its assessment of the Prague Spring, that the CPSU officially followed suit. This time, it was definitely too late.

"Partiinost"? "Party Spirit," without a doubt? It was not to Jakes, but to the Czechoslovak Communist Party that Gorbachev remained faithful until the end, just as he remained faithful to the CPSU until the last. But at what price—for his policies and for himself.

INACTION AS THE BEST POSSIBLE POLICY?

Even if the members of Gorbachev's reformist entourage desired a greater activism on his part with respect to Czechoslovakia, that does not mean that they all foresaw much more accurately than their boss the course of events to come in that country. So, even at the beginning of November, Aleksandr Yakovlev, the one considered to be the most "enlightened" among them, bet a bottle of champagne with the deputy director of the Central Committee's International Department that Ladislav Adamec would soon emerge as the new strong man in Czechoslovakia.[23] If one can speak of a very brief emergence, it certainly was not that of a "strong man."

The large demonstration on November 17 which gave the initial push to the "Velvet Revolution" marked the occasion of the last gesture of "authority" by the regime in place. It was as much, and perhaps even more so, its brutal repression than the demonstration itself which launched the process that quickly led to the regime's ultimate collapse.[24] During the entire following week, the government seemed

23. First interview with Valerii L. Musatov, Moscow, 4 November 1991. Yakovlev incidentally himself acknowledges that he believed in Adamec's authority.

24. In the months that followed, due to the ultimate consequences of the repression, there were reports taken up by the Western press that suggested that the police brutality (and a report that there had been one death—news that turned out to be false) had been planned by the KGB, in concert with collaborators of the Czech secret police, precisely with the goal of destabilizing the Jakes regime and preparing the terrain for a new, Gorbachev-style government. According to information broadcast by the BBC, the demonstrator who had supposedly simulated his death was a KGB agent. (On this last point, see Radu Portocala, *Autopsie du coup d'État roumain.* Paris: Calmann-Lévy, 1990, p. 48.) These reports were examined and rejected by a special commission of the Czechoslovak Parliament, which concluded in 1991 that there had been no foreign involvement in the November 17 events.

paralyzed by its own action and its consequences. On the other side, calls for a strike and popular demonstrations multiplied while the opposition organized itself. It was in that process that the Civic Forum was created on November 19, regrouping, on Vaclav Havel's initiative, the groups which had gravitated around Charter 77 and, notably, "Obroda," the movement of Communists excluded after the Prague Spring. What Shakhnazarov feared, a worry expressed in his note to Gorbachev, was becoming reality. The polarization was pushing all of the currents of opposition—if not to unification, then at least toward very close concerted action.

During this time, the regime, internally divided, did not succeed in redirecting itself in a decisive manner. Ladislav Adamec established cautious contacts with the opposition, but was not able to assert himself. His conservative comrades kept holding on. At this point, the exclusion of another recourse to repression was largely due to Soviet "interference." In fact, a very clear "recommendation" was sent from Moscow to warn against any use of force.[25] For Adamec, that was not enough, and he would have preferred a more substantive intervention by Moscow. In order to have himself supported formally and officially, he telephoned Gorbachev, but the Soviet leader refused to take the call.[26]

On November 24, the confrontations and soul-searching within the Communist Party produced their first results at the conclusion of a Central Committee meeting. Shortly before, on the same day, Alexander Dubcek, who had just joined the Civic Forum, received a triumphal reception from the crowd, and could again appear to be the political alternative for the future. He was, however, soon eclipsed by Havel, who did not then see himself as a candidate for the presidency. The Central Committee meeting ended in the removal of Jakes and the former conservative Party leadership. The entire Politburo and Secretariat resigned. Those responsible for the "invitation" given to the Soviet troops in 1968 were even excluded from the Party. Adamec did not, however, succeed in carrying off a complete victory and establishing his domination over the rest of the apparatus. It was Karel Urbanek, a person from the third ranks, relatively young and without great authority, who was elected the new head of the Party.

From then on, Adamec sought to free his government from the Party's tutelage and, on November 26, he had a first one-on-one meeting with

25. Second interview with Valerii L. Musatov, Moscow, 26 April 1993.
26. Ibid.

Vaclav Havel. At the same time, he still looked for official and explicit support from Moscow, but again in vain.[27] Various Soviet emissaries started to arrive in Prague soon thereafter, but apparently without any specific mandate for action. They gathered information, made contacts with all of the political circles, expressed more or less strong sympathy for Adamec, but held themselves back from giving "advice." On November 27, a delegation from the Bogomolov institute, sent by the Soviet government, arrived in Prague and contacted Dubcek, in particular. The next day, a Central Committee delegation, directed by Falin himself, accompanied by Musatov, arrived for an official visit. Falin met with Adamec and Urbanek.

On November 29, a member of Falin's delegation, D. Prasolov, went to the "Magic Lantern," Civic Forum's headquarters, accompanied by J. Sedlak. He met Dubcek, Vaclav Klaus, and other leaders of the Forum there; Havel was then in Bratislava. Prasolov insisted that he had come "as a private person" to find out about the Forum's political positions. He was assured that it was favorably disposed to maintaining Czechoslovakia's international obligations, notably to the Warsaw Pact. He was, however, told that the Forum wanted the departure of Soviet troops stationed in Czechoslovakia.[28] It should not be concluded from this that Moscow had "chosen its side" and was betting on a Civic Forum victory. The Forum was in touch with the Soviet embassy and would have desired a direct contact at a higher level, but the Soviets remained very reserved.

At the very beginning of December, upon his return to Moscow, Musatov was asked by Yakovlev if he thought that Zdenek Mlynar, one of the leaders of the Prague Spring and Gorbachev's roommate at Moscow State University in the 1950s (who was shortly thereafter invited to Moscow) could represent a political alternative. In fact, with all that was happening at the time in the GDR and the preparation of the Malta summit, Gorbachev and the main officials responsible for foreign affairs were inundated and found themselves in a state of disarray and confusion. In these conditions of uncertainty, pressure and multiple, contradictory solicitations, Gorbachev's most instinctive reflex, one might say, was to hold even more firmly to his fallback position—the rule of nonintervention—which was applied more strictly in Czechoslovakia than anywhere else.

27. See the memoirs of his assistant, Krejci, *Proc to prasklo?*, pp. 16–17.
28. Sedlak, "Road to the Velvet Revolution," pp. 37–38.

Adamec introduced his new government on December 3. Despite the contacts he had with Civic Forum, which had given him the benefit of the doubt, he revealed a grave error in his appreciation of the situation. Of the twenty-one ministers in his new government, sixteen were Communists. Civic Forum protested sharply and threatened to organize a general strike. Adamec then left for Moscow, with Urbanek, for the Warsaw Pact meeting that followed the Malta summit, and at which an official apology for the 1968 invasion was made. During his stay in Moscow, Adamec met with Gorbachev. Beyond the sympathy which Gorbachev expressed to him, he wanted an explicit, firm show of support from the Soviet leader for the government which he had just formed. Adamec believes that he had not received it.[29]

Shortly after his return from Moscow, on December 7, he and his government resigned. Following rapid negotiations between the Communist leaders (in complete disarray) and the Forum, a new government was formed four days later. This time, the balance of power had changed hands. Of the now twenty-two ministers, only ten were Communists. The new prime minister, Marian Calfa, freed his government and himself from the Communist Party, resigning from it shortly thereafter. Vaclav Klaus became finance minister, and Jiri Dienstbier was chosen to be the new foreign minister.

That left the question of the presidency to be settled. Dubcek readily (albeit with some bitterness, it is reported) agreed to bow out in favor of Havel. It was decided that he should be nominated for the position of president of Parliament and was duly elected on December 28. The next day, Havel was elected president of the Czechoslovak Republic by the Parliament. A few days before, on December 22, Adamec had finally been elected head of the Communist Party, which had by then completely lost power and had been deserted in droves by its members.

Adamec's close collaborators believe that, throughout his struggle, he was never really supported by the Soviets. They conclude from this that Gorbachev wanted to rid himself of Czechoslovakia and the other "fraternal states."[30] Other former Czech Communists and political actors are much harsher in their assessment of Adamec than of Gorbachev. They reproach him for having totally lacked authority and having acted too reservedly toward the Prague Spring veterans. According to them,

29. Still according to his assistant Krejci, *Proc to prasklo?*, p. 27.
30. Interview with Oskar Krejci, Prague, 4 May 1993. See also his memoirs, *Proc to prasklo?*

he received encouragement from the Soviets on several occasions, but wanted more, something like a media campaign in Moscow or a full mobilization of the Soviet embassy in Prague in his favor. According to his critics, he was unable to comprehend that, in the context of Soviet policy in 1989, this was impossible.[31]

Obviously, Gorbachev's former assistants in Moscow are much closer to this point of view. Even today, several years after the fact, they defend Soviet behavior in 1989 toward Czechoslovakia with vigor. When they are asked why they did not really support the reformist elements in the CCP, which counted on their encouragement, Vadim Medvedev responds with vehemence: "But certainly, we supported them. They knew very well that we wanted to see reforms undertaken in their country. We did not stop telling them so. But we couldn't do it in their stead."[32] When he is asked why the USSR took a position of apparent neutrality during the November and December events, as if it had no interests at stake in Czechoslovakia, Aleksandr Yakovlev justifies himself by pointing to what could be called the syndrome of 1968.[33] "The USSR had already burnt its fingers in Czechoslovakia. The consequences of our intervention were disastrous. It was a terrible lesson for us. More so than elsewhere, we could not permit ourselves to interfere."[34] Medvedev adds: "The memory of our intervention, which was still very present in Czechoslovakia, gave rise to such a level of distrust toward us that if we had pronounced ourselves heavily in favor of a given leader, that would have been enough to ensure his failure."

It is not in the scope of our analysis to assign blame here between Gorbachev and Adamec and the other Czechoslovak leaders. We have simply sought to establish what the USSR's objectives were and with what degree of coherence and efficiency they were pursued. In that respect, it is probably correct to believe that, by the end of November and early December 1989, it was too late for a different Soviet course of action (apart from military intervention) to be able to substantially alter the course of events. Nonetheless, if the USSR had unilaterally and officially denounced its 1968 intervention just a few months earlier in 1989, one can believe that the conservative leaders of the CCP would have been

31. That is the opinion, it should be noted, of people from Strugal's clan. Interview with Jaromir Sedlak, Prague, 4 May 1993; see also his report, "Road to the Velvet Revolution."

32. Interview with Vadim Medvedev, Moscow, 10 November 1994.

33. This is, of course, a different 1968 syndrome than that which the Soviet reformers attributed to Jakes for explaining his paralysis in the face of reforms.

34. Interview with Aleksandr Yakovlev, Moscow, 8 November 1994.

sufficiently delegitimized and disarmed to ensure the preeminence of the reformist elements, timid as they were. The rehabilitation of Dubcek and his fellow veterans of the Prague Spring would have permitted, and even rendered it necessary, for the Party to deliver itself to them. And even until November, Dubcek would have easily won totally free elections.[35]

In the domestic sphere, and especially in economic matters, it is difficult to see how a government dominated by the Prague Spring protagonists could have taken any other course of action than a rather rapid transition to the market, under the cover of reconstructed socialism. In the area of foreign, and especially European, policy, however, Gorbachev would have had an important ally for some time, and the Warsaw Pact would have disintegrated much less rapidly.

35. In December, Vaclav Havel's supporters in the Civic Forum preferred he be elected president by the Parliament rather than by a quick election with universal suffrage, which they were not sure of seeing him win easily. For exactly the same reason, the Communists wanted a quick election.

CHAPTER ELEVEN

Romania

The Tangle of Plots and Mysteries

We *knew* that a coup was inevitable because the regime was
not only rotten, but intransigent. . . . When a critic of the
regime like Silviu Brucan came to Moscow in November, we
were asked to understand the fact that Romania had no other
way out. As a result, we *very carefully watched the developments within the Romanian armed forces* and the increase in
resistance against the regime, from November until the end of
the year.

Valentin Falin (1990)[1]

A NOT SO EMBARRASSING
NEGATIVE "IDEAL TYPE"

Even if it was the most anachronistic of all, there is obviously nothing
surprising in the fact that Romania was the very last country to rid itself
of its pre-Gorbachev regime, almost missing, by just a few days, the great
historical rendezvous of 1989. The nature of the regime and of Ceausescu's dictatorship are sufficient to explain the delay. First, let us mention two peculiarities of the regime's change. It was the only bloody transition, and the only one which took place completely outside of the top
institutions of the state and Party. But, in fact, everything was particular and unique in what was both a revolution and a coup d'etat at the
same time; the contours and interactions of the two still remain considerably obscure.

If the longevity of Ceausescu's regime is explained, essentially, by its
repressive nature, it must be mentioned that, at least until December
1989, the Soviet Union did not do much to help Romania rid itself of
his dictatorship.

---

1. "The New World Disorder?" *New Perspectives Quarterly,* 7 (2), 1990, pp. 22–26;
emphasis added.

Well before Gorbachev's accession to power, the Romanian regime was already largely impervious to Soviet political influence. The only declared opponent of *glasnost'* and *perestroika,* from 1986 on, Nicolae Ceausescu sought to reinforce this imperviousness, systematically reducing to a strict minimum all political, social, and cultural exchanges between the USSR and Romania through organizations like the friendship societies, official trade unions, and academic institutions such as the Academy of Sciences and the universities. So, while Gorbachev clung to his conviction that change would come from within the leadership circles of the Parties everywhere else in Eastern Europe, that illusion did not exist concerning the Romanian case. Gorbachev's entourage expected that a change would come to Romania either after Ceausescu's death (he turned seventy in 1988 and was reported to be in poor health) or through a real coup d'etat. The only means for the USSR to directly influence a political change would have been through fomenting and encouraging such a coup. That meant a form of interference that would have been more compromising and risky than the more political means of involvement that Gorbachev refused to use elsewhere. Incidentally, even before Gorbachev came to power, in 1984, under Chernenko, the Soviet intelligence services refused to give direct assistance to a coup that failed even before it was executed.[2] (It was organized, among others, by General Militaru, who reappeared in 1989.) The Soviets had estimated that the uncertainties and risks were too numerous.

If the relative neglect and passivity Gorbachev showed with respect to Czechoslovakia is difficult to understand, the same cannot be said for Romania, and not only because of the much tighter limits on his capacity to influence events there. We have seen that, from his first trip to Bucharest in 1987, Gorbachev had made every effort to publicly disassociate himself from the Ceausescu regime by publicly formulating open critiques of the latter. Romania was also the last East European state to which Gorbachev chose to pay an official visit. Faced with an international pariah like Ceausescu, the Soviet leader found it useful to openly keep his distance, particularly during official visits, in order to ensure the credibility of his new foreign policy. He did not, however, have great difficulty in having that distance acknowledged by the international community. Given the conflictual relationship between Bucharest and

2. According to testimony from General Militaru and from the former leader of the Securitate, Ion Pacepa (see *Red Horizons,* Washington, D.C.: Regnery Gateway, 1987), and various other sources carefully analyzed by Nestor Ratesh, *Romania: The Entangled Revolution* (New York: Praeger, 1991), pp. 93–98.

Moscow which had existed, albeit with varying degrees of intensity, since the 1960s, Romania was considered in the West as an autonomous nation within the Soviet alliance system. In other words, for Western governments and political circles, the USSR was not held responsible for the policies pursued in Bucharest; this was not the case in the other countries of the region, and notably in Poland and Czechoslovakia. On the other hand, contrary to the GDR in particular, Romania could not become an important obstacle to the advancement of the USSR's European policy. These were the reasons for not inciting Gorbachev to pay special attention to promoting political change in Romania.

In these conditions, some believed that Gorbachev had found a certain utility in the existence of the Romanian pariah which permitted *perestroika* to be put in brighter perspective for the rest of the world.[3] Others have even deduced a certain degree of complacency of Gorbachev's Soviet Union toward Ceausescu, explaining it through the evolution of economic relations between the two countries. Indeed, Romania's economic independence from the USSR and the other CMEA countries, which Ceausescu had sought to establish and reinforce obstinately for a number of years, was considerably weakening. While he had succeeded in reducing the socialist states' share of Romanian foreign trade from 65 percent in 1965 to 33.8 percent in the early 1980s, that tendency was subsequently reversed. The reversal had even gained momentum after 1985, to the point that the CMEA's share had reached 60 percent by the end of 1988.[4] Trade with the USSR alone represented 33 percent of Romanian foreign trade in 1988, up from only 17 percent in 1980. This tightening of economic relations with the USSR and its partners was notably due to Ceausescu's obsession to eliminate Romania's foreign debt, by reducing imports from the West which were consuming hard currency. It was the drastic reduction of consumer goods and the quality of life of the Romanian people which had financed the rapid repayment of the debt, and which contributed, to an important extent, to balancing out the import of energy from the USSR. Romania had, in fact, become the USSR's largest provider of meat.

Were these sufficient reasons to motivate a certain Soviet complaisance toward Ceausescu?[5] It seems difficult to confirm this with certainty. Of

3. This is what François Fejtö suggests (*La fin des démocraties populaires*. Paris: Le Seuil, 1992).
4. See Édith Lhomel, "L'économie roumaine en 1988: toujours à contre-courant," *Le Courrier des Pays de l'Est*, 341, June-July 1989, pp. 64–72.
5. That is what Édith Lhomel suggests ("Gorbatchev face au cas roumain," *Les Temps modernes*, 522, January 1990, pp. 83–95).

course, the Gorbachev leadership was sensitive to the chronic food short-
ages, which began to become more serious in 1989. However, Romanian
imports were financed by exports that could have been fairly easily reori-
ented toward the world market for hard currency. As the case may be,
even if it is true that the Soviet press was not very critical about the goings-
on in Romania, the same was true for the other conservative-ruled socialist states. In fact, the reports on the GDR and Czechoslovakia were considerably more complacent than those concerning Romania. One specific
case of complaisance toward Romania, which has frequently been
invoked, may merit being mentioned. It is the awarding in 1988 of the
Order of Lenin(the highest Soviet decoration) to Ceausescu on the occasion of his seventieth birthday. We were told, as an explanation for the
event, that it was the Romanian Party leadership which had written to
the CPSU Central Committee, asking that the distinction be awarded
him, as was normally done for foreign Communist leaders in similar circumstances.[6] So, it was supposedly for reasons of bureaucratic inertia
that he was awarded this distinction, and it is obviously not the only case
of contradictory Soviet behavior in Eastern Europe. On the other hand,
inversely, it must be noted that in Party-to-Party negotiations the Soviets
constantly insisted that the Romanians reestablish and broaden contacts
of all kinds that had been restricted by Ceausescu and that they permit
the distribution of Soviet newspapers and magazines.[7]

THE ENIGMAS OF DECEMBER 1989 AND THE KGB

If it is generally agreed that the fall of Ceausescu at the end of 1989 was
the result of the conjuncture of a popular insurrection and a coup, there
is still no consensus on the relative importance of the two aspects of the
December 1989 events. Among those who insist on the decisive role of
the coup, certain observers even go as far as to see the popular insurrection as having been the result of manipulation and a simple element
in a vast plot.

Due to an entire series of troubling and mysterious facts, which for
the most part have not been cleared up in a satisfactory manner to this
day, the December 1989 events in Romania have been the subject of the
most abundant literature relating to that year in Eastern Europe, with

    6. Second interview with Valerii L. Musatov, Moscow, 26 April 1993.
    7. See notably Vadim Medvedev's account of one of his conversations with Ceauses-
cu, in Vadim A. Medvedev, *Raspad: kak on nazreval v "mirovoi sisteme sotsializma" (The
Collapse: How It Happened in the "World Socialist System")* (Moscow: Mezhdunarodnye Otnosheniia, 1994), pp. 196–201.

the exception of the East German events. For the same reasons, a significant part of that literature is based on highly speculative reconstructions of plots that compete to be the most Machiavellian. This literature is found in Romania as well as abroad. Some of these works attribute the most important role in these events to the USSR; outside Romania, it is particularly in France that this version has been most popular and found its most eloquent representatives.[8]

The theses of the USSR's key role are basically founded on two sources of reasoning: the presumed or demonstrated links between the Romanian leaders who emerged in December 1989 and those of the USSR; and the activity attributed to the KGB as the coordinator of various actors, or as the only rational explanation of troubling coincidences. Therefore, it is above all circumstantial evidence or claims that are difficult to verify which are put forth to support these theses.

Let us mention some examples. The reports and horrifying images of the mass grave "discovered" in Timisoara are still a vivid memory; they came several days after the repression of the mid-December demonstrations against the reassignment of the ethnic Hungarian pastor Laszlo Tokes. The demonstrations were followed by riots, which gave the initial push to the Romanian "revolution." The newspapers reported that 4,630 corpses had been discovered. Several months later, it was learned from doctors' accounts that some thirty of the corpses shown "exhumed" by television around the world had been stolen from the city morgue and hospitals in the night of December 21–22. Disconcertingly, the "mass grave" may have been constituted *after* its discovery was announced the day before by East German and Hungarian press agencies. To this day, no one has been able to establish firmly who organized this staging, and precisely to what ends. As far as the purpose of the "grave" is concerned, several interpretations were put forth and supported: to bring about a revolt in the country; to raise the greatest possible indignation on the international level in order to make the leaders of the coup accepted and acclaimed; or to make the Securitate, which was blamed for the carnage, the incarnation of all the Ceausescu regime's evils, in order to better clear the army and its leaders, who joined the side of the new government, or essentially constituted it. It was later learned that it was the army, and not the Securitate, which opened fire

8. That is notably the case with two books: Michel Castex, *Un mensonge gros comme le siècle: Roumanie, histoire d'une manipulation* (Paris: Albin Michel, 1990); and Rado Portocala, *Autopsie du coup d'État roumain* (Paris: Calmann-Lévy, 1990); and with one extensive report, "Les cinq actes d'une manipulation," *Le Point*, 922, 21 May 1990.

on the crowds in Timisoara. General Stanculescu, who commanded the army, faked a broken leg and was taken to the hospital in order to be able to claim that he had not himself given the order to open fire. This is the same General Stanculescu who put Ceausescu on board the helicopter with which he escaped on December 22. It was also Stanculescu who organized the incredible "trial" of the dictator several days later, and who became, at the beginning of 1990, after the (aptly named) General Militaru, the new regime's defense minister.

The thesis that the KGB "orchestrated" events is based on the fact that most of the information which was later shown to be false—such as the reports on the mass grave in Timisoara, the ridiculous figure of 63,000 casualties in the "combat" which followed the dictator's escape, and the "discovery" of Securitate troops disguised as military personnel—was disseminated by East European press agencies, especially from Hungary, but also from the GDR and Yugoslavia, before reaching the West. In those countries, where the intelligence services customarily worked very closely with the KGB, it was the "Gorbachevites" who were in power. That seemed sufficient for a number of observers to state that the key to the Romanian mysteries lay in Moscow, where it was decided to put Romania into line with "Gorbachevism."[9]

The thesis of a KGB-organized plot obviously has developed a certain number of variants. One of those is based on attributing an autonomous, or at least equal, role to the Hungarian intelligence service. The hypothesis is tempting, in the sense that relations between Hungary and Romania had been extremely tense for two years, due to the Hungarian minority's fate and the fact that it was an incident in the heart of that community which was the element unleashing the regime's demise. Father Tökes's resistance was carefully followed by the Hungarian media well before December 1989. For Ceausescu, the destabilizing and initiating role of the Hungarian intelligence service was not a hypothesis, but a fact. During the December 17 Timisoara riots, he stated during a meeting of his executive political committee (the Romanian equivalent of a politburo) that the events were the result of action by "foreign espionage groups, beginning with Budapest."[10] But that seems to have been simply a belief on his part. Incidentally, as if the entire world had joined against him, he added that "East and West have united to destroy socialism, because what they want is a capitalist and human socialism."

9. That is the central thesis of Castex's work, *Roumanie.*
10. Transcript of the meeting's minutes in *Romania libera,* 10 January 1990, cited by Ratesh, *Romania,* p. 26.

If the last part of his statement could be considered as a rather accurate definition of Gorbachevism, the first is largely attributable to paranoia.

Elements of direct proof to support these and similar claims are very rare. As an example, one can cite the rare testimony of an imprisoned Securitate colonel who was freed in 1991. He writes that the Securitate had noted the arrival of "numerous false Soviet tourists" in Timisoara in early December, coming from Soviet Moldavia.[11] He also reports that a convoy of several Lada cars, with Soviet license plates and containing three to four men each, had refused to stop at a police checkpoint in Craiova. After the Romanian police opened fire and killed several men, he claims that the Soviet authorities recovered the bodies without issuing an official protest. To the extent that this information is absolutely correct, it would tend to prove the presence of Soviet agents in Romania (which no one doubts), without, however, indicating to us their exact role in the course of events.

It was not only the initiating events in Timisoara which were, and remain, shrouded in mystery; far from it. The strangest of them followed Ceausescu's flight from Bucharest on December 22, in a context of widespread rioting and after the formation of the National Salvation Front (NSF) government led by Ion Iliescu. Immediately afterward and in the days which followed, the entire world witnessed what appeared to be a civil war, pitting on one side the new government, the army (which had joined it), and the population against what was presented to be thousands of cold-blooded, fanatical terrorists, emerging out of the Securitate, fighting for Ceausescu. It was during this period that the 63,000 casualties were reported and that Radio Budapest mentioned the presence of Syrian and Libyan mercenaries fighting side by side with the terrorists.

Who were these terrorists, and on whose account were they operating? If the answer seemed clear at the immediate moment, it became extremely problematic by the end of December when order was restored. The realization sunk in that if the terrorists had indeed fired on the demonstrators, they seemed to have studiously avoided the government's strategic points. For example, it was clearly visible that the buildings surrounding the Party Central Committee headquarters were riddled with bullet holes. The headquarters itself, however, from the balcony of which the new leaders made their appearances, was spared. The same is true

11. Filip Teodoresu, *Un risc asumat (An Assumed Risk)* (Bucharest: Editura Viitorul Romanesc, 1992); passages translated for this book by Andrei Stoiciu in a research report: *La révolution roumaine de décembre 1989 et le rôle des puissances étrangères,* Montréal, December 1993.

of the siege of the main television station, which remained relatively intact while the adjacent buildings suffered significant damage. It is true that a very important part of the destruction resulted from the army firing on the terrorists. But the most Machiavellian interpretation of the facts argued that the terrorists' actions were a massive diversionist exercise, to keep the crowds away until the new government could get itself in order. Another reading suggests that their actions were designed to permit different forces of the old regime to negotiate the conditions of their adhesion to the new regime. The head of the Securitate, General Vlad, did join the new government very early, only to later be arrested and accused of having played a double game in order to keep his options open. His trial did not help shed light on these affairs.

Very few terrorists were captured. To add to the mystery, several of them escaped, apparently benefitting from the "new" intelligence services' complicity; others were released for lack of evidence. As such, no substantive, satisfactory analysis can be given of their numbers, their masters, or their mission. Even though certain observers have gone as far as to doubt the real existence of the terrorists—given their "flightly" character, they most definitely did exist, if only for the simple reason that they left behind victims. The number of casualties, however, has been proved to be closer to 600 than 60,000.

The Ceausescus' "trial," shown around the world on most television stations, was itself a microcosmic meeting point for the intrigues and disinformation of the December 1989 events. It was on the basis of the outlandish figure of 63,000 deaths that they were accused of genocide and sentenced to death, to be immediately executed on December 25. In addition to this main charge, all of the other information or accusations which later turned out to be fabrications were held against them, notably the use of foreign mercenaries from Arab countries and the disguising of Securitate forces as military personnel. Were the organizers of the trial victims of disinformation or the authors of it? Was Ceausescu's rapid execution designed chiefly to keep him from speaking out and incriminating several of the individuals associated with the new government? Was it to make him take exclusive responsibility for the regime? Or was the goal to put an end to the civil strife, by depriving the terrorists of all reason to engage in it, as the new leaders claimed? Indeed, the fighting did stop practically immediately after the news was announced. But that can also serve as an additional "proof" of the government's manipulation.

The role attributed to the USSR and the KGB after Ceausescu's flight depends, to a proportional extent, on the cohesion and closeness of coordination attributed to the new leaders and the magnitude of manipulation for which one holds them responsible. Whatever the role of the USSR was, it does not seem that their coordination could have been optimal. Iliescu himself believed in the importance of the threats against the new government enough to call for Soviet military aid. We shall return to this point.

To take up a hypothesis advanced by Iliescu, if one can speak of a plot, then it seems very likely that there was not one, but a multitude of plots, intrigues, and intended goals. Their precise interaction remains to be determined in a satisfactory fashion, and it is be doubtful that the mystery will ever be fully unravelled.[12]

ROMANIAN AND SOVIET GORBACHEVITES

The ideological and political kinship between the new Romanian leaders of December 1989 and Gorbachev's team was immediately and particularly remarkable. From his first public utterances, Ion Iliescu declared himself in favor of a renovated socialism, and the brief program of action which was published by the National Salvation Front Council on December 23 committed itself to promoting the "common values of humanity." On the international level, the NSF promised to make Romania a catalyst "of the process of constructing a unified Europe and a common home for all the peoples of the continent." It obviously also affirmed that Romania would fulfill all its international obligations "and, in the first place, those stipulated by the Warsaw Pact and the Helsinki accords."[13]

It was in large measure on the basis of this political lineage that Moscow's action was supposed to have put power in the hands of the new Romanian leaders. As for direct relations and contacts between Iliescu and the Soviet leaders, they are impossible to reconstruct, at least for the few years preceding 1989. Suspected, and not without reason, to have had contacts with the organizers of the 1984 abortive coup,[14] Iliescu was closely watched, even if he was not imprisoned; he held the

---

12. For a particularly sober evaluation of the purported conspiracies, the hypotheses which were formulated, and the difficulty of drawing convincing conclusions from them, see Ratesh, *Romania*.

13. Text of the program cited by *Izvestiia*, 24 December 1989.

14. See James F. Burke, "Romanian and Soviet Intelligence in the December Revolution," *Intelligence and National Security*, 8 (4), October 1993, pp. 26–58. It should be noted that General Militaru's actual participation in that plot is probably more suggested than established, since he was retired and only watched but not incarcerated.

position of a publishing house director. As he had been at Moscow State University in the 1950s at the same time as Gorbachev, it was frequently said in early 1990 that he had been a personal friend of the Soviet leader. This was never established, and both parties deny it. However, under Ceausescu, Iliescu could be considered politically close to Gorbachev—to such an extent, in fact, that during the latter's visits to Bucharest in 1987 and July 1989 (for the Warsaw Pact summit), Iliescu was removed from the capital to avoid any contact, be it on his initiative or at the Soviets' behest.

The only new Romanian leader of December 1989 certain to have had contacts with the Soviet leadership in the months before is Silviu Brucan, considered the NSF's *éminence grise*. His testimony and several concomitant facts reveal Soviet behavior that resembles rather remarkably the policy established in the case of other East European states.

Brucan—former editor in chief of the Party daily, former Romanian ambassador to the UN, polyglot, who maintained various connections in the United States, the USSR, and Eastern Europe—was able to continue travelling until 1989, even if he had fallen from grace in the early 1980s. In November 1988, he went to Moscow, where he had discussions at the Kremlin. As he had contacts with several Romanian leaders removed by Ceausescu, he told his Soviet interlocutors of their willingness to rid themselves of the dictator and sought the Soviets' assistance.[15] They apparently listened very attentively and with much understanding, but they also seem to have told him that they could not take the risk of acting directly to try to oust Ceausescu and that it was not up to them to do so. They did, however, promise, according to Brucan, to intercede in order to ensure his personal safety.[16]

Four months later, in March 1988, the BBC in London received and broadcast a political manifesto against the Ceausescu regime signed by six former Romanian leaders living in Romania, including Silviu Brucan, who was its author. Among the other signatories was Gheorghe Apostol, head of the Party for a brief period in 1954 and 1955,[17] and Corneliu

15. Interview with Silviu Brucan, Bucharest, 11 June 1991.
16. Ibid. Brucan relates the same things in his memoirs: Silviu Brucan, *Generatia irosita (A Ruined Generation)* (Bucharest: Universul Calistrat Hogas, 1992), pp. 184–190; translated for this book from Romanian by Andrei Stoiciu.
17. The true political leader of Romania at the time was Gheorghe Gheorghiu-Dej. But, in 1954, to put Romania on schedule with Moscow, where the virtues of collective leadership were being extolled, Gheorghiu-Dej ceded his position as head of the Party to Apostol, leaving himself only with the post of prime minister; that position, then occupied in Moscow by Malenkov, seemed, as a consequence, to be more important. In 1955, Gheorghiu-Dej took back the official leadership of the Party, abandoning his post as prime

Manescu, a former foreign minister. The manifesto denounced the nepotistic and monstrous dictatorship of Ceausescu as being foreign to socialism, accusing the dictator of bleeding the Romanian people dry. It underscored the European character which Romania had lost and which it should pick back up to "progress in the framework established in Helsinki." The appeal, which was widely rebroadcast on an international level and clandestinely distributed in Romania, had as its goal to sound a rallying call to all known and potential Ceausescu opponents. Due to the nature of the regime and the absence of a significant Soviet initiative, the Brucan manifesto had no notable effect in the months that followed. The Soviets showed their sympathy, but in a minimal fashion, by publishing the text in a secondary journal and well after its broadcast.[18] Like the other signatories of his manifesto, Brucan was put under house arrest. He attributes the moderation of this "punishment" to an intervention by the Soviet leaders, just as they had promised him.[19] Later, he was even allowed to receive the *Pravda* correspondent in Bucharest for a visit, and in November, a few weeks before the fall of the regime, doubtlessly benefitting from some act of complicity, he was able to escape his surveillance and made his way to Moscow. His new requests for support were received there "with reticence," according to him.

Even if Brucan's credibility, like that of the other Romanian leaders of December 1989, can be doubted,[20] his statements concerning Soviet attitudes seem altogether reasonable in the light of what we have seen in the preceding chapters of the USSR's behavior. In fact, one would wonder why the Soviet leaders, who finally did very little and always acted with the greatest circumspection and reserve in the other East European countries, would have used all of their organizational means and international coordination (as they are alleged to have done) to destabilize Ceausescu's Romania and to bring it over to Gorbachevism. That would be all the more surprising since, with the possible exception of Bulgaria, Romania was the least important country for them within the entire region. And that is true in all spheres and on all levels.

What was it about the Romanian case which made such a change so much more urgent in December 1989 that so many means not used

---

minister, and hence again put himself in step with Moscow, where Khrushchev had clearly become the strong man.

18. *Sovetskaia Molodezh'*, 14 June 1989.

19. Interview with Silviu Brucan, Bucharest, 11 June 1991.

20. For example, he gave contradictory information about the level of contacts he had in Moscow, as well as about the spontaneity and plots of the December events.

elsewhere, particularly in Czechoslovakia, were all of a sudden to have
been deployed? In fact, much more so than any direct action by the
USSR, it was the new international conjuncture in December 1989 which
led to the disintegration of the Ceausescu regime. After the opening of
the Berlin Wall, the fall of Todor Zhivkov, and the collapse of the regime
in Prague, Ceaucescu's days were numbered. A large number of high-
level officials in the state organizations and the apparatus of repression
were only waiting for the opportune moment to jump ship and turn
against the despot they hated. More than a very complicated vast plot,
the twisted web of intrigue reveals the confusion of maneuvers in a free-
for-all that was poorly (if at all) coordinated and made up of mutual distrust cultivated by the atmosphere of dictatorship.

It was possible to observe this poor coordination in public at the very
top of the new regime. After Ceausescu's departure from Bucharest on
December 22, General Militaru appeared on television and asked the
audience to find Iliescu and request that he come to the television station. He arrived shortly thereafter. In the meantime, he had not been
inactive, because he announced on television that he had just contacted
(though he did not yet have any formal authority whatsoever) General
Stanculescu, then acting defense minister,[21] and that the latter had
assured him that the army was "on the side of the people." Still through
the use of television, Iliescu asked other persons to come to the seat of
the Central Committee to participate in the founding of a National Salvation Committee.

All of this does not mean that the USSR was totally inactive in Romania. As the quote from Falin at the beginning of the chapter indicates well,
the Soviets, through their intelligence services, knew much and could
closely follow what was going on in different circles. On what the KGB
might have done, beyond informing the Soviet leaders, nothing is known
that could be verified, and the opinions of Gorbachev's collaborators
diverge on the question. Andrei Grachev, who underscores that he has no
personal knowledge of the situation, says he is persuaded that the KGB
was instructed not to take the risk of implicating itself in an attempt to
oust Ceausescu. But, he says, "once the regime started to shake, I believe
that the KGB forces on the ground did everything they could in order to
tilt the balance in favor of the emerging new government."[22] Aleksandr

---

21. The defense minister had committed suicide shortly before. As with every Romanian political event of December 1989, his suicide has been put in doubt.
22. Interview with Andrei Grachev, Paris, 2 March 1993.

Yakovlev says he is convinced of the opposite.[23] Given the segregation of information, only Gorbachev and Kriuchkov, among Soviet leaders, could tell us with certainty if they wanted to.[24] Asked about this, Gorbachev, intentionally or not, avoided the question.[25]

Without wanting to go very far into speculation, which the Romanian case seems particularly to invite, one can, nonetheless, indicate what seems to be reasonable in light of the other cases. Before the events of Timisoara, it is possible and even probable that the KGB shared some of the information it had with its close Romanian interlocutors and that it served as an intermediary between certain of them. It is unlikely, though, that it went very far or played the role of an instigator. In brief, if it was able to assist the conspirators, it was undoubtedly in a way that was least compromising for itself. In fact, Grachev's and Yakovlev's words are not really contradictory unless they simultaneously concern the period that goes from the Timisoara riots to Ceausescu's flight from Bucharest. From the formation of the National Salvation Council, the USSR immediately recognized it as the legitimate government of Romania and, after that, the KGB no longer had any reason not to do all it could to help it consolidate its power.

A diplomat from the Soviet embassy in Bucharest even proposed Soviet military assistance to the new government.[26] This incident fed into the thesis that the Kremlin had envisaged the option of a military action to support the new regime, but finally decided to put it aside. On this question, as far as he is concerned, Gorbachev is categorical and states that "personally" he "could not and would not have had such ideas." He adds that "a military intervention would have contradicted the entire logic of our policy from the first days of *perestroika*."[27] In fact, it seems that it was only assistance in the form of military equipment that the USSR was willing to provide, in response to a much larger request

23. Interview with Aleksandr Yakovlev, Moscow, 8 November 1994.

24. In an interview given to a journalist from French television, Maurice Najman, Kriuchkov was uncooperative, refusing to say anything about these questions.

25. This author's question to Gorbachev had several elements, and he chose to answer only the part of the question which referred to the reported Soviet intention to provide military support to the new Romanian government (see below).

26. The proposition was even made publicly, without the knowledge of the Soviet diplomat who was making it. Television cameras happened to be in the office of General Guse when he received a phone call from someone speaking Russian. The general, who does not speak Russian, gave the phone to an interpreter, who translated the Soviet diplomat's imprecise proposition in front of the cameras.

27. M. S. Gorbachev, *Otvety na voprosy professora Zh. Leveka (Responses to Questions from Professor Jacques Lévesque)*, Moscow, 12 July 1995.

for military assistance made officially by Iliescu[28] and rendered public shortly thereafter.

On that subject, a revealing event merits being highlighted. Apparently because of the international media frenzy surrounding the Romanian "civil war" and the outrage it aroused, U.S. Secretary of State James Baker declared on December 24 on American television that the United States would not make any objections "if the Warsaw Pact judges it necessary to intervene" in Romania. Some observers saw this as an extraordinary gaffe, which would have given unprecedented legitimacy to the Warsaw Pact and allowed Moscow to then resist the withdrawal of its troops from Eastern Europe.[29] Others saw in this the most spectacular success of the disinformation orchestrated by Iliescu and Moscow, "certainly the greatest in the whole 'Romanian affair'."[30]

In Moscow, things were seen differently. The United States had just sent troops to Panama in order to chase out General Noriega. The Soviet press and leaders saw in Baker's implicit invitation a way of legitimizing the United States's unilateral behavior. One of the few benefits that Gorbachev could draw from the debacle in Eastern Europe was to be able to claim with greater credibility the moral leadership of the USSR and its "new thinking" in world affairs. It was hence with a certain arrogance that Shevardnadze told the American ambassador to Moscow that the USSR was "categorically opposed" to any foreign intervention in Romania[31] and that the Soviet press took a similar line. One of his deputy ministers tartly remarked to the ambassador that it was somewhat paradoxical that now, at a time when the USSR had abandoned the Brezhnev Doctrine, that the United States was making itself the advocate of the policy.

On one quite important point, one could say that Romania was the greatest success story of Gorbachevism, even more so than Bulgaria. Of all the Gorbachevite leaders of the Communist world, Ion Iliescu is the only one to have stayed in power uninterrupted from 1989 until now, and to have won two free elections. But, in 1990, given the relative unimportance of Romania in Europe, that could not be of great help for Gorbachev's foreign policy. It would have been different if Egon Krenz or Hans Modrow could have kept themselves in power, even if it had just been for two or three years.

28. See Burke, "Romanian and Soviet Intelligence in the December Revolution."
29. Ibid., note 150.
30. Portocala, *Autopsie du coup d'État roumain*, p. 143.
31. M. R. Beschloss and Strobe Talbott, *At the Highest Levels* (Boston: Little, Brown, 1993), p. 171.

PART III

The Great Project's Ruin

CHAPTER TWELVE

After the Earthquake

The last time I was to meet Ceausescu was on December 4, 1989. The representatives of the Warsaw Pact had gathered on my initiative. . . . There were many new faces. . . . I said (to Ceausescu) that the process we were living through at the moment had a clearly democratic character, despite all of its contradictions and the pain it was engendering. Due to this fact, there was no reason to fear the collapse or the end of socialism.

Mikhail Gorbachev (1995)[1]

A DIFFICULT RECONCILIATION WITH REALITY

Most of Gorbachev's collaborators and the entire Soviet leadership, just like the Western world, were caught unprepared by the rapidity and breadth of the earthquake which shook Europe at the end of 1989. In that context, the attitude which guided their behavior in the following several months was marked by three general characteristics. It consisted of refusing, to a certain extent, to see and admit the depth of the change which had taken place and the consequences which could arise from it. Soviet attitude was also characterized by some attempts to slow down the course of events. But, despite that, the dominant and most remarkable aspect of its behavior was its attempt to adjust to the new situation which had been created.

The first characteristic fulfilled a necessary function for the third. In other words, in order to be able to adapt themselves (with great difficulty) to the changes which had taken place, the Soviet leaders needed to deny, or at least to minimize somewhat, the depth of these transformations.

At the beginning of 1990, and for several more months, the main Soviet media and most Soviet leaders continued to speak of the "socialist countries" of Eastern Europe.[2] It is true, technically, that the economic

---

1. Mikhail Gorbachev [Michail Gorbatschow], *Erinnerungen (Memoirs)* (Berlin: Siedler Verlag, 1995), pp. 925–926; translated from German for this book by Laure Castin.
2. See A. Bogaturov, M. Nosov, and K. Pleshakov, "Kto oni, nashi soiuzniki?" (Who are they, our allies?), *Kommunist*, 1, January 1990, pp. 150–114.

structure and property relations had not changed from one day to the next in the region. And, for the next few months, the reformist Communists continued everywhere, albeit to varying degrees, to have a share of power. But for the Soviet leaders, educated in the school of Leninism and used to seeing the primacy of political factors, it must have been particularly difficult to downsize the radical character of the political transformation which was taking place in front of their very eyes. Even if the term "revolution" (and, *a fortiori,* "counterrevolution") was systematically avoided,[3] that was exactly what was happening.

The fall of the Honecker regime, followed by that of the Berlin Wall, and their acceptance by the USSR burst the main valve holding back changes elsewhere and limiting them from turning into a disaster. We have seen the result in Czechoslovakia and Romania, even if, in the latter case, the ultimate result was satisfactory for Moscow. In the case of Poland, the preservation of General Jaruzelski as head of state and of the armed forces and the presence of Communists at the head of the "power ministries" lost their meaning. On October 3, during a PUWP Central Committee meeting, one could still hear calls from its leading circles for a reconquest of power. But, as Georges Mink points out, "if the PUWP members did not immediately realize the irreversibility of the situation, the revolutionary wave which swept the East managed to destroy their morale. . . ."[4] In the weeks that followed Honecker's ouster, the PUWP disintegrated. In various places, the cells declared their own dissolution. In January 1990, in confusion and disarray, the remnants of the PUWP, which dissolved itself, gave birth to two new parties which defined themselves as social-democratic. Even the more important of these two, the Social-Democratic Party of Poland (despite the dynamism of its new head, Alexander Kwasniewski) did not appear, in the conditions of the time, to have a future.

In Hungary, as planned, the Communist Party had held a congress in October to complete its transformation into a social-democratic party. The leaders committed a serious error in judgment in asking the HSWP members to formally apply for membership in the new party. They

---

3. Later in 1990, some authors were to use the term "democratic revolution," but still in terms of linking it to a renewal of socialism. See Iurii Kniazev, "Demokraticheskie revoliutsii v Vostochnoi Evrope" (Democratic Revolutions in Eastern Europe), *Kommunist,* 14, September 1990, pp. 106–115.

4. Georges Mink, "Pologne: le paradoxe du compromis historique," p. 58, in Pierre Kende and Aleksander Smolar, eds., *La grande secousse: Europe de l'Est, 1989–1990* (Paris: Presses du CNRS, 1990).

expected to gather together about 70 percent of the 720,000 members still remaining, at that moment, in the HSWP. In fact, in the political context of fall 1989 and despite the fact that the new party still remained in power through its leaders, only 50,000 supporters had applied by the end of 1989. The setback was all the more bitter since those who, under the political leadership of Karoly Grosz, had refused to transform the HSWP and decided to maintain it, succeeded, for their part, in gathering 100,000 members. This was not the only disappointment for the new party. Denouncing the accord between the Hungarian Democratic Forum and the reformist Communists designed to favor Imre Pozsgay's election to the presidency, the radical, minority faction of the opposition succeeded in obtaining the holding of a referendum. The goal of the referendum-seekers was to push back the presidential election (which was to be held by direct popular vote) until after the election of a new Parliament, which would then elect the president. It was meant to assert the political primacy of the Parliament. On November 29, by a very narrow vote, the presidential elections, which Pozsgay was still sure to win just a few weeks earlier, were cancelled. While opinion polls had given the HSWP on the road to transformation 40 percent of decided votes in the summer, at the end of November, after the opening of the Berlin Wall, they were only estimated to have 16 percent support.[5]

Certainly, Soviet commentators close to the dominant ideology recognized that "world socialism" and the East European Communist Parties were undergoing new, and very serious, difficulties and that their relationship to power was changing fundamentally. But, in a more social-democratic than Communist perspective, they stated that, by developing their relations with the other Leftist parties, they could remain one of the essential, determinant political forces within their respective societies, if they knew how "to stay on the 'train' of processes common to all civilizations."[6] Others insisted on the objective resistance which the socioeconomic structure and property relations in Eastern Europe posed to a pure and simple changeover to capitalism.[7] In early 1990, a report of the Bogomolov institute, while recognizing that several Communist

5. See Zoltan D. Barany, "The Hungarian Socialist Party: A Case of Political Miscalculation," *Radio Free Europe Research* (RAD Background Report-227, Hungary), 22 December 1989.

6. See S. Kolesnikov and G. Cherneiko, "V stranakh sotsializma: dostizheniia, problemy, poiski. Vremia peremen" (In the Countries of Socialism: Realizations, Problems and Research. The Time of Changes), *Kommunist*, 18, December 1989, pp. 73–77.

7. See L. Shevtsova, "Kuda idet Vostochnaia Evropa?" (Where is East Europe Going?), *Mirovaia Ekonomika i Mezhdunarodnye Otnosheniia*, 4, April 1990, pp. 86–105.

Parties would be ousted from power, stated that, apart from Poland, there were "strong chances that the GDR, Czechoslovakia, Hungary and Bulgaria will successfully embark on a social-democratic road of the type taken by Sweden. . . ." Whatever the outcome, the report underlined that the changes taking place in the region "cannot adequately be characterized by the old bipolar categories of a 'capitalist-socialist' view of the world."[8]

The efforts made by *perestroika*'s leaders and ideologues to downsize the upheavals going on in Eastern Europe can be explained in several different ways. They were aimed at not ceding too much ground to their political adversaries within the USSR. But it also simultaneously helped them to rationalize what was happening and not to lose, all of a sudden, the compass which had guided them up to that point. Between rationalization and belief, the border is often very fine or even impossible to draw, and we are touching here on the complex issue of the role of ideology in political action. Soviet leaders still needed to give a meaning to their actions, even when these began seriously slipping away from them. This writer asked Gorbachev, in light of the remarks (cited at the beginning of this chapter) he had made to Ceausescu in early December 1989, well after the fall of the Berlin Wall, if he really believed that reformed socialism still had a chance in Eastern Europe or if it had been statement of convenience, given his interlocutor. He answered: "Yes, at that moment, we believed that the guarantee of real freedom of choice and of real sovereignty in Central and Eastern Europe would act in favor of socialism."[9]

In a speech given to a foreign audience at the end of December 1989, Eduard Shevardnadze made remarks in this regard that must be considered significant. Speaking before the European Parliament in a slightly defensive tone, he warned against "the eagerness to make declarations about the end of History and of socialism." What was necessary, he said, was to make "a distinction between a specific model of socialism . . . and the idea of socialism as a component of the global process of civilization." Speaking of Eastern Europe, he declared himself "convinced that socialist-type orientations will continue to guide these societies." He

8. Marina P. Sil'vanskaia and Vyacheslav Dashichev, *Preobrazovaniia v Vostochnoi Evrope i pozitsiia SSSR (The Transformations in Eastern Europe and the Position of the USSR)*, nonpublished report to the Central Committee; text presented to the author by Marina Sil'vanskaia.

9. M. S. Gorbachev, *Otvety na voprosy professora Zh. Leveka (Responses to Questions from Professor Jacques Lévesque)*, Moscow, 12 July 1995.

chose to see the recent events as proof of the compatibility between Western values and those defended by Gorbachev in the USSR, and of East-West convergence: "Now, while socialism is undergoing an evolutionary process, it is legitimate to dream and to speak of the future as a time when, on the basis of new, common, universal values, a synthesis of the best and most generous realizations of political and social thinking on a world scale will become reality."[10]

Still abroad, but this time in private during the Malta summit, Gorbachev made similar remarks to George Bush. Joined by Yakovlev, he asked his American counterpart, with some irritation, "Why are democracy, transparency and the market [!] 'Western' values?" Bush responded that this was "because they have long been those of the United States and Western Europe," to which Gorbachev retorted, with insistence, that "they are also ours" and that "they are universal values."[11] It was as if he feared that the USSR might be in the process of losing its own identity.

His illusions about the preservation of a certain form of socialism in the region seemed to be supported by the new leaders there, or maybe by how he chose to understand what they were saying. He relates, for instance, that during a meeting with President Vaclav Havel in February 1990, the latter had told him that it was erroneous "to believe that Czechoslovakia will return to capitalism."[12] Havel supposedly even added that "if the Soviet press were to state that I want to liquidate socialism, they would be mistaken."

Nearly one year later, at the end of 1990, when Communist reformers had been ousted from power nearly everywhere in Eastern Europe, and the new governments were doing everything in their power to eradicate the entire Communist and socialist legacy, Yakovlev (who at that time had been totally marginalized within Gorbachev's entourage) told Lilly Marcou:

> Despite the confusion of the current situation, I believe that the Left will win. Through the return to universal values and the process of European integration, the socialist idea is taking root in Europe. The way out of this dead end that was the Cold War will be through *perestroika* in the USSR and through the evolution in the other East European nations. In the middle range, a great

10. *Pravda*, 20 December 1989.
11. Transcript of the conversation reprinted in Mikhail Gorbachev, *Avant Mémoires* (Paris: Odile Jacob, 1993), p. 127.
12. Gorbachev, *Erinnerungen*, p. 887.

process of positive reappraisal of what has been rejected is inevitable; in the long range, the Left will rediscover other horizons. For the moment, the people are refusing socialism: the idea has stumbled on the real conditions of East European countries; it was destroyed by the Stalinist counterrevolution. Now that the Stalinist model has been eliminated, we will see the emergence of a post-Thermodor socialism. This new socialism, which will no longer know bureaucratic oppression, will be made in the name of mankind.[13]

Several years later, in 1994, the entourage of Gorbachev, with the exception of Yakovlev, who was no longer part of it, could take some consolation from the return of the reformed Communists to power in Poland, Hungary, and Bulgaria, and to see in it "a positive reappraisal of what has been rejected." But in 1990, the crest of the wave had yet to come—and it was to come for the Soviet Union itself.

THE CPSU'S ADAPTATION

If the whole Soviet political world was caught unprepared, to varying degrees, by the collapse of the East European regimes, it must be said that Gorbachev and his team were able to recover more quickly than their conservative adversaries. This fact is all the more striking since the conservatives, without having been able to predict the pace, had not stopped warning in private about the disastrous consequences which the Party leadership's policy risked engendering. Nonetheless, it took them several months before they were able to offer Gorbachev's policies a resistance that was relatively efficient and sustained. This opposition only began to be felt as such from September 1990. The chronic incapacity of the conservative forces to reverse Gorbachev's policies, if not to overthrow the leader himself, constitutes one of the most remarkable characteristics of the political process that lasted from his accession to power until the end of the USSR. It is notably due to their strongly ingrained habit to operate under a clearly identified command and in solidly established institutional framework and rules.[14] But this subject, in itself, would merit an in-depth study.

---

13. Aleksandr Yakovlev, *Ce que nous voulons faire de l'Union soviétique, Entretiens avec Lilly Marcou* (Paris: Le Seuil, 1991), p. 104.

14. Ligachev's memoirs bear eloquent witness to his continual loyalty to the cadre and to the leading bodies of the Party, and ultimately to Gorbachev himself, despite the continual political divergences with him and his circle. See Yegor Ligachev, *Inside Gorbachev's Kremlin* (New York: Pantheon Books, 1993).

In the months that followed the collapse of the East European regimes, and in large measure as a result of it, the reformist camp in the Soviet Union fragmented, with the most radical elements abandoning the Party and even the idea of reformed socialism itself.

In a surprising way, it was Gorbachev and his immediate entourage who succeeded in getting back on track most quickly. As he had been able to do with success in the past under difficult conditions, the Soviet leader again managed to retake the initiative in order to accelerate changes within the USSR. It somewhat resembled the aftermath of the March 1989 elections for the Congress of People's Deputies (CPD), when, faced with the unexpected extent of the apparatus's defeat, he had seized the opportunity and demoted a considerable number of Central Committee members—something he had not been able or dared to do before.

If the Soviet leadership had great difficulties recognizing the new realities in Eastern Europe and adapting itself to them, it was still, overall, adjustment which won out over resistance, in its global political approach and its "program," even if this term, which presupposes an articulated, structured vision, cannot truly be adequate. Tangible proof of this is offered by the Central Committee's adoption in early February 1990 of a resolution, which Gorbachev succeeded in pushing through, abandoning Article 6 of the Soviet constitution, which guaranteed the Communist Party's leading role. At the same time, he had the principle of political party pluralism adopted, with the conditions of accreditation remaining to be fixed by a new law. This was a crucial step in the process of social-democratization which the CPSU never fully achieved. The decisions pushed through by Gorbachev actually meant the abandonment of the "dictatorship of the proletariat" (in reality, the dictatorship of the Party), which had been the main traditional line of demarcation between Leninism and social democracy. They sought to give a new legal, definitive form to the slogan of *perestroika,* according to which power for the Party ought to be gained and preserved through political means. These decisions did not, though, signify an admission of socialism's possible defeat in the USSR. On the contrary, they were aimed at assuring its viability through its adaptation to the "universal values." On the other hand, the preservation of a certain number of safeguards, notably on the ownership of land, were to continue to be ensured by law.

One can see a dialectic relation between the evolution of Gorbachev and the CPSU, and the events in Eastern Europe. On the one hand, it was marked by a willingness of the Soviet Union to adapt, to a certain extent, to the new realities which had been created in Eastern Europe. On the other, as we have seen in chapter 7, the issue of party pluralism had already been debated, behind closed doors, in the CPSU leadership during the summer of 1989. That is why the Gorbachev leadership was able to accept, even though with considerable reluctance, the transformations which took place in the region in late 1989. In a certain way, one can agree with Karoly Grosz when he says: "It is not the collapse of the East European regimes that led to the collapse of the USSR. . . . It is the opposite which took place."[15] If the USSR's collapse is understood as being the erosion of Leninism, then it is indeed due to this that the Soviet leaders accepted and encouraged the political changes which led to the earthquake of 1989.

The opposite of Grosz's proposition nonetheless remains true as well. Just as the fall of the Berlin Wall precipitated the collapse of the East European regimes, the latter also gave a formidable accelerating push to the USSR's implosion, which had hardly begun in 1989. And just like the countries of Eastern Europe flooded through the breach which opened up in the Berlin Wall, Lithuania would seek, as of early 1990, to escape through the enormous chasm which had suddenly been formed to the west, in its immediate neighborhood.

THE BALTIC REPUBLICS: A DOMESTIC MICROCOSM OF EASTERN EUROPE

Mikhail Gorbachev's policy toward developments taking place in the Baltic republics in 1989 is extremely revelatory about Soviet policy in Eastern Europe during the same period and helps to illuminate it. The parallels in the Soviet leadership's approach and behavior are striking on several levels. But the parallels stop in 1990. However, the parallels of 1989 as well as Soviet behavior of 1990 and 1991 with respect to the Baltic states allow for rejecting the thesis that the Soviet leaders had wanted to abandon or get rid of Eastern Europe.

The creation of the Popular Fronts in the Baltic republics in the summer and fall of 1989 was perceived in Moscow by Gorbachev and his reformist assistants as a positive development. In fact, the Lithuanian front "Sajudis" ("the Movement"), which was to become the most radical of the fronts, had taken as its full name "the Movement for *Perestroika.*" Clearly nationalist from the beginning, it did not immediately

15. See chapter 7.

advocate independence or separation. As we have already underscored, at least 50 percent of its members were also members of the Communist Party, and the latter's first secretary had participated with benevolence and consent at its founding congress. In both Moscow and among the reformist leadership of the Lithuanian Party, a relationship of osmosis between the two organizations was expected to emerge. In this way, the Party was to be "revitalized," becoming more sensitive to national aspirations and giving a more nationalist content to its actions. On the other hand, by joining and enveloping Sajudis, the Party could help to keep nationalism within acceptable limits. We know what happened. From the end of 1988 into 1989, Sajudis became openly pro-independence. Without going that far, the Lithuanian Party, in order to adjust to and follow the general trend, used an increasingly nationalist discourse, concentrating on the demand for sovereignty in various spheres. Despite this, Gorbachev, according to one of his most important lieutenants, bristled on several occasions against Ligachev's alarmism on these questions and his insistent desire to reestablish order there.[16]

In the March 1989 federal elections, Sajudis had won 75 percent of the seats reserved for Lithuania in the USSR Congress of People's Deputies. In addition, if the Lithuanian Party's first secretary, Algirdas Brazauskas, was elected to the CPD, it was because Sajudis did not field an opponent against him. Certainly, the presence of a group of pro-independence deputies in the CPD of the Soviet Union did not modify Lithuania's status. Moreover, Sajudis had not yet set a date for realizing independence. Nonetheless, these events made it possible to predict the turn that the situation in Lithuania could take at the next elections at the level of the Union republics. Two months later, in May, a Politburo meeting, of which we now know the contents, was dedicated to the situation in the Baltic republics. The heads of the Communist Parties of the three republics had been called to Moscow, and a report prepared by six Politburo members was discussed. The report found that a "disaster" (*razgromnaia*) situation existed and underscored that power was in the process of slipping into the hands of the Popular Fronts. At the end of the discussion, Gorbachev outlined the conclusions he had drawn and simultaneously set the course of policy to be followed. Addressing the heads of the Baltic Parties, he told them: "We have confidence in the three

16. See Anatolii Cherniaev, *Shest' let s Gorbachevym: po dnevnikovym zapisiam (Six Years with Gorbachev: From Journal Notes)* (Moscow: Progress Kul'tura, 1993), pp. 249–250.

of you, and it cannot be otherwise. . . . It is impossible that the Popular Fronts, to which 90 percent of the people in the republics adhere, could be considered extremists. We must learn how to have discussions with them."[17] He expressed his conviction that "if we hold a referendum there, none of the three, not even Lithuania, will leave." He recommended delegating governmental responsibilities to the leaders of the Fronts, in order to give them the opportunity (or responsibility) of matching their words to their actions, presuming that it would not be the inverse which would occur. He added that there was no need "to become anxious about a differentiation in their use of sovereignty."

One is struck here by Gorbachev's serenity and the faith he could have in *perestroika*. A given republic's secession seemed to him absurd, and hence unthinkable. He totally underestimated the force of nationalism, persuaded that a number of concessions and adjustments would be enough to appease it. Certain of the Soviet Union's fundamental solidity, he was convinced that it possessed sufficient powers of retention to circumscribe and manage this type of problem, which he visibly did not believe to be a priority. Beyond Yakovlev, he was not the only reformer to see things in this way.[18]

Just as when confronted with other problems, Gorbachev saw in *perestroika* as much a necessity as a panacea. This explains why he added, under the cover of a conclusion, that it was necessary "to ponder and ponder again on how to transform our federation in practice. Otherwise everything will, indeed, disintegrate."[19] Yet, a special Central Committee plenum on the nationalities question, long announced, kept being put off. We also see here Gorbachev's ascendancy in the Politburo at the time, given the way he was able to shrug off rather easily a report of six of its members.

17. See a report of Gorbachev's conclusions in Cherniaev, *Shest' let s Gorbachevym*, p. 295.

18. In February 1989, upon returning to Moscow from a stay in Vilnius, the author of this book had a discussion with the economist Nikolai Shmelev about the situation in Lithuania and the political preponderance that Sajudis and its pro-independence option had secured there. I asked him if he did not believe that this was the most difficult problem which the USSR would have to face in the near future, barring a resort to the mechanisms of repression, with all the consequences that would engender. He expressed the opposite opinion. Speaking of the Lithuanians and the Baltic peoples, he said: "These are civilized people, with whom we will necessarily find common ground. The demands for independence are a bargaining position to gain the maximum possible, but a compromise will certainly be found. The most vexing and dangerous problem is the absence of economic reform taking off."

19. Cherniaev, *Shest' let s Gorbachevym*, p. 295.

Several months later, quite soon after the debacle in Eastern Europe, on December 20, 1989, the Lithuanian Communist Party, despite warnings from Gorbachev, declared its independence from the CPSU. It understood this as a move to adjust itself to the ongoing evolution. Moscow hence formally and definitively lost all control over the Lithuanian Party and therefore over the principal political lever it counted on to retain and circumscribe nationalism in that Baltic republic. Rather courageously, Gorbachev personally went to Vilnius on January 11, 1990, in order to try, by persuasion, to reverse the course of events. It was the first time that a general secretary had gone to the small Lithuanian capital while in power. He mixed with the crowds and harangued them, using all imaginable arguments to convince them of the absurdity and dangers of secession. He expressed thinly veiled threats of economic reprisals. At the same time, he promised a law which would specify the procedures for exercising the right to secession enshrined in the constitution since Stalin's days. The law which was to be promulgated contained enough rules and constraints to make secession practically impossible.

In early March, Sajudis easily won the Lithuanian Supreme Soviet elections. Despite warnings from Moscow and the United States (communicated to the leader of Sajudis by the American ambassador), the new Supreme Soviet unilaterally declared Lithuania's independence on March 11, 1990. This was the first attempt at secession and the first proclamation of independence on the territory of the Soviet Union. Without the collapse in Eastern Europe, Sajudis would still have won the Lithuanian elections, but it certainly would not have dared to defy the center's power so rapidly and totally nor would the Lithuanian Communist Party have dared to leave the CPSU.

Just as in the case of Eastern Europe, Gorbachev's behavior toward Lithuania until the end of 1989—the encouragement given to the Lithuanian Party in its transformations, his permissiveness, the refusal to listen to warnings, and his neglect—might have led to the belief that he had decided to abandon the Baltic republics. His later behavior clearly proved the contrary. Indeed, after having had the Lithuanian declaration of independence voted illegal and without standing by an overwhelming majority of the USSR Supreme Soviet, he used all of the legal, economic, and political means, including the threat of using force, to stop its independence, without going to the ultimate end of his threat. He never accepted the secession of Lithuania and the other Baltic republics.[20] It was only after the August 1991 coup, when he had lost all real power and was under pressure from Yeltsin and the United States, that he was obliged to resign himself to the fait accompli.

In the case of Eastern Europe, which belonged to the sphere of international relations, the means for stopping the course of events were more limited and the possible consequences of their use much more costly. That is why adjustment and adaptation won out over resistance, even if both components remained present. Even if they had to progressively bury their idea of a reformed socialism in Eastern Europe, Gorbachev and Shevardnadze continued to cling, as much as they could, to their project of a new European order. They did so through a constant, forced process of rationalization and adjustment that, at the end of the day, resulted in emptying the project of its initial meaning.

In December 1989, they could state with superficial calm, and not without reason, that a giant step had been taken toward ending the division of Europe and that the Cold War belonged to the past. But the configuration of Europe's possible future was likely to be very different from that which they had envisaged and sought. They began to feel it shortly after the fall of the Berlin Wall. They believed, however, that they had given enough proof of good behavior, and that they still had enough political instruments and guarantees from their foreign partners, to be able to save the essence of their European policy.

The policy which they followed until the summer of 1990 with respect to the process of German reunification gives eloquent testimony to the efforts they deployed to defend the European project which had so conditioned and permeated their policy in Eastern Europe and which continued to do so, even more than before.

20. In his memoirs, Cherniaev recounts how he was harshly dressed down by Gorbachev for suggesting to him in a private conversation that it might be better to let the Baltic republics go (ibid., p. 338).

CHAPTER THIRTEEN

The Reunification and Status of Germany

The Last Battle for Europe

The current position of the Soviet Union formally excludes
the possibility that a united Germany could be a member of
NATO. That opposition does not, of course, signify that the
Soviet leaders do not see the importance for Germany to be
firmly integrated into an international security framework.
The entire question concerns what kind of framework it
will be.

Yuri P. Davydov and Dimitri V. Trenin[1]

Independently of what is now said about NATO, for us it is a
symbol of the past. . . . And we will never be willing to assign
it a leading role in the construction of a new Europe.

Mikhail Gorbachev[2]

HOW TO PREVENT GERMAN REUNIFICATION?

In order to understand the Soviet position on the question of German
reunification at the end of 1989 and in January 1990, we must first of
all put the events into their proper sequence and context.[3] In studying a
period both of acceleration in history and of a telescoping of major
events such as those which interest us here, this is a difficulty with which
we are constantly confronted.

1. Iurii P. Davydov and Dimitrii V. Trenin, "German Unity: The View from Moscow,"
The European Journal of International Affairs, Spring 1990, pp. 75–92.
2. Interview with *Time* magazine, 4 June 1990.
3. Contrary to what is the case concerning the other East European countries, an
enormous literature was published, especially within Germany, but elsewhere as well, on
Soviet policy towards East Germany and German reunification. I therefore do not intend
to embark here upon a detailed study of the facts, gestures, and meanderings of Soviet
behavior on the question. However, I do want to reconstruct its main outlines and display
how they can better illuminate what are, according to me, the objectives which guided the
Soviet approach to all of Eastern Europe in 1989.

One can say today that the fall of the Berlin Wall made German reunification inevitable. But in the context of the event, even if the opening seemed to render it possible, no one among Western or Eastern leaders envisaged reunification as probable or desirable in the near future. Even Chancellor Kohl, who was the first to call for it openly in his November 28 speech, did not foresee its realization before many years.

In a conjuncture where everything in Eastern Europe was slipping away from them, the Soviet leaders very rapidly saw this reunification not as a probability, but as a danger, full of negative consequences, which needed to be immediately prevented. As we have seen, it was not the process, but their loss of control over it, which they feared. The precipitating events and their lack of control did, indeed, risk costing them the various benefits which they had expected from it. They first hoped to forestall the danger of an early reunification by refusing to talk about it. Contrary to Kohl, who said that he wanted to calm the situation by evoking the prospect of German reunification, they stated that this would "destabilize" it. Believing, correctly, that the USSR was an important and absolutely essential actor with respect to this question, they thought it possible to limit Kohl's expectations by rejecting a discussion, and even the idea, of intermediate formulas which might be susceptible to accelerating the process.

Their calculations and expectations did not, however, depend only on an "ostrich strategy." Helmut Kohl's November 28 speech and his ten-point plan had surprised and irritated his Western allies, who had not been consulted. Having remained entirely silent about the foreign or international aspects of the steps which were to lead to reunification, Kohl had, to varying degrees, sown anxiety among everyone, in both East and West. Gorbachev and the other Soviet leaders therefore counted on the reticence and objections of West Germany's allies concerning reunification to help slow down the events.

Only a few days after Kohl's famous speech, Gorbachev had the opportunity, at the Malta summit of December 2, to query his American counterpart with a view to developing a minimal common approach on the question. Bush told him at the time: "We will not engage in any imprudent action and we will not make any attempt to accelerate a solution to the question of reunification. . . . As strange as it may be, you are in the same boat on this question as our allies in NATO. The most conservative among them approve your approach. At the same time, they must think about a moment when the notion of West Germany and East

Germany will have entered the annals of History. On this question, I am going to act prudently. And let our Democrats accuse me of being timid, if they want."[4]

Gorbachev chose to interpret these reassuring words in his own way, and said, notably to his Polish allies, during the Warsaw Pact summit which followed the Malta meeting, that Bush and he shared the same views on the reunification question and that it was not on the agenda.[5] Yet, it was Bush who was the first to rally around his West German ally's approach.[6] For a time, though, things were quite different for France and Britain, who feared the possible consequences of the emergence of a great Germany on the European scene.[7]

On December 6, François Mitterrand met Mikhail Gorbachev in Kiev, and even in his public remarks, the French leader supported his Soviet counterpart's approach.[8] At the end of December, he undertook an official visit to the GDR, with the clear goal of recalling and consolidating its legitimacy as a state. In Britain, Margaret Thatcher more than empathized with France's deep reticence. Given that they were the Federal Republic's allies, they could not offer resistance to Kohl's project that was as open as Gorbachev's. But they did say enough about it to the Soviet leaders that the latter became convinced that "they wanted, evidently, to slow down the process of German reunification, with Gorbachev's hands."[9] In private conversations with his advisers, Mitterrand could not have been more explicit about that. After Kohl's surprise speech of November 28, advocating reunification, Mitterrand said angrily, "He did not tell me anything! Nothing at all! I will never

4. From notes taken by Gorbachev's assistant: Anatolii Cherniaev, *Shest' let s Gorbachevym: po dnevnikovym zapisiam (Six Years with Gorbachev: From Journal Notes)* (Moscow: Progress Kul'tura, 1993), p. 310.

5. Interview with M. Rakowski, Warsaw, 3 March 1993.

6. It has now been very well demonstrated and documented that Bush not only supported Kohl but also played a very active and crucial role in neutralizing British and French opposition. See Philip Zelikow and Condoleezza Rice, *Germany Unified and Transformed* (Cambridge: Harvard University Press, 1995), pp. 102–148.

7. Gorbachev gave instructions for Soviet policy to be "more closely coordinated with that of France and Britain." Mikhail Gorbachev [Michail Gorbatschow], *Erinnerungen (Memoirs)* (Berlin: Siedler Verlag, 1995), p. 715; translated from German for this book by Laure Castin.

8. In a joint press conference in Kiev, after having recalled that France was Germany's ally, François Mitterrand declared that "no European country can act without taking into consideration the others' opinions . . . and the situation inherited from the Second World War" (*Pravda*, 7 December 1989).

9. Those are the words of his international affairs assistant; see Cherniaev, *Shest' let s Gorbachevym*, p. 310.

forget it! Gorbachev will be furious: he will not allow that to happen. It is impossible! I will not need to oppose that, the Soviets will do it for me."[10] That is, more or less, what Bush had understood and said to Gorbachev in Malta.

Again, it was the dynamics of events on the ground that upset the political leaders' calculations. In mid-January, the Modrow government's intention to preserve a "reformed" Stasi provoked riots and the occupation of its offices. Even the East German army showed signs of disintegration while emigration continued. If the East German regime had already collapsed, this time it was the state which began to crumble. Modrow was obliged to open his government to all political forces while awaiting the results of elections initially scheduled to take place in June but finally brought forward to March 18. For his part, in order to limit an immigration which threatened to grow even more, Kohl decided that a monetary union had to be achieved rapidly by extending the West German mark to the East.[11] It was a step which was initially planned to come about much further down the road toward unification. In fact, it was the entire process which he found appropriate to accelerate.

The Soviet leaders realized that they had to adjust to the new situation. They did it so grudgingly that they found themselves thereafter constantly out of step with the dynamics of the events. During a visit to Moscow at the end of January, Hans Modrow restated the Soviet-approved project of a "contractual community" between the two Germanys. On February 2, Gorbachev sent Kohl a message in which he gave his approval to "a contractual community as *a step on the way* to a Confederation between the two German states."[12] The Soviet leader was starting from Kohl's point of departure on November 28. To the great relief of his German interlocutor, Gorbachev told him clearly, eight days later, during a face-to-face meeting, that he accepted the principle of German unity.

Nonetheless, the Soviet leaders still envisaged that its realization should take place over a number of years. Even at a later stage, Shevardnadze still spoke of ten years.[13] There was certainly in this an inten-

10. Jacques Attali, *Verbatim III* (Paris: Fayard, 1995), p. 350.

11. "If we do not want them to come to the DM, then the DM must come to them," was the pithy formula of Kohl's principal adviser on reunification, Horst Teltschik. See excerpts from his diary in *Der Spiegel*, 30 September 1991, pp. 118–140; translated from German for this book by Laure Castin.

12. See Teltschik, ibid.; emphasis added.

13. *Izvestiia*, 20 June 1990.

tion to slow things down and a lack of farsightedness. But, here again, their approach was not without foundation in political reality. They had very good reasons to count on an SPD victory in the elections that were to take place in the GDR in March. All of the polls showed the party would be victorious.[14] The SPD, for its part, foresaw a much less rapid reunification than Kohl's party. Fearing for the survival of the majority of East German enterprises and the social consequences of a brutal transition to the market economy, it envisaged longer stages.[15] In addition, it favored negotiations by the GDR on the conditions of creating a new German state, rather than, as was in fact to happen, its absorption by the Federal Republic.

At the end of January, during a meeting of what Falin called the "crisis committee"[16] on the German question created by Gorbachev, Cherniaev suggested that it was necessary to seek an understanding with Kohl rather than with the SPD. Shevardnadze, he says, was in agreement, but Falin, Yakovlev, and Shakhnazarov thought it expedient to bet on the SPD.[17] Gorbachev, unsurprisingly, believed that both ought to be cultivated. He did, nonetheless, reject a suggestion from Cherniaev, who had gone so far as to propose cancelling Modrow's planned visit, arguing that the latter no longer represented anything.

The head of the SPD, Oscar Lafontaine, came to Moscow himself on the eve of the elections, and Gorbachev told him of his hope that the Social Democrats would win the East German elections. More than any other item, it was on the crucial question of a future unified Germany's international status that the convergence of views between the USSR and the SPD was strongest and most important for the Soviet leaders.[18] And so, its unexpected defeat was received as a new shock in Moscow.

14. In his diary entry dated 14 March, Teltschik mentions one poll that gave 20 percent of the vote to his party and 44 percent to the SPD, which could therefore hope to win an absolute majority of the seats in the GDR Parliament (*Der Spiegel,* 30 September 1991).

15. *Izvestiia,* 21 February 1990.

16. Valentin Falin, *Politische Erinnerungen (Political Memoirs)* (Munich: Droemer Knaur, 1993), pp. 489–490; translated from German for this book by Laure Castin. The members of this committee, in addition to Gorbachev, were Yakovlev, Shevardnadze, Iazov, Kriuchkov, Cherniaev, Shakhnazarov, and Falin himself.

17. Cherniaev, *Shest' let s Gorbachevym,* pp. 346–347.

18. See Daniel Dignard, *Analyse d'une prise de décision: l'acceptation de l'unification allemande par l'URSS en 1989–1990* (Master's thesis in political science, Montréal, Université du Québec à Montréal, 1992).

WHERE AND HOW TO "ANCHOR" A UNIFIED GERMANY?

From the moment that Helmut Kohl made his famous speech on November 28, 1989, even if he did not say a word about it, the principal and most troubling problem that it posed for the rest of the world was, obviously, the place of a greater Germany in the international system. This was the question that Gorbachev immediately raised in the flood of reproaches he addressed to Kohl through the West German foreign minister, Hans-Dietrich Genscher.[19] The European system which Gorbachev had envisaged was far from being sufficiently developed to incorporate German reunification into it, and the rapid realization of the latter could imperil the former's premises and foundations. It was first of all, and mainly, this danger the Soviet leaders had wanted to prevent by refusing to discuss even the principle of reunification.

With a lesser sense of danger, but nonetheless with anxiety, this was the same question that Western leaders immediately asked themselves. Very shortly after Kohl's speech, George Bush demanded, as the only condition, that the new Germany be a part of NATO. Before seeking to reassure the Soviets, Kohl obviously needed to reassure his own allies, and he rapidly gave them the demanded guarantee, without wondering about its consequences. His European allies were far from being entirely convinced, fearing the place a unified Germany would take in NATO and the configuration the organization would have as a result.

For seven months, from December 1989 to July 1990, the question of a united Germany's membership in NATO became the principal international nightmare for the Soviet leadership. The opposition which they maintained with obstinacy during this period seemed like some kind of ultimate combat to save something of their grand design for a new international order in Europe and the place which they saw the USSR occupying in it.

Let us first of all distinguish the respective importance of their problems. The prospect of the incorporation of a unified Germany into NATO clearly implied a very serious modification of the military equilibrium in Europe, and an equal reduction in the USSR's relative military power. Gorbachev was sufficiently preoccupied with the USSR's international power to be sensitive about this aspect of things. Even if

19. See chapter 8.

he was ready to considerably downsize the meaning and foundations of strategic parity, it was still a notion to which he remained attached. However, this was an area of concern that was much more troublesome for the military and the conservative political leaders than it was for Gorbachev's inner circle. Cherniaev, Gorbachev's adviser on international affairs, for example, reports that Ligachev, during this period, did not cease to "scream" that "NATO is drawing closer to the USSR's borders."[20] Even publicly, he evoked the danger of a new German threat.[21] And military leaders, of course, underscored the serious change which would result for the balance of forces from the integration of a greater Germany into NATO.[22]

On several occasions, Gorbachev invoked the security problems which would result from this for the USSR. But, for leaders like himself, Shevardnadze, and Yakovlev, who were the most pro-Western Politburo members, another question of different importance than military balance and security was at stake. If Germany became integrated into NATO, then the Warsaw Pact's raison d'etre and survival would be seriously threatened, as we did in fact witness; the same would be true of CMEA. The Warsaw Pact was the USSR's main structural affiliation with Europe and the most important framework for its influence in European affairs. If NATO were to become larger, while the Warsaw Pact disappeared and nothing emerged to replace it, the USSR risked being completely marginalized in European political affairs, and hence relegated to the fringes of Asia. And yet, as we have often underscored, one of *perestroika*'s principal objectives was precisely to integrate the USSR into Europe structurally, and as solidly as possible.

The disarray and obstinacy which the Soviet leaders demonstrated throughout all the discussions and negotiations surrounding German reunification must be understood in this context.

This is an opportune point at which to open a parenthetical note that underlines the contemporaneity of this problem and its resurgence in a very different context, but one that presents several analogies. After the disappearance of the Warsaw Pact and of the USSR itself, it is the East European states' adhesion to NATO which began to appear on the agenda, as early as 1993. The radical pro-Western Russian leaders, who had chased Gorbachev out of power and wanted to dissolve

20. Cherniaev, *Shest' let s Gorbachevym*, p. 347.
21. *Pravda*, 7 February 1990.
22. See the article by I. Vladimirov in *Krasnaia Zvezda*, 15 March 1990.

the USSR so as to better integrate Russia into the "civilized world," still occupied the most powerful political positions in Moscow. The Eastern European countries' potential membership in NATO has been the subject of vehement opposition from the nationalists, the "centrists," and the radical pro-Western group, here again for very different reasons. The nationalists, military, and centrists have seen in the extension of NATO up to the borders of the former Soviet Union a Western penetration into Russia's traditional sphere of influence and a threat to its strategic and geopolitical interests. The radical Westernizers, including former Prime Minister Yegor Gaidar, understood it as a new structuring of Europe that still excluded Russia and put it even more on the outer periphery of the continent. They saw it as a disavowal and a rebuff of their foreign policy, the prime objective of which had been, at any price and as rapidly as possible, to link Russia to Western international institutions. That rebuff, according to them, can only delegitimize their policy and abet the nationalists and those pining for the old regime. In order to dissuade their Western partners from proceeding, they used the "blackmail" threat of nationalism on them, somewhat as Gorbachev had "warned" François Mitterrand in Kiev that the West would soon see a general taking his place if German reunification happened "prematurely."

Gorbachev's fundamental preoccupation with respect to a unified Germany's inclusion in NATO is easy to discern, since it appeared in the private and public declarations of the Soviet leaders, even before they had accepted the principle of German unification.

In his speech to the European Parliament on December 20, 1989, Eduard Shevardnadze, while firmly insisting on the preservation of the GDR, stated that the future of the two German states would later be determined "in the framework of the pan-European process's development."[23] He reaffirmed that such a process should take place on the basis "of a decisive dismantling of the structure of military confrontation, parallel to the planning and construction . . . of structures of integration in different spheres which will advance the formation of a truly unified Europe."

At the beginning of March, after the USSR had been compelled to accept the principle of German reunification, Gorbachev stated, and not for the first or last time, that the integration of the future Germany into

---

23. *Pravda,* 20 December 1989.

NATO was "absolutely out of question."[24] He recalled that "progress toward reunification" ought to take place "stage by stage," and that this process "should be linked to the process of European rapprochement, which also needs to be accelerated." The most eloquent and clear terms used to express the Soviet position were those of a *Pravda* commentator: "The process of German unification should be *organically linked and synchronized* with the European process and the creation of an essentially new security structure in Europe, a structure which would replace the alliances. That is the official Soviet position."[25]

The new security structure, as mentioned by Gorbachev in his press conference, was to be put in place through the reinforcement and institutionalization of the Conference on Security and Cooperation in Europe (CSCE). This organization was to surpass and replace the alliances threatened in the future by German reunification. In this structure for coordinating European security, the USSR would have occupied an important place. But it was still only embryonic and its "operationality" was still far from being in place. That is why the United States preferred the more familiar and reassuring framework of NATO.

From the Soviet perspective, the whole problem lay in the synchronization. To achieve it, it would have been necessary to slow down the pace of German unification on the one hand and to accelerate the establishment of a new European security system on the other. Both were of course very difficult tasks to achieve.

When the Soviets accepted the principle of German unification at the end of January, they did so in the framework of the Modrow plan, which foresaw the neutrality of a future single Germany. That was the position to which the USSR held until after the March 18 elections in East Germany. The Soviet leaders knew very well that the prospect of a greater neutral Germany was one of the most worrisome scenarios for Western governments, as it also was for them. Germany's neutrality would have called into question the existence of NATO just as much as that of the Warsaw Pact,[26] not to mention the negative images that the idea of a greater Germany, totally free in its foreign and military policies, evoked

24. Remarks made at a press conference given on the occasion of another visit by Hans Modrow to Moscow (*Pravda,* 7 March 1990).
25. Yuri Solton, 21 February 1990, Foreign Broadcast Information Service, FBIS-SOV-90–039, 27 February 1990; emphasis added.
26. That was precisely the meaning of Gorbachev's warning to Genscher on December 5, 1989 in opposing the idea of premature reunification: "What would NATO mean without the Federal Republic?" See chapter 8.

in the West. That is why the Soviet demand for a neutral Germany must be seen less as a serious proposition (which, incidentally, was not relevant for the near future) than as a way of upsetting the West and pressing it to put in place a new collective European security system to better tie down Germany, with the USSR's participation. Moreover, it was also the approach favored by Germany's Social Democrats.

After the East German elections of March 18, this entire approach, fragile from the beginning, was untenable. The possible stages and potential allies slipped away completely. Several weeks later, a victorious Helmut Kohl stated his intention to realize unity before the end of the year. Even the SPD rallied to the idea of integrating a united Germany into NATO. France, which had until then itself sought to slow down the process, reluctantly decided to support Kohl's policy, in exchange for his assurance of the implementation of a political construction which would reinforce the European Community. This could only accentuate the difference between the two parts of Europe.

Despite these setbacks, it would take another four long months before the Soviet Union brought itself to accept a united Germany's integration into NATO.

AN ERRATIC BATTLE FROM BEHIND

Despite its long duration, and the permanence of the preoccupations which we have just indicated, the struggle against a united Germany's membership in NATO was far from being coherently organized by the Soviet leaders. It was also not led with equal conviction on their part. This is not surprising given the extremely difficult and changing conditions in which the battle took place and the disarray to which they necessarily gave rise.

Valentin Falin reports that as early as the end of November 1989 and the first meeting of the "crisis committee" on the German question, some of Gorbachev's advisers already had a defeatist attitude, suggesting that Moscow needed to accept the idea that a united Germany would join NATO and to find a way of "saving face."[27] He himself, supported on this by Yakovlev, strongly opposed such an approach. Falin, who accuses Shevardnadze and Gorbachev of being soft and reproaches the latter

---

27. Falin, *Politische Erinnerungen,* p. 489. In his own memoirs, Cherniaev (*Shest' let s Gorbachevym*) confirms that he indeed had such an attitude.

for having ultimately capitulated before the demands of Kohl and the
West, reports that, at the meeting, the general secretary did not take a
very firm position.[28] This was often his habit and a way of keeping the
middle ground. But as we shall see, beyond his public positions already
cited, he would much later show an attitude of categorical refusal behind
closed doors, in the Politburo for instance.

Publicly, among high-level leaders close to Gorbachev, it was indeed
Falin who expressed the most hard-line position, threatening that the
USSR would veto reunification "if the Western alliance holds fast to its
demand to integrate all of Germany into NATO."[29]

In order to reinforce its bargaining position, the USSR sought as much
as possible to have the negotiations take place within the framework of
the victorious coalition which triumphed over Hitler's Germany. As is
common knowledge, the 1945 Yalta and Potsdam accords required una-
nimity for fixing the conditions of reconstituting the German state and
of a peace treaty with it. In addition, the massive presence of its troops
in East Germany gave the USSR a de facto veto right, which it avoided
invoking openly. That is precisely where the paradox in the Soviet position on Germany's future lay. It was very strong on the legal and military level, but very weak in the political sphere not only because of the
unraveling of the GDR, but also due to the crucial importance Moscow
attached to good relations with the Western powers, and especially with
West Germany, of which it became, progressively, *volens nolens,* a
hostage.

When the United States proposed the formula "2 plus 4" (the two
Germanys for the internal aspects and the four Potsdam signatories for
the international issues) as the framework for negotiations on reunification, the Soviet leaders insisted that the formula be reversed.[30] In proposing to call the negotiations "4 plus 2," they intended to underscore the
primacy of international arrangements and the rights of the four victorious powers. Yet, on February 14, on the fringes of the "Open Skies"
conference in Ottawa, which brought together the foreign ministers of
the two alliances' twenty-three members, an agreement was announced
on the calling of a "2 plus 4" conference. In his memoirs, Falin accuses

28. Ibid.
29. *Boston Globe,* cited by Hannes Adomeit, "Gorbachev and German Unification:
Revision of Thinking, Realignment of Power," *Problems of Communism,* 39, July-August
1990, pp. 1–23.
30. Falin, *Politische Erinnerungen,* pp. 490–491.

Shevardnadze of having, on his own authority, altered the Soviet position in order to please Genscher and of having minimized the importance of the question.[31] Indeed, Genscher had insisted on the "2 plus 4" formula precisely to avoid the Federal Republic's appearing to be a power under trusteeship. After the Christian Democrats' victory in the East German elections of March 18, it was the two Christian Democrat Germanys, or rather Bonn, which set the terms and conditions of the process. As one observer noted, the "2 plus 4" formula hence became a "5 against 1" formula.[32]

From then on, the USSR's lonely struggle was kept up in an impulsive fashion, without a very clear vision of what it wanted and hoped to truly, concretely obtain by preserving objectives that were becoming increasingly less realistic.

At the end of March, a Politburo meeting endorsed a list of directives for Shevardnadze, who was to go to Washington and meet President Bush at the beginning of April. We obtained a copy of this list in Moscow. The document begins with a remarkable admission of weakness. Shevardnadze is first told to emphasize to the American president "the utility of overcoming the temptation which is showing in his administration to use the difficulties we are undergoing in Eastern Europe and in our country in order to obtain unilateral advantages. . . ."[33] The minister is instructed to "show the illusory character of the idea that the USSR could, under pressure, reconcile itself with the de facto Anschluss of the GDR" and "to make it clearly understood to the president that we cannot be in agreement with a united Germany's joining NATO." The Politburo's instructions did not demand German neutrality any more. But, at the same time, they also did not propose any precise alternative, visibly as a result of the lack of a clear and realistic consensus among the leaders themselves. The document simply stipulated, still to Bush's attention, that it "is necessary to seek solutions acceptable to all" and "to develop concrete ideas," without formulating any. Even if its realization seemed ever more difficult, the Politburo still insisted on "synchronization with the pan-European process" and, in order to do so, on the "institution-

31. Ibid., p. 492.
32. Walter Schütze, "Les aspects extérieurs de la réunification allemande," *Allemagne d'aujourd'hui*, 119, October-December 1990, pp. 6–21.
33. "Ukazaniia dlia besedy Ministra inostrannykh del SSSR c Prezidentom SShA, Dzh. Bushem" (Instructions for the meeting of the USSR Foreign Affairs Minister with the U.S.A. president, George Bush), Archives of the Ts Kh S D, 89 kollektsiia, perechen' 9, dokument 100 (*sekretno*).

alization of the Helsinki process."[34] Without making it a necessary condition, the Politburo stressed that the best approach was "a peace treaty which would draw a final line under the last war and would define Germany's politico-military status." In any case, and this represented a toughening of the Soviet position, the document clearly affirmed that "until the creation of new European security structures, the rights and responsibilities of the four powers in German affairs, including the presence of military missions, should be fully preserved."[35]

As Falin points out in his memoirs, and is also underscored by our source for this document, Shevardnadze sometimes took his liberties with the Politburo. Benefitting from the confusion which had settled into relations between the Party and the state, he often only answered for his actions to Gorbachev, who left him a significant margin of action. This later allowed Gorbachev to let his minister suffer the sting of conservative criticism. Therefore, it was bit by bit that the Politburo recommendations appeared in Shevardnadze's position during the first "2 plus 4" meetings.[36] In the first place, in Washington, he put forward, as a "concrete idea" likely to be the most "acceptable to everyone," the not entirely new notion of a united Germany's simultaneous membership in NATO and the Warsaw Pact.[37] This became the principal proposal of the various formulas advanced by Moscow. The United States immediately refused it, stating that this was simply a proposal for neutrality in a new guise. This was absolutely incorrect from a military security point of view, as Germany would have hence been doubly tied or "anchored." It was, however, true from a political perspective, to the extent that the formula would have permitted the USSR to influence the foreign policy orientations of a united Germany rather than leaving it to an international framework which was entirely foreign to Moscow.

At the beginning of May, on the eve of the first official session of the "2 plus 4" conference, there was a "very tense" Politburo meeting, according to Cherniaev.[38] He tells us that Gorbachev got carried away and exclaimed: "We will not let Germany join NATO, and that's that. I

34. Ibid.
35. Ibid.
36. See notably his speech at the opening of the "2 plus 4" conference (*Izvestiia*, 7 May 1990).
37. While simultaneously stating that there could be other scenarios and that double membership could appear to be naive. See *Izvestiia*, 8 April 1990.
38. Cherniaev, *Shest' let s Gorbachevym*, p. 347.

would even go so far as calling off the Vienna arms negotiations, but I will not allow it." Intimidated, Yakovlev, Kriuchkov, and Yazov who, with Shevardnadze, had signed a working document which was less rigid (Cherniaev does not specify its content), did not dare to make any reply. We see here that Gorbachev was not, or at least not always, as "indecisive" as Falin suggests. His intransigent words could be explained by Ligachev's presence in the Politburo and by the growing pressure of the conservatives. But they equally reflect Gorbachev's own objections and his difficulty in accepting defeat on this issue.

The only concrete "reprisal" which was made against Western obstinacy was the announcement, in May, of the suspension of the partial Soviet military withdrawal from the GDR, which was part of the unilateral measures announced before the United Nations by Gorbachev in December 1988.

Given the impossibility of finding a quick solution on the basis of the Soviet bottom-line demand, Shevardnadze decided to propose a decoupling of the internal and international aspects of unification. In other words, unification could go ahead as rapidly as the Germans wanted, and the difficult determination of the new state's international status would be put off until later. In the meantime, Germany would temporarily remain in both alliances. This situation would have favored the transformation of NATO and the Warsaw Pact, and their fusion into a new collective security system.[39] But the Germans were the most opposed of all to any decoupling that would have left the new Germany a state with limited sovereignty.

Parallel to double membership, Moscow was also putting forward, gropingly, other options which reflected a certain confusion but which always had in common its refusal of a full German integration into NATO. This is how, notably, the proposal came about of giving Germany a status in NATO similar to that of France; that is, it would be a member of the alliance but not a part of its military organization. Such a solution would have given a measure of satisfaction to the Soviet military and conservatives. At the same time, it would have sufficiently weakened NATO and threatened its existence, making the establishment of a new European security structure an urgent priority. The United

---

39. See E. Shevardnadze, "Towards a Greater Europe—the Warsaw Treaty Organization and NATO in a Renewing Europe," *NATO's Sixteen Nations,* April-June 1990, pp. 18–22; cited by G. Wettig, *Changes in Soviet Policy towards the West* (Boulder: Westview Press, 1991), p. 163.

States was not hostile to a certain pan-European structure and to an institutionalization of the CSCE, but on the strict condition that this not be a step toward the dissolution of NATO and that the latter not be subordinated to any new structures or organizations. Beyond that, they—just like the Germans—were prepared to make a whole series of concessions permitting Gorbachev to save face.

This issue was the subject of much debate during Gorbachev's visit to the United States in early June and in his meetings with George Bush. In Washington, it had been hoped that the summit would produce an agreement on the main point of contention. That was not to happen. Yet, from various signals they received, the Americans had the impression that Gorbachev was getting ready to give way. On this score, a controversial episode was later reported. At a given moment, during a conversation with Bush, Gorbachev reportedly declared that the Germans themselves should have the right to decide the alliance of their choice. Bush, surprised, asked him if he would be willing to repeat that remark. Gorbachev responded by an affirmative sign, but the exchange was interrupted by a long declaration from Falin against any notion of Germany's integration into NATO.[40] In his memoirs, Falin states that this is an incorrect interpretation and that Gorbachev's nod was addressed to him, indicating that he (Falin) should express and elaborate the reasons for Soviet opposition.[41] It does, in fact, seem unlikely that he would have permitted himself to interrupt Gorbachev in the presence of the U.S. president. But the Americans saw in other signals evidence of a weakening of the Soviet leader's opposition.[42] Curiously, but mistakenly, Gorbachev, for his part, also had the impression that Bush would end up giving in. Immediately after one of his meetings with his American counterpart, Gorbachev confided to Falin, as the latter reports in his memoirs, "We were right not to listen to Eduard [Shevardnadze]. It is difficult to estimate what will happen, but, in any case, the Americans do have in reserve alternatives to Germany's participation in NATO."

If Gorbachev was not yet ready to resign himself to that option, he was already thinking up all sorts of imaginable (and less imaginable)

---

40. See M. R. Beschloss and Strobe Talbott, *At the Highest Levels* (Boston: Little, Brown, 1993), p. 220.

41. Falin, *Politische Erinnerungen*, p. 493.

42. See Zelikow and Rice, *Germany Unified*, pp. 277–279.

scenarios. This is how he, in hypothetical form, asked Bush about the idea of the USSR joining NATO. George Bush responded with a quip, stating that he doubted the Soviet military was ready to serve under American command. The meaning of Gorbachev's question is quite clear. In desperation, membership of the Soviet Union in NATO would have transformed the latter into a new European security structure of which it would have been a full member.[43] Here again, it is the same dilemma which faced the Russian leaders in 1993 when the question of extending NATO to the other East European countries first arose.

After the Bush-Gorbachev summit, the Soviet position seemed to harden, to the extent that the 28th (and last) CPSU Congress in July approached and that it seemed as if an offensive by the conservatives there would score an important victory. To everyone's surprise, the opposite occurred. Gorbachev's dramatic counteroffensive ended in an unexpected success. Ligachev, who put his name up as candidate for the post of deputy general secretary, was defeated by Gorbachev's candidate and retired from public life. This was the last, and very ephemeral, victory of Gorbachev over the conservatives. The room to maneuver which he reconquered allowed him to settle the German question, but practically against all the objectives which had been the most important of his foreign policy.

IN THE ABSENCE OF EUROPE, GERMANY

It was not in the framework of the "2 plus 4" negotiations and conference, designed for this purpose, that agreement was reached on the international conditions of German reunification. Instead, it was at the Kohl-Gorbachev summit in mid-July, and to the surprise of the entire world, including Kohl himself. This manner of proceeding was intended by Gorbachev to be highly significant.

As we have seen in the preceding chapters, the Soviet leaders had believed at the beginning of 1989 that, on the entire gamut of important questions, the Federal Republic was becoming the USSR's main interlocutor and closest partner in Europe. Therefore, if it wanted to use its

---

43. This hypothesis was discussed at the time in the USSR. It had been publicly presented to Shevardnadze, who declared that it was not on the agenda. See his interview in *Novoe Vremia*, 20, May 1990, pp. 5–7.

veto to block the conclusion of an international agreement or to do so by threatening not to withdraw its troops, it would have been first and foremost its good relations with Germany, more so than with any other country, which would have seriously deteriorated. Gorbachev would have largely lost the enormous credit he had gotten from the German public. By lifting the last obstacle to reunification directly with Kohl, he could hope to gain even more from it in the future. Obviously, the political cost of the investment was enormous.

While remaining very firm on the question of NATO membership, Kohl and Genscher had constantly sought to maintain a privileged relationship with Moscow and to present to it prospects for a bright common future. The Soviet leaders had made small tests in that regard, notably in the economic sphere. So, in January, before the USSR officially accepted the principle of unification, Shevardnadze had sent Kohl a message, recalling the terms of his conversation with Gorbachev in June 1989, in which the Soviet leader had asked if the USSR could count on West Germany in case of emergency, and asking if Kohl's positive response at the time still held.[44] The delivery of 100,000 tons of meat was rapidly organized by the Bonn government. In April, while the difficult negotiations on Germany's international status were on-going, Shevardnadze asked for a DM 5 billion credit, which he quickly obtained. All of this caused Kohl to say, privately and a bit presumptuously: "For the USSR, the question of future economic relations is more important than that of a united Germany's membership in NATO."[45] Even larger sums were committed during the Kohl-Gorbachev summit and in the course of the negotiations which followed.

It would be, at the very least, an exaggeration to say that the economic price paid by Germany was the most decisive factor in Gorbachev's final decision.[46] This price was, anyway, very small, given Soviet needs and with respect to what Bonn was ready to invest in

44. See Teltschik, diary, *Der Spiegel*; Horst Teltschik, *329 Tage, Innenansichten der Einigung (329 Days, Unification Seen from Inside)* (Berlin: Siedler Verlag, 1991); cited by Timothy Garton Ash, *In Europe's Name: Germany and the Divided Continent* (London: Jonathan Cape, 1993), p. 350.

45. Teltschik, *329 Tage*, p. 204; cited by Laure Castin, "L'URSS et la question allemande de 1985 à 1991 (Doctoral thesis in international relations, Université Paris 1, 1992), p. 126.

46. On the importance attributed to this factor, see A. A. Akhtamazian, *Ob'edinenie Germanii, ili Anshlius GDR k FRG (German Unification, or the FRG's Anschluss of the GDR)*, vol. 2 (Moscow: MGIMO, 1994), p. 75.

restoring the GDR.[47] At the same time, it was certainly an important consideration in a context where the USSR's economic difficulties were seriously worsening. But, above all, Germany was the only Western country it could count on for economic aid, however insufficient. After the Malta summit, the United States had, for the first time, promised aid to the USSR. But, in the months that followed, it was blocked and became conditioned on a negotiated settlement between Moscow and Lithuania.

The consolidation and the elevation of political relations with Bonn to a new, higher level promised to continue and accentuate the partnership and its economic advantages. As of April, Bonn had proposed the negotiation of a major friendship and cooperation treaty to the USSR, in order to manage German-Soviet relations after unification. The proposition had been welcomed enthusiastically by the Soviet ambassador in Bonn, Kvitsinski, and by the Soviet leaders. Kvitsinski dreamed of a renaissance of the Russian-German partnership of the Bismarck era, which had formed the dominant duo in Europe.

It was very much a small remake of Rapallo that Gorbachev wanted to accomplish by reserving for Kohl his ultimate concession and by fixing with him the final terms of reunification. The surprise and irritation of Kohl's Western allies was expected and desired in order to emphasize the Soviet leader's diplomatic triumph. As Andrei Grachev pointed out to us, France and Britain had counted on the USSR to stop, or at least slow down, reunification; they themselves, meanwhile, did very little and finally dropped the Soviets.[48] Anatolii Cherniaev recounts the same bitterness. After having said that France and England wanted to hold back the course of events "through Gorbachev's hands," he adds they had "underestimated Gorbachev's capacity to adapt himself to the realities."[49]

Even if the German-Soviet treaty "on partnership and cooperation" was only formally signed in the fall, after reunification, its terms were set during the Kohl-Gorbachev summit in July. It is useful to cite one of them: "If one of the two parties is the object of an attack, the other side will not

47. The direct costs assumed by the German state in compensation and indemnities given to the USSR and other CMEA is estimated at DM 20 billion, whereas they had to invest DM 200 billion per year up to 1995 in the reconstruction of the GDR. See Schütze, "Les aspects extérieurs de la réunification allemande."

48. Second interview with Andrei Grachev, Paris, 27 February 1995.

49. Cherniaev, *Shest' let s Gorbachevym*, p. 310.

furnish the aggressor military aid nor any other form of support."[50] Taken at its letter, this clause could be interpreted as ensuring German neutrality even in case of conflict between the USSR and NATO. Only one year earlier, it would have provoked enormous political commotion in the West. But with the Cold War ended, and Germany having just done so much for NATO, the specter of Rapallo seemed much less menacing.

The prospect of a close and promising relationship with Germany obviously was not the only compensation which Gorbachev obtained for lifting his objection to its full membership in NATO. There were others, and of all kinds. Most of them had already been offered to him before this summit in the Caucasus, either by Kohl or by his Western allies. Several of them were essentially designed to permit him to save face on what had been the main preoccupations of his foreign policy.

The most recent had come at the NATO summit which had taken place in London in early July. At it, a declaration was adopted announcing the alliance's intention to emphasize, from then on, its political, rather than military, component, and the beginning of a revision of its "forward defense" doctrine. The declaration also accepted the institutionalization of the CSCE and proposed measures to this effect. However, there was no question of the CSCE being called on in the future to replace NATO.

Already a signatory to the nonproliferation treaty, the Federal Republic solemnly pledged that a unified Germany would renounce the possession of nuclear, chemical, and biological weapons and confirmed as definitive the existing external borders of the two Germanys.

It was on the military level that the concessions obtained by the USSR were most tangible. Kohl agreed that the armed forces of a united Germany would not exceed 370,000 men; the West German *Bundeswehr* alone had over half a million men under arms at the time. The measure meant a 40 percent reduction of the forces then in place in both parts of Germany. So that Kohl's obligation would not seem to be a restriction imposed on the sovereignty of the new German state, the Kohl-Gorbachev agreement indicated that it should be formulated and take force in the framework of the future multilateral treaty on the reduction of conventional forces in Europe, then being negotiated in Vienna. Kohl accepted that the Soviet troops stationed in the GDR

50. "Traité entre la République fédérale d'Allemagne et l'Union des républiques socialistes soviétiques sur les relations de bon voisinage, le partenariat et la cooperation," *Politique étrangère*, 1, 1991.

would remain on German soil for a period of "three to four years" (that imprecisely) and at Germany's expense. It was also agreed that Germany would finance the construction of housing in the USSR for the repatriated soldiers.

Finally, Chancellor Kohl pledged that no NATO installations and no foreign forces or nuclear weapons (under U.S. control) would be deployed on the territory of the GDR. On this issue, Kohl's assurances were stricter and went somewhat further than what NATO had been willing to concede. They gave rise to tensions between the Federal Republic and its allies before the finalization of the accords reached in the framework of the "2 plus 4" conference, of which the last meeting took place in Moscow on September 12. The USSR had therefore obtained a denuclearized and neutral former GDR.

To the Soviet military and the conservatives, Gorbachev could claim that, on the military level, NATO would not emerge strengthened in any way from reunification, and would even be somewhat weakened by the reductions imposed on the *Bundeswehr.*

However, as far as it was concerned, the USSR was to emerge from German reunification dramatically weakened, both militarily and politically. The terms of German unity spelled the end of the Warsaw Pact and of the Soviet military presence in Eastern Europe.

The Caucasus summit was Gorbachev's last foreign policy triumph. One can understand why, contrary to those which preceded it, the summit did nothing to strengthen his political position within the USSR.

CHAPTER FOURTEEN

The Agony and the End
of the Warsaw Pact

There is no question, therefore, of dissolving the Warsaw
Treaty Organization in the course of the next several years.
If, as everything would lead us to believe, its military importance is diminishing, its political role remains. . . . But this
treaty is above all important as a tool for restructuring European policy, for East-West rapprochement, and for regulating
arms reductions. . . .

Sergei Karaganov (1990)[1]

One of the greatest illusions of the Gorbachev leadership and its reformist advisers was to believe that the Warsaw Pact could survive the loss
or diminution of power by the East European Communist Parties. As we
have seen over the course of the preceding chapters, from the summer
of 1989 onward, although the Soviet leaders accepted and even favored
an evolution of the region's regimes and of "renovated" socialism into
ever more uncertain directions, the only constant rigidity in their stated
position and the only condition they made was the continued adherence
of these countries to the international organizations which linked them
to the USSR, first and foremost among them being the Warsaw Pact.

They were convinced that the flexibility and tolerance they had shown
toward the domestic evolution of these countries were the best guarantees for the future and the preservation of the alliance. One could even
say that their restraint in the face of what they considered to be dangerous excesses is explained by their desire not to mortgage the Pact's future,
to which they attached the greatest importance. It may be recalled that
the Bogomolov institute's report of early 1989, which had presented the
most pessimistic scenarios concerning the future of the East European
regimes, and which had even then envisaged a form of Finlandization

---

1. Sergei Karaganov, "Les problèmes de la politique européenne de l'URSS," *La Vie
internationale*, 7, July 1990, pp. 75–83.

for the states of the region, considered the maintenance of the Warsaw Pact as its principal characteristic. It saw in this a minimal recognition of the USSR's most legitimate geopolitical interests as a matter of course—and even more so if Moscow was prepared to accompany the inevitable process of change in these countries.

The Soviet leaders' certainty did not rest simply on incorrect political calculations. As we have seen, they had demanded and received a formal guarantee from all of the new leaders who took power in Eastern Europe in 1989, that they would respect the international obligations of their countries toward the USSR. The freedom to act which these new leaders had acquired on the domestic level was so unexpected that the Soviet demand seemed a small price for them to pay.

In his speech before the European Parliament on December 20, 1989, Eduard Shevardnadze stressed that "it is significant that all of these countries have confirmed their obligations as allies, at the heart of the Warsaw Pact."[2] He saw in it a guarantee for the preservation of stability in Europe.

It is easy to understand Soviet insistence on the preservation of the Warsaw Pact. At the risk of being repetitive, let us recap the main reasons. In addition to being the USSR's main structure for membership in Europe, it was one of the essential attributes of its international power. In European affairs, it ensured a certain symmetry between the Soviets' strategic position and that of the United States. It was also the framework and principal instrument of its political weight in Europe and in the negotiations concerning the European military balance and its political future.

Preventing German reunification, and then its integration into NATO, had been one of the USSR's major attempts to save the Pact. It was not the only one. In fact, even after accepting Germany's membership in NATO—and although their hopes were singularly reduced as a result—the Soviet leaders did not, as a result, renounce saving the Pact. However, the problems did not only come from Germany.

SOVIET MILITARY WITHDRAWALS IN ORDER TO SAVE THE PACT

Without calling into question the existence of the Warsaw Pact, Vaclav Havel, shortly before he became president of Czechoslovakia, had clearly

2. *Pravda,* 20 December 1989.

signalled to Moscow his intention to obtain the withdrawal of Soviet troops from his country. He had at first stated that the withdrawal should be part of the process of conventional forces reductions in Europe and be synchronized with it. Therefore, he was taking a position that was in perfect accord with that of the Soviet Union. He was, however, to change his position very rapidly. Following the Velvet Revolution, several mass demonstrations took place demanding the immediate and complete withdrawal of the 75,000 Soviet troops. Havel's advisers pointed out to him that the introduction of Soviet troops in 1968 had had nothing to do with the military balance in Europe and that, in any case, they were not deployed on its Western borders.

Beyond that, the presence of Soviet troops in Czechoslovakia was based on bilateral agreements between Prague and Moscow and had never been the subject of multilateral accords made in the framework of the Warsaw Pact. Foreseeing the problems that could result from this situation, the Soviet authorities had rushed emissaries to Prague at the beginning of December 1989—after the Velvet Revolution had begun but before the change of regimes—charged with renegotiating the status of Soviet troops in Czechoslovakia to place them in the Warsaw Pact framework.[3] Nothing could be concluded before the fall of the regime. The Soviets came back to the issue when the new authorities in Prague asked to negotiate the troop withdrawal. For nearly two weeks, they insisted on having the negotiations center on the status of the troops, rather than on their complete withdrawal. They were ready for a partial withdrawal, but demanded that a complete withdrawal be part of negotiations with NATO and be eventually compensated by equivalent reductions in U.S. in Western Europe. Prague was obliged to threaten Czechoslovakia's unilateral withdrawal from the Warsaw Pact for Moscow to accept its position. On January 15, 1990, official bilateral talks to negotiate the modalities of a Soviet troop "withdrawal" began.

In order to facilitate negotiations with the Soviets, the new Czech foreign minister, Jiri Dienstbier, had asked the U.S. administration as of late December 1989, through semiofficial, confidential channels, to propose lower ceilings on U.S. and Soviet troops in Europe in the framework of the Vienna talks; he suggested the numbers be reduced by at

---

3. Interview with Zdenek Mateika (Czechoslovak deputy minister of Foreign Affairs and general secretary of the Warsaw Pact's consultative political committee in 1990), Prague, 27 April 1992.

242   The Great Project's Ruin

least 75,000 men.[4] The United States had previously proposed a ceiling of 275,000 troops for each side. In January 1990, shortly after the Czechoslovak request, Washington altered its position and suggested a ceiling of 195,000 men, respectively, in Central Europe, while asking to be allowed to keep 30,000 more outside of this zone.[5] At first, the Soviets insisted on the principle of symmetry and equality in the ceilings. But they rapidly changed their minds. Against the backdrop of problems that were beginning to loom with the other allies, and especially with Germany, the American proposition had the value, in the context, of giving legitimacy to the preservation of a Soviet military presence in Eastern Europe.

On February 26, 1990, only a bit more than a month after negotiations had officially begun, an accord was reached between the USSR and Czechoslovakia. Despite objections from the military, who invoked logistical problems, particularly that of finding housing for the officers and soldiers in the USSR (which did in fact prove to be very serious), Shevardnadze was able to speed up the negotiations and an accord was concluded under which the withdrawal was to be completed by June 1991. The Czech side had insisted that the departure be completed before the end of 1990, and it took Gorbachev's personal intercession with Havel for the time period to be prolonged by six months. The Czechoslovak demands were met; and ironically they were met exactly in order to preserve the future of the Warsaw Pact.

In Hungary, even before 1989, the government had been conducting discreet negotiations with its Soviet counterpart aimed at obtaining, initially, a partial withdrawal of the 50,000 Soviet troops stationed on Hungarian soil. From 1989 onward, with the prospect of free elections looming and the concomitant necessity to improve its image among the Hungarian public, the Communist government in Budapest showed itself to be in a great hurry. In December 1989, all the while trying to present the move as being part of its European conventional disarmament policy, the Soviet defense minister, General Yazov, announced the "unilateral" withdrawal of 6,000 soldiers from Hungary. The Hungarian government, however, thought this insufficient. It asked for and received a complete and very rapid withdrawal. A definitive agreement

4. Interview with Jaroslav Sedivy (Czechoslovakia's ambassador in France in 1992. He was assigned this mission by J. Dienstbier in 1989), Paris, 9 April 1992.
5. On January 1,1990, Soviet troops stationed in Eastern Europe numbered 544,400 men.

was finally announced on March 10, just a few days before the Hungarian elections. The departure of Soviet troops was to begin the next day, and be completed by June 1991, just as in the case of Czechoslovakia. The Hungarian government would have liked a tighter schedule, but it was difficult for a Communist government to demand and obtain more than Vaclav Havel. Here again, the Soviet Union was trying to preserve the future of the Warsaw Pact in the two countries where it evoked the darkest memories.

Beyond the GDR, the only other country of the Pact in which Soviet troops were stationed was Poland. The new Polish government was much less rushed to see them leave, at least as long as the conditions of German reunification were not set. This was even more the case since Helmut Kohl, for electoral reasons, had committed the serious blunder in February 1990 of introducing an element of ambiguity into a definitive recognition of Poland's western borders, proposing to put the question to the future Parliament of a unified Germany. The USSR had immediately and vigorously supported its ally,[6] and Prime Minister Tadeusz Mazowiecki publicly underscored "the importance of this alliance for the question of our borders' security."[7]

Despite all of the uncertainties taking shape on the horizon, the commander of the Pact's armed forces, General Lushev, stated in May 1990, on the occasion of the thirty-fifth anniversary of the treaty, that the withdrawal of the troops from Hungary and Czechoslovakia was being made on the basis of bilateral agreements with those two countries and not as a collective decision of the Pact; consequently, "it certainly does not signify the liquidation of its unified armed forces."[8] Affirming his confidence in its future, he forcefully recalled that all of the new leaders of the member states had committed themselves to "pursuing the fulfillment of their countries' obligations to the Pact." At the most, he admitted the necessity of introducing certain elements of democratization which had already been envisaged at the political level for the past year, such as changes in the command structure and the rotation of positions previously reserved for the Soviets alone.

---

6. See Horst Teltschik's comments on the matter. See excerpts from his diary in *Der Spiegel*, 30 September 1991, pp. 118–140; translated for this book by Laure Castin.

7. Press conference on 21 February 1990 in Warsaw, cited by Hannes Adomeit, "Gorbachev and German Unification: Revision of Thinking, Realignment of Power," *Problems of Communism*, 39, July-August 1990, pp. 1–23.

8. "Varshavskomu Dogovoru—35 let" (The Warsaw Pact—35 Years), *Krasnaia Zvezda*, 13 May 1990.

NEW MISSIONS FOR THE WARSAW PACT?

Quite rapidly, from early 1990, some political leaders and theoreticians of *perestroika* understood that the Warsaw Pact no longer had many prospects as a military system, and it was particularly on the importance of its preservation as a political organization that they began to insist. Taking up several arguments he had already formulated in the fall of 1989, Andrei Kortunov, one of the brilliant intellectual reformers at the Institute of the U.S.A. and Canada, enumerated several reasons which he estimated to be the most appropriate for maintaining a reformed and transformed Warsaw Pact, especially as an organization for international political coordination.[9] Among these, he stated that the countries of Eastern Europe, as much as the USSR, were having difficulties gaining acceptance on an equal footing with their partners in Western countries and in West European institutions. Consequently, he wrote that they had an interest in remaining together and collectively negotiating, with more weight and efficacy, the terms of their integration into West European structures and institutions.[10] The argument was certainly very valid from the point of view of Soviet interests. The countries of Eastern Europe, however, did not share this perspective. They rapidly realized that the enormity of the USSR's economic and political problems could only be a burden they would be bringing with them into their negotiations with Western Europe. The group that held to this view was composed of Poland, Czechoslovakia, and Hungary, which considered themselves in a better position than the others to rapidly obtain more advantageous conditions. Contrary to what was to happen, the deputy director of the Institute of Europe stated that, in their relations with the West, the countries of the region, "weaker in the political and economic spheres," were "much more in need of the USSR than the USSR of them. . . ."[11]

Bezrukov and Kortunov also affirmed that a "unilateral liquidation" of the Warsaw Pact "could exert a destabilizing influence on East-West relations."[12] In support of their argument they found it useful to rely on an article written by the American alliance theoretician, Stephen Walt,

---

9. See M. E. Bezrukov and A. V. Kortunov, "Nuzhna reforma OVD" (The Necessary Reform of the Warsaw Treaty Organization), *S Sh A-EPI*, 3, March 1990, pp. 30–35.

10. See M. E. Bezrukov and A. V. Kortunov, "What Kind of an Alliance Do We Need?" *New Times (Novoe Vremia)*, 41, 1989, pp. 7–9.

11. Karaganov, "Les problèmes de la politique européenne de l'URSS."

12. Bezrukov and Kortunov, "Nuzhna reforma OVB."

published in the USSR.[13] Here again, the Pact's dissolution could only be more inauspicious for relations between the USSR and the West, and much less so for relations between Eastern Europe and the West. If the United States and NATO could fear a destabilization in Europe as a result of a possible resurgence of conflicts between East European states, these no longer wanted the USSR as the only, or even the main, arbiter of such conflicts.

Nonetheless, there was a certain convergence on this question which emerged between the USSR and Vaclav Havel's Czechoslovakia. Apprehensive about the structural vacuum which would result from the erosion of the Warsaw Pact, Havel became one of the principal advocates, in 1990, of establishing a new European security structure, notably through accentuating a reinforcement of the CSCE. He even stated that the new collective European security system should replace NATO and the Warsaw Pact. However, this seemingly perfect convergence of views rested only on the long-term objective. Czech diplomats did not insist on having the dissolution of NATO and the Warsaw Pact be synchronized, and it was more for the replacement of the latter that they were pressing for a new collective European security system. In the meantime, they had no objection to the continued existence of NATO and preferred a united Germany that was integrated into it, rather than being neutral. Such a prospect also raised anxieties in Poland. During a meeting of the foreign ministers of the Pact's member states, held in Prague in March 1990, the Soviet Union received very little support from its allies on this fundamental question. Only Bulgaria abstained from taking a position against German neutrality. Skeptical about the realism of the double membership option for Germany, its "allies" refused to rally behind the USSR on this issue.

Despite the denial from most Soviets, the interests which the USSR and the new regimes in Eastern Europe had in common on which to found an alliance were quite limited and fragile. The common problems in the transition to a market economy were evoked. But, in that respect, the gap between the partners' objectives, and even more so the pace of their transition, was to widen considerably. Moscow also underscored the importance of economic relations between the USSR and the East European states, but those were to collapse rapidly. At the beginning of

13. Steven (sic) Walt, "Sokhranenie mira v Evrope: podderzhanie status-kvo" (The Preservation of Peace in Europe: Support for the Status Quo), S Sh A-EPI, 2, February 1990.

1990, a Soviet economist wrote that "one has the growing impression that the Soviet side continues by pure inertia to hold to the point of view that it is essential to preserve CMEA at any price."[14] But the Soviet leaders were to come to terms with CMEA's failure more easily than with that of the Warsaw Pact. Interestingly, it is on the Pact as a political alliance that they seemed to count as the framework for coordinating integration into the Western economic institutions.

For its part, the Soviet military argued that all of the East European armies' equipment was Soviet, that the USSR's partners did not have the hard currency to reequip themselves from the West, and that therefore military cooperation with the Soviet Union remained in their interest.[15] The Soviet military was the slowest to realize that the Pact was rapidly losing its substance.[16]

In fact, one of the main reasons why the new leaders in Eastern Europe accepted not calling in question the Warsaw Pact's existence for several months was out of "recognition" or "gratitude" toward Gorbachev for the tolerance the Soviet Union had shown during the revolutions in the region in 1989. They also hoped thereby not to harm the process of transformations which he had introduced into Soviet internal and foreign policy. This was a very thin basis for preserving an alliance.

TOWARD DISSOLUTION

The erosion and dissolution of the Pact came about in two stages. First, it was its military organization that was targeted by Eastern Europe's leaders. To reach their objectives on this point more easily, they proposed maintaining the Pact as a political organization, hence seeking to take Gorbachev, who had stressed the importance of this function, at his word.

The new Hungarian government of Jozef Antall, which replaced the reformist Communists in April 1990, demonstrated the greatest haste in wanting a dissolution of the Pact. From the beginning of June, it spoke

---

14. A. Nekipelov, "Zavtra—novyi SEV?" (Tomorrow—A New CMEA?), *Eko-nomicheskoe Sotrudnichestvo Stran-Chlenov SEV*, 3, 1990; cited by Marie Lavigne, "Economic Relations of the (Former) CMEA Countries: Past, Present and Future," p. 120 in United Nations Economic Commission for Europe, *Economic Integration in Europe and North America*, Economic Studies 5 (New York, Geneva: United Nations, 1995).

15. See the analysis by Colonel Markushin, "Vostochnaia Evropa i my" (Eastern Europe and Us), *Krasnaia Zvezda*, 26 October 1990.

16. See also "Sud'ba Varshavskogo Dogovora," *Krasnaia Zvezda*, 17 June 1990.

openly of the need to do away with its military structures.[17] Nonetheless, at a meeting of the consultative political council (the Pact's supreme organ), which met in Moscow on June 7, Antall did not achieve his goal, and it was Gorbachev who won—at least for the moment, to the satisfaction of the Soviet military. It was agreed, though, that an intergovernmental commission would be created, charged with examining possible paths for its transformation so that it could become a more political than military organization. Having not yet given in on a united Germany's membership in NATO, Gorbachev still needed both a military and a political organization. To his satisfaction, the common declaration at the end of the meeting called for the replacement of the two blocs through a new pan-European security system.[18]

Even after the Kohl-Gorbachev summit in mid-July, the Soviet leaders continued to hold firm to the Pact's existence, and to their desire to see it continue, still hoping for something in exchange for its dissolution. Knowing that the CSCE was a very large organization with unwieldy mechanisms for functioning and that its transformation into a working collective security system would take a lot of time, Soviet authors also introduced formulas other than its institutionalization to replace the threatened Pact. These options were often made without great elaboration, in a last ditch, desperate style. For example, the deputy director of the Institute of Europe took up the (more philosophical than concrete) proposal by Franççois Mitterrand for a European confederation and also suggested the creation of new "pan-European politico-military organs."[19] Two higher officers from the armed forces proposed the establishment of an "European Security Alliance (ESA)" through the fusion of NATO and the Warsaw Pact, and enumerated several duties and sketched out the contours of such an alliance.[20]

If the military organization of the Warsaw Pact was not dissolved at the June 1990 summit, this was not only the result of the East European leaders' deference to Gorbachev. The signals coming from Washington and NATO were not encouraging them in this sense. On the contrary: the West, for very tangible reasons, did not want to see a breakup of the framework in which the Vienna negotiations on conventional arms

17. See Andrew A. Michta, *East Central Europe after the Warsaw Pact* (New York: Greenwood Press, 1992), p. 137.

18. Text in *Krasnaia Zvezda*, 8 June 1990.

19. Karaganov, "Les problèmes de la politique européenne de l'URSS."

20. A. Vladimirov and S. Posokhov, "A European Security Alliance," *International Affairs*, October 1990, pp. 80–83.

reductions in Europe (begun before the 1989 revolutions) were taking place. It was therefore largely through inertia that the Pact continued to exercise its military functions until the conclusion of the CFE (Conventional Forces in Europe) accords in the fall of 1990. The last phase of negotiations proved to be a very painful experience for the Soviet military and political leaders.

After the Kohl-Gorbachev summit, which foresaw the departure of Soviet troops from Germany, there could no longer be any question of some kind of parallel between the presence of U.S. and Soviet forces in Europe. It was in part to avoid this problem, which became increasingly embarrassing for the Soviets, that the treaty finally left aside, with the exception of Germany, the question of fixing a ceiling on the number of troops; this constitutes one of its main weaknesses.

However, on other issues, the framework and the appearance of symmetry continued to be maintained in the last phase of negotiations. This created a paradoxical situation which clearly demonstrated the Warsaw Pact's anachronism. A tacit alliance emerged between the members of NATO and the non-Soviet Warsaw Pact signatories to have the USSR assume the greatest part of the reductions assigned to the Warsaw Pact as a whole.[21]

In 1989, the USSR accepted the principle of equality in the quantity of armaments possessed by the two alliances and the fixing of ceilings very close to the current level of NATO armaments. This was a considerable concession long sought by NATO, and it was on this basis that the treaty led to withdrawal of 4 percent of NATO stockpiles, compared to 39 percent for the Warsaw Pact.

One can easily understand why, in the second half of 1990, Gorbachev and Shevardnadze had lost much of their interest in these negotiations. The major concessions which they had earlier accepted were designed to bring the two blocs closer politically and to attenuate the division of Europe. The West held two cards with which to press Moscow to conclude the treaty. First, the accord was a necessary condition for the limitation of forces in a future Germany, as agreed between Kohl and Gorbachev in July. Second, the West had made the holding of a CSCE summit conditional on the conclusion of a treaty. It was in the framework of that summit that the institutionalization of the CSCE, so much desired by Moscow, was to be begin. It had also been agreed that

21. See Douglas L. Clarke, "The CFE Talks: One against Twenty-Two," *Report on Eastern Europe,* 5 October 1990, pp. 41–44.

the CSCE, and not the two alliances, would be the framework for negotiations which would follow the conclusion of a CFE treaty.

For the Soviet military, less sensitive to political considerations, the treaty was even more difficult to accept for obvious reasons. Given the very small amount of total reductions required of NATO, the Soviet top brass saw it as a unilateral disarmament measure on the part of the USSR. Already at the moment of its conclusion, Gorbachev had begun to move closer to them and to the conservative forces as a result of his domestic difficulties. Therefore, it was concluded by "snatching" it from them. One month after it was signed, on December 20, 1990, Shevardnadze resigned before the mounting tide of criticism from military leaders and conservatives. The implementation of the treaty's terms took place under the greatest possible Soviet reluctance, which had, moreover, begun to show itself even before the signing. When he resigned, Shevardnadze warned against the imminent danger of a dictatorship without specifying if the danger came from Gorbachev, or to him. He made it clearly understood that the Soviet leader had been on the verge of sacrificing him to the conservatives.[22]

In the months preceding Shevardnadze's resignation and the conservative turn in Soviet policy, the Hungarian, Czechoslovak, and Polish leaders had limited themselves to asking for a dissolution of the Pact's military structures and for its transformation into a consultative political organism. A summit meeting of the Pact's member states to that effect was to take place in early November. The USSR had apparently resigned itself to the change, and one of Gorbachev's advisers, G. Batenin, had declared that the Pact's joint command and staff would be dissolved and new political structures put in place.[23] The summit meeting was put off until early December at the Soviets' request; they preferred to wait until after the end of the CSCE conference in November in order to present themselves at the latter in a better institutional position, which became more a matter of appearances. The Warsaw Pact summit did not take place in December, having again been put off at the USSR's request.

During this time, events took a worrying turn. Several weeks after Shevardnadze's resignation, in mid-January 1991, the danger he had described seemed to manifest itself with the brutal repressive measures launched against Lithuania and Latvia, which resulted in several deaths.

---

22. See the text of his speech in *Izvestiia*, 21 December 1990.
23. See Vladimir V. Kuzin, "Security Concerns in Central Europe," *Report on Eastern Europe,* 8 March 1991, pp. 25–40.

These events caused a strong reaction in Eastern Europe. A military coup in the USSR was feared, and the East Europeans wondered if the Warsaw Pact would not be used as an instrument or pretext, if not for an attempt to regain control over the region, then at least for efforts to intimidate or exert pressure. The Polish government, reassured by Germany and the guarantees from the "2 plus 4" conference, chose that moment to demand an immediate agreement on the rapid withdrawal of Soviet troops on Polish soil. To that, the commander of those forces, General Dubinin, responded that they would leave when the USSR was ready to go, and "on its conditions."[24]

In this context, the foreign ministers of Hungary, Poland, and Czechoslovakia gathered in Budapest on January 21,1991. Threatening a unilateral withdrawal of their countries from the Warsaw Pact, they demanded that the summit meeting, already put off several times, be held at the latest by mid-March 1991, and that it proceed with the immediate dissolution of its military structures and fix a date for its complete disbandment. They wanted the disbandment to happen at the latest in March 1992, at which time a CSCE conference was to take place in Helsinki. The date proposed was seen as a final concession to Gorbachev, so that a link could be made between the disappearance of the alliance and a pan-European institutional reinforcement which, in reality, remained weak and symbolic.

Given the danger of unilateral withdrawals which would have considerably damaged the USSR's prestige, Gorbachev was obliged to accept that a meeting of the all the Pact's foreign and defense ministers take place in Budapest on February 25 to dissolve its military structures. In the meantime, he still hoped to convince his partners to keep the Pact as a political organization. However, at the February 25 meeting, it was decided to get rid of the military structures at the end of March and to hold a summit meeting on July 1, 1991, to fix the terms and dates for the complete disbandment of the remaining political structures.

In order to avoid a personal humiliation, Gorbachev did not attend the July 1 summit in Prague where a protocol on the Warsaw Pact's complete dissolution was signed. He was represented by his vice-president, Gennadi Yanaev, who was to preside over the coup against him a month later. Asked via telephone by Russian television on July 1 about the significance of the Prague summit, the defense minister, General Yazov

24. *Znamia Pobeda*, 15 January 1991.

(himself one of the main actors in the attempted coup), declared that "the military had nothing to do with this event," and refused to give any interviews.[25]

Some weeks earlier, it was the CMEA which had been officially disbanded. The principal structures and instruments of the USSR's European policy had disappeared. The USSR itself was not to survive very much longer—less than six months, in fact.

For over a year, the dream of European multilateralism along the lines envisaged by Gorbachev and his entourage had gradually dissipated. By continuing to advance it, Gorbachev could depend only on the Western leaders' benevolence rather than on the constantly declining means of the Soviet Union.

25. Foreign Broadcast Information Service, Soviet Union (Daily Report), 5 July 1991, p. 1.

Conclusion

Rarely in history have we witnessed the policy of a great power continue, throughout so many difficulties and reversals, to be guided by a such an idealistic view of the world, based on universal reconciliation, and in which the image of the enemy was constantly blurring, to the point of making it practically disappear as the enemy.

Let us again guard here against thinking that the Soviet leadership did not have other options and that its policy was somehow the inevitable product of the impasses in which the USSR found itself. If Gorbachev's policy could be considered by some as a desperate adventure, history provides too many examples of impasses which led to adventures, or simply policies, that were of a completely different nature. Indeed, that is why the world did not cease, between 1987 and 1991, to be surprised by Soviet foreign policy.

This is not, of course, to say that this policy was the product of chance. As we have seen, it was a social-democratic transformation that the Soviet leadership underwent, under impulses from an intellectual elite that had already been largely "social-democratized." This social-democratization is far from being an accident in the history of Marxist, and later Leninist, parties. It has been the result of the quasi-permanent relative success of parliamentary democracy and the liberal economy, and of their capacity to adapt. From the beginning of the century, reformism began to win over revolutionary parties based on Marxism. The polarization resulting from the apparition of Leninist parties contributed to accentuating the process. To the extent that one of their main reasons for being was the struggle against social democracy as it had become, the Leninist parties' conversion to social-democratization was much slower to come. In the West, the most remarkable case was that of the Italian Communist Party. In the East, it first won over the most European of Communist Parties in power, those of Poland and Hungary in 1956, and of Czechoslovakia in 1968. The process there had been interrupted, as we know, by Soviet pressure or military intervention. While there was nothing inevitable about the moment that it took place, the USSR's leading party finally enlisted social-democratization to help lead it out of its impasses and to bring it closer to Europe.

The critical phase of a Communist Party's social-democratic transition is often the one marked by the strongest dose of political idealism, and this is not a matter of chance. Initially, the social-democratic change is rarely recognized as such by those who are engaging in it. Shaped by a global, articulated vision of the world and social processes, as well as imbued with an heroic mission, a Leninist Party cannot abandon its old standards without pursuing new, more promising objectives that are as mobilizing as those which have become out of reach or discredited. Without being completely abandoned, these are continually diluted into new "syntheses," seen as being both promising and new. This explains the Italian Communist Party's proposed "historic compromise" of the 1970s, which was supposed to fundamentally transform Italy's political life and put it on a qualitatively new track, very different from a banal social-democratization. In the same way, the Prague Spring intended to reconcile socialism and democracy, the plan and the market, into a new synthesis which would renew the attractiveness of socialism. The project of European and global reconciliation put forward by the USSR in 1988 and 1989 was all the more impressive since it came from a nuclear superpower and was centered precisely on disarmament.

Paradoxically, despite these messianic ambitions, which were indeed pursued with determination and conviction, it was still essentially a more or less rapid process of adaptation that they matched and that accompanied them. That is why we have termed the world view and the vision of social processes which were articulated a transitional ideology. We have seen how, for Gorbachev and his circle, the socialist idea became constantly more open, elastic, and eclectic. In the search for a new synthesis, the osmosis was first made with a social democracy perceived to be increasingly less foreign. As we have discussed, this is what made it easy to accept the formal transformation of the Hungarian Party in the summer of 1989, before the CPSU itself had integrated a greater number of characteristics of social democracy.

Between the conquering, promising phase of Gorbachev's grand design, when his project of a new synthesis could seem on track, and its rapid ruin in the first several months which followed the opening of the Berlin Wall, the space of time was very short—extremely short, in fact. Consequently, the adaptation was very painful, difficult, and traumatizing for the Soviet leaders. But it was still adaptation that carried the day. We have seen how a whole range of reasons limited the Soviet leadership's option at the end of 1989. The events were rapidly closing in from all sides, the leaders had burnt their bridges, and all kinds of costs practically prevented them from any attempt at reversing the course of events through the use of force. But the ecumenicalism, the conviction that the former adversary would be at least partially transformed by the new relationship, the certainty that ultimately something from the initial project would be saved—all these contributed significantly to the refusal of resorting even to demonstrations of force, to the choice not to block an international agreement on German reunification, and to the pursuit of the process of adaptation.

Mikhail Gorbachev remains convinced, even after all the setbacks he endured, of the viability of reformed socialism in Eastern Europe and its fundamental incompatibility with the use of force. He wrote (to this author) that he continues to believe that "the socialist idea, as the idea of freedom, democracy and social justice, cannot die or disappear." He added that, "the objective course of events, including the most recent elections in a whole series of East European countries, fully confirms this conclusion."[1] He sees in these elections the supreme vindication of his refusal to envisage any recourse to or threat of using force.

It is quite clear that Gorbachev's policy toward Eastern Europe from 1988 to 1991 sheds considerable light on the nature and meaning of his global political undertaking. Its examination has allowed us, among other things, to see how the particular ideology, the expectations and illusions which accompanied it (and which accompany any ideology) structured the representation of Soviet interests and the manner of pursuing them; this all resulted in policy choices being pursued in the way we have witnessed during the debacle which ensued.

1. M. S. Gorbachev, *Otvety na voprosy professora Zh. Leveka* (Responses to Questions from Professor Jacques Lévesque), Moscow, 12 July 1995.

Without having, of course, exhausted the subject, we think that, without being too presumptuous, we have been able to render Soviet behavior, which so surprised the world during the great historic changes of 1989, less enigmatic. It is easier to understand the various foundations of that behavior. If their understanding sheds light on the entire Soviet experience under Gorbachev, it is still far from any kind of complete account. Not only does it leave various spheres in the dark, but it makes Gorbachev's long political survival even more enigmatic, given the way in which the disaster in Eastern Europe was managed in 1989. As indicated above, the mobilizational character and promises of the great international design initiated by Gorbachev, as well as the successes of his foreign policy, were able to neutralize the conservative Soviet forces in a first phase. But the rapidity with which it disintegrated should have also just as quickly increased the vulnerability of its promoter. If Gorbachev and his reformist entourage were able to internalize and downsize the debacle more or less successfully, the same cannot be said for their conservative adversaries, who should have been able to regain control faster than them. It remains extraordinary that it was, finally, the liberals and the radical Westernizers who chased him from power. One can be certain that the historic importance of this phenomenon's consequences will not be left without a search for explanations—explanations that go beyond the scope and analysis of this book.

Throughout the course of this work, I have sought to illustrate how the Soviet leadership's international political project, and more specifically its European policy, determined, or at the least considerably influenced, its expectations and its behavior toward Eastern Europe in 1989 and, to an equal degree, in 1990. It would, however, be exaggerated to speak of an organic link between the European policy and that which was directed at Eastern Europe, in the sense that, in practice, the disconnections were frequent and sometimes flagrant, even as late as autumn 1989, albeit much less so afterward.

In general, these inconsistencies were principally due to Gorbachev's personal approach and behavior. At the beginning of my research, I had the tendency to reduce the importance of Gorbachev the individual, dissolving him into the project for which he made himself the standardbearer and champion. Alas, I had to conclude that, in the case of the policy pursued in Eastern Europe, the importance of his personal role (which was very strong, due to the structuring of Soviet power) was clearly larger than in other areas.

It was not Gorbachev personally, but a vast circle of intellectuals who elaborated the new Soviet vision of the world, the policy in the area of disarmament, and the European political project. But he made himself their staunchest defender and their most zealous and persistent promoter; he personally "melted" with the policies advocated. However, in the case of Eastern Europe, somewhat as in the area of domestic politics, he was, if not in contradiction, then at least much more frequently out of step with his reformist entourage's recommendations and the imperatives of the global project he ultimately defended. In short, he was more centrist in his domestic policy and in regard to Eastern Europe than in the area of general foreign policy, which became his favorite policy area. In the first two spheres, he was sometimes more carried away by the project than acting as its carrier. But he was not always carried away—and that had very important consequences.

We have seen how Gorbachev's behavior toward the East European conservative leaders was marked, despite occasional, important indirect pressure, by caution, patience, neglect, and hesitation; this was constantly justified by the principle of noninterference. Certainly, he gave advice and encouragement for reforms, but in a nonimperative and rather "philosophical" way, as the deputy director of the Central Committee's International Department, Valerii Musatov, underscored. Except for those who were in power, the East European reformers only received indirect support and encouragement that was almost in code, and several of them still reproach Gorbachev for it. Consequently, he found himself in contradiction with one of the fundamental slogans of *perestroika,* which considered taking the initiative to be crucial. He waited for the initiative to come from the leading circles, and it did finally come, but, in most cases, under the worst possible conditions.

If he had acted differently, the course of events would certainly have been very different. But in which direction? Comments on this subject are risky and hypotheses impossible to verify. But, beyond resigning one's self to considering history to be inevitable, we cannot desist from making some hypotheses and comments.

Many observers (and Gorbachev himself) believe that in the sphere of domestic politics, his centrism, deals, and zigzags not only assured his relative political longevity, but above all resulted in the August 1991 coup not happening at an earlier moment when it might have been able to succeed. The argument seems quite solid and convincing, though it may wrongly imply that Gorbachev's centrism was merely a tactical stance. On at least one point, however, greater boldness in the direction of democratization would have produced better results for Gorbachev. If he had had himself elected by a popular vote in 1987 or 1988, in a true election, rather than having himself designated president, he could have resisted the attacks from the conservatives and Yeltsin much longer. He might have even been able to translate his victory in the March 1991 referendum on the preservation of a reconstructed Union into deeds by pushing through the implementation of the new Union Treaty (sharing sovereignty between the republics and Moscow), which was on the verge of being signed at the moment of the August coup.

As far as Eastern Europe is concerned, there is no doubt that the deepest tendency was toward the dismantling of the regimes. But not necessarily in the form of such a precipitated disaster as the one which occurred. One could argue that more interventionist action by Gorbachev in favor of reforms would have only accelerated their collapse. Perhaps. However, as was shown in a convincing manner above in the case of Czechoslovakia, a reevaluation of the Prague Spring by Moscow, which Gorbachev had constantly been advised to undertake, would have almost immediately caused the CCP to do the same, and would have brought Dubcek and the 1968 leaders back into the circles of power. Even in 1989, it seems certain that they would have easily won free elections. There would have been, therefore, a regime in Prague for several years with a social-democratic orientation, much more in tune with Gorbachev's foreign policy. The same is true for the GDR, where a Roundtable and elections, had they taken place in 1988, would have undoubtedly meant a considerably different course of events. We may recall that the opposition groups which existed at the time were in favor of preserving a "social-democratized" GDR, and remained so until the end of 1989. The logic of dismantling the old regime would have nonetheless without a doubt led to reunification. It would have happened less hurriedly, though. Moreover, even an SPD victory in the East German elections of March 1991 would have slowed down the process. It is clear that a slower, precisely more controlled, reunification would have taken place under conditions more favorable for Soviet policy.

In short, a somewhat slower transition in Prague and Berlin, which a more activist Soviet policy could have supported, would have allowed Gorbachev to better push ahead with his European policy. His prospects were excellent in the summer of 1989. What he did miss was time, and above all the credibility and a minimal viability of the alliance on which he relied to advance it. Certainly, such an ambitious and messianic project could not have been realized in its totality. But, albeit messianic and ambitious, this project was far from being devoid of realism and corresponded to political aspirations that had currency in West and East. It was only after the fact—after the failure—that the illusions turned out to have been just that. Therefore, was it illusory to expect Mazowiecki's Poland to remain in the Warsaw Pact? As we have seen, it was essentially the precipitancy of German reunification which led to its dissolution, without the Pact being replaced by anything else.

Leninism's departure from the European stage could have left a more solid European order in its wake, one that would have been worthy of the historic occasion which 1989 represented. The question of a new order remains on the agenda and still awaits its solution.

Undoubtedly, however, the most important fact remains that Leninism left so easily and peacefully. This remains the most remarkable event of 1989 and a legacy of hope for the future of mankind.

Index

Compositor: Braun-Brumfield, Inc.
Text: 10/13 Sabon
Display: Sabon
Printer and binder: Braun-Brumfield, Inc.